Practical Lock Picking

Practical Lock Picking
A Physical Penetration Tester's Training Guide

Deviant Ollam

Shane Lawson, Technical Editor

ELSEVIER

AMSTERDAM • BOSTON • HEIDELBERG • LONDON
NEW YORK • OXFORD • PARIS • SAN DIEGO
SAN FRANCISCO • SINGAPORE • SYDNEY • TOKYO
Syngress is an imprint of Elsevier

SYNGRESS.

Acquiring Editor: Rachel Roumeliotis
Development Editor: Matthew Cater
Project Manager: Paul Gottehrer
Designer: Alisa Andreola

Syngress is an imprint of Elsevier
30 Corporate Drive, Suite 400, Burlington, MA 01803, USA

Notices
Knowledge and best practice in this field are constantly changing. As new research and experience broaden our understanding, changes in research methods or professional practices, may become necessary. Practitioners and researchers must always rely on their own experience and knowledge in evaluating and using any information or methods described herein. In using such information or methods they should be mindful of their own safety and the safety of others, including parties for whom they have a professional responsibility.

To the fullest extent of the law, neither the Publisher nor the authors, contributors, or editors, assume any liability for any injury and/or damage to persons or property as a matter of products liability, negligence or otherwise, or from any use or operation of any methods, products, instructions, or ideas contained in the material herein.

Library of Congress Cataloging-in-Publication Data
Application submitted

British Library Cataloguing-in-Publication Data
A catalogue record for this book is available from the British Library.

ISBN: 978-1-59749-611-7
ISBN: 978-1-59749-619-3 (DVD)

Printed in the United States of America
10 11 12 13 14 10   9 8 7 6 5 4 3 2 1

Working together to grow
libraries in developing countries

www.elsevier.com | www.bookaid.org | www.sabre.org

ELSEVIER   BOOK AID International   Sabre Foundation

For information on all Syngress publications visit our website at www.syngress.com

To my Mother and Father

My father taught me to take pride in the things that I own, to treat them with care, and use them properly so that they serve me well. It is because of him that I own a 10-year-old truck and a 30-year-old jeep, both of which run just fine with half a million miles between them. I also cannot thank him enough for teaching me to shoot at a young age.

My mother taught me the value of getting the most out of the equipment you own by learning how it functions, inside and out, so you can fix it if the need should arise. I can remember a time when I was all of about 9 years old and the iron in our house stopped working. My mom explained to me that you don't throw something away just because it is old. Fiddling with the cord, she was able to determine where a break existed in the wire; it was down near the plug.

I stood there, wide-eyed, as she cut the line, stripped the wire ends, and inserted them into an aftermarket replacement plug. She let me hold the screwdriver and tighten the contact points where electricity would again flow to the appliance. I never forgot what it felt like to take something you owned and get more out of it using your own skills and tools. You never can quite tell when you first become a hacker, but for lack of a better point on the calendar I will always believe it started for me on that Sunday afternoon.

...My parents still own that iron to this day.

Contents

Foreword

I feel somewhat like an old man remarking in this fashion, but this book is a great example of the wonderful time in which you currently find yourself. To be alive and learning right now—when there are accessible resources such as this about lockpicking, with beautiful illustrations and lessons written with passion visible on every page—that is truly something.

I reflect back and compare the state of things now with how they were when I was young. I dreamed of being able to open locks. I knew it could be done, but I did not know how. In the 1980s, when my hunger for this knowledge was getting quite powerful, the state of educational materials was very different. Through ads in magazines I found a small publisher in the United States offering a book called *The Complete Guide to Lockpicking by Eddie the Wire*. This book was an inspiration, both for paying close attention during my English lessons in school (all the better to understand Eddie's every word) and for obtaining pick tools (which could only be found at an expensive spy shop for the equivalent of $200 at the time).

It was with great excitement that I sat down at home with my first proper tool set, my book, and some locks from the store. However, it took an entire long and frustrating day before the first padlock clicked open. You know (or you will soon find out!) how it feels your first time; you will always remember that moment! The rush was amazing and addictive. From then on I was hooked and tried to pick any lock I could (legally!) get my hands on.

In the following decade, I published articles on my passion for lockpicking and have since presented many hands-on demonstrations at security conferences. It wasn't long before interested parties began forming sport picking clubs. A group of lockpickers in Germany formed SSDeV; 2 years later I was among those who formed a group in the Netherlands. In 2001, our organization became TOOOL—The Open Organisation Of Lockpickers. Whenever anyone asks why our name is spelled with three O's, we remind them that to be good at picking there is no other path than to practice Over and Over and Over again. TOOOL has continued to grow and today we are pleased to be able to introduce new people to the topic of locks and security all around the world.

I first met Deviant Ollam when presenting about lockpicking on a trip to the United States. I was attempting to spread the idea that knowledge of physical security matters should be spread much like the details and reports of computer security matters, any industry that encourages open, honest discussion will always have better products, more informed consumers, and better security for everyone overall. When someone showed me slides from one of Deviant's lectures, I immediately understood that he could be quite an ally. He not only totally grasped the concepts when it came to locks, but he also understood the bigger picture regarding the state of the security industry overall.

Deviant believes in the right of the people to understand how their hardware works in order to properly evaluate it and use it. He now sits on the Board of Directors of the U.S. division of TOOOL and dedicates much of his time to teaching, traveling, and making certain that those who wish to learn can truly understand and follow along with this knowledge. He has also put a *lot* of energy into developing his illustrations, diagrams, and training materials. The images that appear in this work are unlike any other that most of us have encountered in reference woks at any other time; it's amazing to compare resources like this book to the ones which have been available up until now.

This book is quite an achievement. It is the first new text to appear in ages showing some more advanced and up-to-date topics. This book is also perhaps the first text ever that is both suitable for beginners and yet also has so much to offer to those seeking advanced, professional training. Deviant explains things clearly with easy, flowing words paired with technical drawings of great precision. An absolute beginner starting out knowing essentially nothing about the subject of locks and lock-picking can be well-versed in this topic in almost no time.

Perhaps you just want to open locks as a hobby, or you may be training as a professional security consultant. It could be that you want to know more about the locks you buy for your own needs, or you may be in charge of advising businesses on their security decisions. No matter what your back-ground is, if you want a new and fascinating insight into this world, I don't think any book will give you a better introduction to this field than this one.

Thank you, Deviant, for writing this book and spreading the knowledge.

Barry Wels
Founder and President,
The Open Organization Of Lockpickers

Acknowledgments

This book was written over the course of one month, during which time I sat at my desk wearing my battered Navy watch cap and drinking hard cider, scotch, and jasmine tea, as the same huge playlist repeated over and over and over again full of songs from Flogging Molly, Girlyman, Emancipator, The Ramones, Billie Holiday, Trash 80, and a guitar-playing goat.

Thank you, Rachel, Matt, and everyone else at Syngress for somehow having the vision to see that such a process would somehow result in a decent book. Thank you to Shane Lawson, Babak Javadi, and Barry Wels, for being so instrumental to this enterprise along with me.

I have to thank Barry Wels, Han Fey, and Mike Glasser for truly opening my eyes about the potential for grasping and understanding lockpicking. TOOOL and the other locksport groups have also been so key in this process. Thank you, Schuyler Towne, Eric Michaud, Eric Schmiedl, and especially Babak Javadi for keeping TOOOL alive and growing here in the United States. To Chris, Jim, Jon, Dr. Tran, Ed, the Daves, and especially Mouse... thank you for making the local TOOOL chapter what it is. Having been with you from the beginning makes me feel amazing. Steve, JVR, Dr. Tran, and Dave Ploshay... you're the greatest ever when it comes to running public lockpicking events on the road with Babak, Daisy, and I. Shea, Scott, Michael, Katie, and everyone else who is showing so much interest and energy in getting local TOOOL chapters started in new places, we all salute you.

Thank you to Renderman, Jos, Rop, Til, Nigel, Kate, mh, Ray, Suhail, Gro, Hakon, Kyrah, Astera, Rene, Mika, Morgan, Saumil, Andrea, Daniele, Federico, and Francisco, and all of our other international friends who make us feel at home no matter how far we travel.

TOOOL would like to thank all of the other sporting, hobbyist, and amateur lockpicking groups who help to spread knowledge and build interest in this fascinating field. SSDeV, LI, FALE, and the FOOLS are full of wonderful people who love to teach and have fun. An extra special thanks goes to Valanx, Dosman, and the rest of the FOOLS for reminding us to not be so serious, even when we have something serious to say. Some other local groups who have been instrumental in spreading interest, enthusiasm, and awareness about lockpicking are:

- DC719—Thank you for starting such awesome lockpicking contests at DEFCON
- DC303—Thank you for making lockpicking look badass on nationwide TV
- DC949—Thank you for making handcuff picking look badass on Closed-Circuit TV

Thank you, Scorche, datagram, and Ed, for your beautiful photos, good advice, amazing collections, and invaluable friendship.

Without Q, Neighbor, Russ, MajorMal, and Zac showing off all of their wickedly fun gadgets over the years, I would never have had the slightest insight into matters of electronic security.

I have to thank my old neighbor Tom for listening to my first rehearsal of my original presentation slides, and my new neighbors Geoff and Heather for being there as I developed new ones.

Thank you to Johnny Long for showing the world that even a highly technical presentation should always be amusing and enjoyable... and for reminding us that we all have a responsibility to do right by our brothers and sisters on this planet. May all that is good watch over you and your family, Johnny, as you continue to help others in foreign lands.

Thank you to Dark Tangent for first suggesting that I turn this content into a proper training course, and to Ping and everyone else who work tirelessly so that Black Hat can keep ticking along.

An extra special thanks to Bruce and Heidi for ShmooCon, where I gave my very first public lecture about lockpicking. You and all those who put in the monumental effort every year are the reason ShmooCon remains my favorite conference to this day.

Thank you as well to everyone behind the scenes at (deep breath)—AusCERT, Black Hat, CanSecWest, CarolinaCon, DeepSec, DEFCON, DojoCon, ekoparty, HackCon (go, team Norway!), HackInTheBox, HOPE, LayerOne, NotACon, PlumberCon, PumpCon, QuahogCon, SeaCure, SecTor, ShakaCon, SOURCE, SummerCon, ToorCon, and all of the other events who have been kind enough to invite me to spread knowledge of this topic to new people.

We wouldn't be the researchers we are without the help of the world's Hackerspaces (particularly PumpingStation:One and the MetaLab) hosting us and helping us reach out to others.

This work would not have been possible had I not met Babak Javadi, who has given endless advice, encouragement, and invaluable constructive criticism of my material.

I offer great thanks to Nancy, who was there as I discovered the extent to which one could do amazing things with Photoshop. So special was my time with Janet, Don, and those who were there when I was finding my voice as a teacher. So invaluable was my time with Jackalope, who was there with me as I was discovering the conference circuit; you made me realize that people actually liked listening to what I have to say.

I cannot express my pleasure and good fortune in meeting Christina Pei while writing this. You reminded me that even teachers of scientific material can be funny and casual in their delivery. Having you in my life makes me feel like I can do absolutely anything.

Most of all, I offer my deepest and most heartfelt thanks to Daisy Belle. You have shown me more kindness, love, understanding, and support than I have ever dreamed one person could give. From running the logistics of TOOOL to managing daily operations for The CORE Group to coordinating all of my travel (all three of those tasks each being practically a full-time job), you are essential to all of the projects I attempt and to my life as a whole. Your love is what sustains me... that, and your awesome sandwiches.

... and a special thank you to those in the hacker community who *get involved*. Those who attend conferences, prepare presentations, research exploits and publicly disclose them properly, those who continue seeking new skills, who want to explore, who want to understand, who want to learn, touch, and do. To anyone who has ever sat in one of my lectures and asked an insightful question or gone home to try out what they have learned... to anyone who has not just watched but gotten up and tried their hand at Gringo Warrior, Pandora's Lock Box, the Defiant Box, ClusterPick, or any of the other contests that I have run over the years... to all those who make the community what it is... I thank you from the bottom of my heart.

About the Author

Deviant Ollam's first and strongest love has always been teaching. A graduate of the New Jersey Institute of Technology's Science, Technology, and Society program, he is always fascinated by the interplay that connects human values and social trends to developments in the technical world. While earning his BS degree at NJIT, Deviant also completed the History degree program federated between that institution and Rutgers University.

While paying the bills as a security auditor and penetration testing consultant with The CORE Group, Deviant is also a member of the Board of Directors of the U.S. division of TOOOL, The Open Organisation Of Lockpickers. Every year at DEFCON and ShmooCon, Deviant runs the Lock-pick Village, and he has conducted physical security training sessions at Black Hat, DeepSec, Toor-Con, HackCon, ShakaCon, HackInTheBox, CanSecWest, ekoparty, and the United States Military Academy at West Point. His favorite Amendments to the U.S. Constitution are, in no particular order, the 1st, 2nd, 9th, and 10th.

About the Technical Editor

Shane Lawson (CISSP, CPT, CEH, NSA IAM/IEM) is a security engineer for a leading systems, solutions, and technical services company. He creates secure network solutions for various commercial and government clients, advises on security policy development, and provides physical security guidance to multiple facility security officers. Prior to this, he was a senior technical advisor for multiple U.S. Navy carrier and expeditionary strike groups, specializing in information security and joint communications. Shane is a U.S. Navy veteran, where he served as an information systems security manager and communications watch officer for over 10 years.

Ethical Considerations

Dear reader, you've picked up quite the interesting book indeed. During its course you will learn many fascinating things about locks and their operation; but before you begin, I pose to you three ethical dilemmas of varying degrees:

SCENARIO ONE

Sarah is driving around town running various errands. As she approaches an intersection where she has the right of way, another vehicle cuts her off, forcing her to swerve in order to avoid a collision. She misses the other vehicle, but runs into the median in the process, damaging one of her front wheels. The other vehicle drives away, and since she has only liability insurance, Sarah will have to pay for the repairs out of pocket. Later in the day, as she waits in the checkout line at her local grocery store, she recognizes the cashier as the driver of the vehicle that cut her off. As her items are totaled up, she considers confronting the cashier about the incident. Sarah decides to let the issue drop and the cashier informs that her total is $76.19. She hands the cashier a $100 bill and receives her change. Now counting her change, Sarah realizes that she received $33.81 in change instead of $23.81, an excess of $10. What should Sarah do?

SCENARIO TWO

It's a beautiful day and Jeremy and his girlfriend Emily decide to visit the local botanical center for a nice walk. As they enter, he realizes he forgot his student ID at home and wonders if the center would still allow him to purchase tickets at the student pricing. A quick exchange with the pleasant lady working at the ticket counter reveals that he would have to pay full price for the tickets. Defeated, he pays for the two tickets and proceeds with Emily inside. As they explore the various areas, Emily mentions that she heard about a new collection of exotic flowers that she wanted to see. Jeremy notes the location of the Special Exhibits area on the map and they begin to navigate their way there. As the couple approaches the area, they find themselves blocked by a roped off area with a sign that reads *"Due to extenuating circumstances, this exhibit is temporarily closed. We apologize for the inconvenience."* Emily is visibly disappointed and Jeremy considers unhooking the rope and entering the exhibit anyway. After all, they paid full price for admission! Shouldn't they have the right to see all of the exhibits?

SCENARIO THREE

While working on a project in his apartment Chad is interrupted by a knock at his door. When opens the door, he finds his friend Zach standing there, flustered. Zach explains that he's left his house keys at the office and needs to get into his apartment. He already tried calling the landlord, but there was no answer at the number. Zach knows that Chad recently read a book about lockpicking and was fairly skilled at opening many locks that he has purchased for practice. Zach wants Chad to open his apartment door so he can get his spare key from within. Should Chad try to open the door for Zach?

So what do you think?

Let's look at the first scenario. How much of the fault and respective liability fall on the cashier? Even though Sarah had the right of way, did she have any other options? Did she have a different direction she could have taken the car? Could she have stopped? Regardless of the level of fault of the cashier in regards to the car accident earlier in the day, many people would return the extra $10 without hesitation. After all, it's not even the cashier's money. It belongs to the grocery store. Even if the scenario was modified and the driver of the offending vehicle was also the owner of the store, many would argue that the issue of the car repair and the accuracy of the grocery transaction are separate, and should be dealt with accordingly.

Now let's move to the dilemma within the botanical center. What's the appropriate course of action to take there? In regards to simply bypassing the rope barrier, one must remember that in this case, the botanical center is legally considered private property. As such, the owner of the property has the right to restrict movement of visitors as they see fit, up to and including removal of visitors from the property. If you had guests in your home and told them that a particular room was off limits, wouldn't you be upset if they entered anyway? It's also important to consider the practical implications of the sign. Even though there wasn't much information available on the sign as to *why* the area was closed off, there are many good reasons for such an action. It's possible that the plants were currently undergoing special care or treatment, or perhaps hazardous chemicals were in use. Maybe the center was just simply short-staffed because an employee called in sick and they didn't have anyone to oversee the area. Regardless of the reason, it's clear a boundary was drawn and it's important to respect that. The best course of action to take would be for Jeremy or Emily to bring up the issue with an employee or a manager, and explain their disappointment. The manager would likely give them some day passes to come back at another time, or might even arrange a supervised tour. Barriers aren't often used without cause and it's important to consider both the ethical and practical implications involved with breaking them.

The ethical significance of locks in our society is a very intriguing matter. Locks have historically had a very important and personal place in our lives. They are used as a means of security. They prevent others from seeing that which we do not wish to be seen, and they keep our property and families secure from intruders. The ethical issues surrounding lockpicking are a bit more clouded for many people. It is not an issue that is dealt with very often, and it is difficult for some to understand.

For many people the interactions with a lock fall into three basic categories:

1. A lock is opened with a key by an authorized user.
2. A lock is picked open or bypassed by a locksmith on behalf of an authorized user.
3. A lock is compromised via picking or physical force by an un-authorized entity (i.e., burglar).

Often times when discussing the hobby of lockpicking with others, you may be asked if you are a locksmith. If you are not, many will look at you oddly and some may think that you have nefarious purposes in mind. After all, if you aren't using a key, and you're not a locksmith, what business do you have opening locks without the key? Most people never think about the fourth scenario:

4. A lock not being used for the purposes of security is treated as a puzzle by an intrigued party.

Many have tried explaining this fourth possibility only to be met with incredulous looks from friends, family, and others. As a result, sometimes the situation is explained as an endeavor of research in the name of better security. However, whether you choose to adopt this hobby simply as a diversionary pastime or as part of a security-related career, it is essential that you are mindful of matters surrounding ethics and law.

In most states possession of "burglary tools" is considered illegal if it can be shown that one had intent to commit a crime using said tools. In such cases, nearly *anything* can be considered a burglary tool, including but not limited to lock picks, crowbars, screwdrivers, pliers, and even spark plugs. However, a couple states now have laws that make mere possession of lock picks without a license a crime. While such laws stem mostly from scammers doing business as "locksmiths" and defrauding the public, such legislation affects the lockpicking community, as well.

It should go without saying that it is *your* responsibility to know your local laws regarding the possession of lock picks, but in general if one remains safe and ethical regarding such things no trouble arises. It is here that I would like to introduce what are commonly referred to in the community as the two golden rules of lockpicking:

1. Do not pick locks you do not own.
2. Do not pick locks that you rely on.

Why the two rules? Well it's actually fairly difficult to get oneself into an undesirable position if one follows these two rules. Let's talk about the first rule.

Do not pick locks you do not own.

In this usage, I refer to ownership in the strictest sense. It's important to note that there is a clear delineation between ownership of a lock and permission to use the lock. When first learning about lock picking, many immediately go to the nearest lock they can find and start practicing. Often times this is an apartment door, dormitory door, or office door. In these examples note that one does not *own* any of the locks. A key is provided by the owner or landlord for authorized access as the lock was designed to be used. Thus, access to the key does not imply ownership. Now let's look at the second rule.

Do not pick locks you rely on.

It may not be immediately apparent why this rule is important, but you must understand that it is possible for a lock to be damaged or even occasionally disabled by picking. Not only does repeated picking of a lock put premature and abnormal wear on the cylinder and pins, in some configurations locks can become disabled or damaged in a way that prevents their normal operation. If this happens to a lock that you own and rely on, you've now disabled or broken part of your own security. You may lock yourself out of your house or prevent yourself from being able to secure the property. Should you accidentally damage someone else's lock, you're now responsible for the damage caused to their property in addition to any labor and repair needed to resolve the problem.

Are there exceptions to these rules? In a way, yes. If someone offers you one of their locks to try (for example, a practice lock from their own collection) that is okay as long as everyone understands that there is always a risk of damage or premature wear. If you get locked out of your own house but do happen to have some picks, you may elect to try to pick your house lock to get back in, with the understanding that if you fail, you may damage the lock and the lock may require replacement. In light of these specific exceptions, I offer the amended rules:

1. Do not pick locks you do not own, except with express permission by the owner of the lock.
2. Do not pick locks you rely on, except when risks of damage are fully considered.

Still, it's much easier to use the original verbiage, as most will understand the implied exceptions noted above.

Now, let us return to our friends Chad and Zach. In this case, neither Chad nor Zach own the lock that is on Zach's apartment door. Additionally, Zach relies on his apartment door lock in order to secure his residence. This means that if it is damaged, they have now damaged the landlord's property *and* broken part of Zach's security. Chad would be violating both golden rules of lockpicking if he picks the lock. The best course of action would be to wait for the landlord, return to the office for the key, or if absolutely necessary, call a locksmith if the landlord allows for it. Proper, trading locksmiths are insured and bonded, which protects both the locksmith and the property should an issue arise regarding damage.

So, dear reader, we come to the close of our ethical discussion, but not to the end of our journey. I ask that you keep in mind all of the topics that were outlined, and keep in mind the implications of being too cavalier with the knowledge you learn. Remain respectful of others' property and boundaries, and have fun. Don't forget the golden rules:

> *Do not pick locks you do not own.*
> *Do not pick locks you rely on.*

I hope you enjoy the magic of lockpicking as much as I do.

Babak Javadi
Director, The Open Organisation Of Lockpickers

Introduction

I have been interested in lockpicking since I was young. Growing up, I enjoyed works in the "espionage" genre, like *I Spy* and *MacGyver*. I was captivated by James Bond's equipment from the Q Labs, and yearned to possess gadgets that would open doors, reveal the contents of safes, and allow for covert and speedy escape from tight situations. Later generations have grown up with films like *Sneakers* or television shows such as *Burn Notice*, but I suspect that this desire to slip past an adversary's defenses tugs at people's imagination now as much as it did back then.

Another rather universal theme that hasn't changed with time, much to my surprise, is the fact that lockpicking is still assumed by most people to be a skill that is somehow beyond their grasp. Individuals tend to believe that what they see or read about is either embellished to make for better narrative or could only be achieved after a lifetime of practice. Now, it is true that the best lockpickers in the world spend years honing their craft, but the *basic principles* of lockpicking can be learned in a very short time. This, along with the fact that the majority of locks in common use lack even the most basic protection and security-conscious designs, means that virtually anyone can learn this skill and apply it in many situations.

This is most likely not the first book about lockpicking that you may have seen. I own popular works on this topic that have been published as far back as the 1970s, but unfortunately most of these texts either suffer from too little detail or they contain a deluge of overly specific information. This book is not a simple hobbyist pamphlet featuring cursory line art drawings and bullet-point advice, nor is it a massive reference work geared towards the locksmithing industry or law enforcement. This book seeks to strike a balance between those two extremes... providing easy-to-follow, step-by-step lessons, and tutorials that will teach *most* security-conscious people how to open *most* of the locks they are likely to encounter during auditing or assessment work.

The penetration testing field is very large and constantly growing, shifting its focus, and evolving. While the bulk of those working in this sector will almost surely always focus on remote testing of networks and applications, more and more companies are realizing that to properly assess their security posture, "blended" attacks are superior. Most security auditing companies, large and small, have started adding some physical security aspect to their assessment packages. These corporations realize that including an on-site attack replicates real-world threats more genuinely and offers a more dramatic impact to the client when results are shown. To better serve this emerging need, major auditing firms will either attempt to retrain existing personnel with this type of knowledge or they will hire additional teams of individuals who have read books like this and are well-versed in this knowledge.

Being able to social-engineer your way into a target facility is one thing, but just how much can you accomplish once you're inside? That is the mission of *Practical Lock Picking*... to educate penetration testers and incorporate an additional level of expertise into their repertoire of skills.

Fundamentals of pin tumbler and wafer locks

INFORMATION IN THIS CHAPTER

- Pin tumbler locks
- Wafer locks

While there are a multitude of lock designs on the market today, produced by many different manufacturers, the bulk of these offerings are not in widespread use. Nearly all of the locks that you are likely to encounter on a day-to-day basis stem from just a few basic varieties, and the mechanisms inside of all of these devices operate in almost the exact same manner. If you can understand the basics of just a few styles of locks, I'm confident in suggesting that you should be able to open with great ease at least three quarters of the locks you're likely to encounter... even more, as you become more skilled with time.

The overwhelming majority of locks that are in use today, particularly in North America, are either pin tumbler locks or wafer locks. A handful of other designs are prevalent in certain international regions. Lever locks, for example, are of an older design originating in the 17th century with keys that tend to be larger and their operation more cumbersome than more recent designs. Such locks are a common sight in Europe, central Asia, and parts of South America. Rotating disk mechanisms are popular in northern Europe and parts of the Pacific Rim, while some locks in Austria and Japan feature magnetic components. However, in all cases—even in the regions outside of North America—it should be understood that these designs are usually not nearly as prominent as basic pin tumbler locks and wafer locks, particularly as far as penetration testing is concerned.

Typical office doors, desk drawers, filing cabinets, and access panels will usually be equipped by default with lower quality locks because they are the easiest to mass produce, the simplest to service, and the most economical to replace or rekey should the need arise. Until furniture manufacturers and hardware stores cease ordering bulk shipments of locks with low production costs and lax quality standards, we are likely to continue encountering them for a very long time.

PIN TUMBLER LOCKS

The style of lock with which the majority of people are most familiar is the pin tumbler design. I realize that many of you may already be somewhat aware of this hardware (and, indeed, diagrams and photographs of all shapes and sizes seem to abound on the internet and in other printed works), but I feel it would be helpful for us to analyze this mechanism briefly, from the ground up, in order to properly understand how it functions and how it can be exploited.

Practical Lock Picking. DOI: 10.1016/B978-1-59749-611-7.00001-5

Pin tumbler locks come in many forms and styles and can be incorporated into hardware that appears in a number of different shapes. Take a look at the locks in Figures 1.1–1.3.

While each lock has clearly a very different form factor, all three function with a traditional pin tumbler mechanism that is operated by means of a simple "blade" style key, shown in Figure 1.4, the likes of which you have seen multiple times before.

The pin tumbler mechanism is one of the oldest lock designs in existence and is still widely used today. Let's take a closer look at how the components of these locks are made and assembled, paying particular attention to how the lock attempts to hold itself shut without the key present. There are two primary large pieces that comprise the bulk of a pin tumbler lock: the housing and the plug. These are the two items that can easily be seen from an exterior perspective and are thus the most understood. We will now walk through the manner in which these two segments are fabricated and how they fit together.

The plug

The plug of a pin tumbler lock is constructed from a cylindrical billet typically made of brass, although occasionally steel is used in high-quality models. Often the first feature to be added, after the metal is cut to the requisite length, is a small divot in what will become the front face of the plug. This helps to seat and align the key during user operation. See Figure 1.5 for a better understanding of how we shall look upon the various components of lock hardware. On the left is a frontal view, what the user would typically see from a straightforward perspective. On the right of the diagrams in Figures 1.5–1.12, we see a perspective from the side.

FIGURE 1.1

A padlock featuring an embedded pin tumbler mechanism.

FIGURE 1.2

A doorknob featuring a key-in-knob pin tumbler core.

FIGURE 1.3

A deadbolt featuring a pin tumbler lock in a mortise cylinder.

FIGURE 1.4

Blade style keys, which feature bitting cuts along their thin edge. Many well-known manufacturers' keys can be identified simply by the shape of the key's bow.

FIGURE 1.5

A blank plug featuring the key-seating divot, ready for milling.

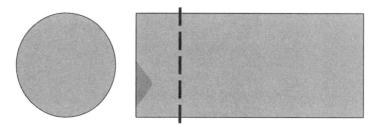

FIGURE 1.6

The left side of the diagrams in this figure to 1.12 will begin to focus on a cross-section slightly inward from the exterior front facing surface of the lock.

Given that the bulk of what concerns us takes place further inside of the lock, we will begin to focus our "straight forward" view (on the left side of these diagrams) further inward. In Figures 1.6–1.12, that image will correlate to a cross-section of the plug (or the lock as a whole) approximately 5 mm inward from the front face.

The plug will be milled with a small lip around the front-facing edge. This serves a dual purpose, in that it prevents the plug from sliding inward through the lock housing and at the same time

FIGURE 1.7

The milled lip at the front of a plug. Note how our "front perspective" on the left side has reduced in size slightly, since we are focusing our attention on a cross-section approximately 5 mm inward from the front face.

FIGURE 1.8

The milled notch in the rear of the plug which will later accommodate a retaining clip. Some lock styles utilize a screw-on threaded end cap instead.

FIGURE 1.9

The keyway has now been milled into the plug. Note that it often extends fully through the bottom of the plug. This will come into play later when we discuss picking techniques and tool placement in Chapter 2.

precluding a potential attacker's insertion of material that could penetrate the front of the lock and interfere with the operation of the pin tumblers within.

It is quite common for this front milling process to be more intricate, involving additional ridges or deeper grooves. Again, this is to prevent pieces of thin metal or other tools from being inserted and worked into the depths of the lock from the outside.

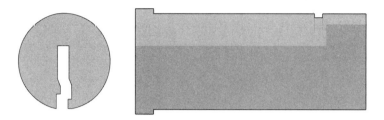

FIGURE 1.10

Some additional milling has been cut into the rear of the plug in order to accommodate a tailpiece.

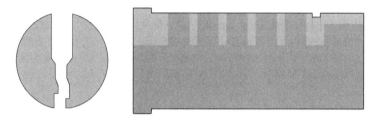

FIGURE 1.11

Five pin chambers have been milled into the plug. Our cross-section (on the left side of this diagram) is still focused on an area approximately 5 mm inward from the front face and thus is showing the first pin chamber as well as the keyway milling.

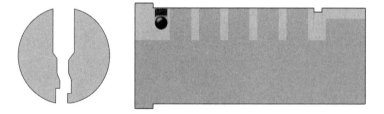

FIGURE 1.12

From the side perspective of our lock plug (on the right half of this diagram), we see the additional hole drilled in front of the pin chambers. It has been filled with both a steel ball bearing and a ceramic block.

In addition to this front lip, the rear section of the plug is also typically milled with either a grooved notch or given a threaded end to accommodate a retaining clip or screw cap, respectively. While threading is typically produced at the end of the process, a clip notch can often appear at this time as represented in Figure 1.8.

The next component to be milled is the keyway. The shape of the slot for the key is called the keyway profile. The primary reason for using more than a simple rectangular slot is the need to help seat and align the key as it is inserted into the lock. The curvature present in nearly all keyways results in protrusions of metal (called wards) that align with deeper cuts and bends on the key. These help keep the key level raised to the appropriate height during operation.

The warding created in the design of a keyway has additional function. As we will see in Chapter 4, the more complicated the curvature of the keyway profile, the more the wards will potentially interfere with the usage of picks, snap guns, and other tools that could potentially be used in attacking a lock.

A third consideration for manufacturers when designing a keyway profile is also one of intellectual property protection. If a specific pattern is unique and unprecedented, the lock manufacturer will enjoy copyright protection of this "new design" for a period of 20 years. This right is typically leveraged not for the prevention of knockoff or copycat *locks* but is in fact used by hardware manufacturers to prevent the availability of unauthorized *key blanks* in the open market. When a design is still relatively new, vendors can claim in the market that their locks incorporate "restricted keyways" for which no widespread supply of blanks is available to third parties.

As you may have seen when having a key duplicated at a hardware store, the large racks or drawers of uncut blank keys are not typically filled with name-brand components. Kwikset and Schlage may be among the most common logos stamped on our locks in North America, but take a look at the actual keys in your pocket. If I were a betting man, I'd wager that many (if not all) of them are embossed with names like Ilco or Hy-Ko (or bear no markings whatsoever). This is because manufacturers of locksmithing components and supplies now primarily handle the production and sale of blank keys to most hardware stores, strip mall kiosks, and key copying centers. While this often results in a savings in cost (passed on to consumers, who can typically copy a key nowadays for one to two dollars), the flood of "unauthorized" key blanks across the market can have security implications.

A number of tactics for defeating a lock are feasible only if the attacker has a supply of blank keys that can be inserted into the keyway. Bump keying and impressioning are two such methods of attack. (Impressioning is a bit beyond the scope of this work, but bump keying will be discussed in Chapter 5.) Even more basic is the risk of unauthorized copies of keys being made without permission. While it is possible to stamp "Do Not Duplicate" onto the bow of a key, this direction is routinely ignored. . . particularly by non-locksmiths.

NOTE

If you have a key that you wish to copy but which has been stamped "Do Not Duplicate," the easiest tactic I have found is to purchase a slip-on "key identifier" cover. These are typically made of rubber and sold in small packs, often in assorted colors. Placing one over the head of the key (perhaps with a dot or two of strong resin or plastic epoxy to prevent its removal) and marking some innocuous label there (i.e., "Grandma's Garden Shed") will often dissuade close scrutiny, even from established locksmiths. I've even made splotches of paint in the right place and once said I was from a school that had just hired a new art teacher who needed a key to the closet where we keep the craft supplies locked up. The locksmith barely noticed that he was cutting a key for a high-security padlock.

At this stage of production, the keyway is typically milled into the plug blank. I have seen this done in person at the Evva factory in Austria and it's an astonishing process. A large pneumatic ram forces the plugs along a track, exposing them to a series of fixed blades in an ornate and intricately arranged jig. As the plugs pass each blade, the slot for the keyway grows deeper and wider and more intricate. The whole process takes mere seconds (Figure 1.9).

Often, additional milling and cutting takes place at the rear end of the plug, in order to accommodate and interface with tail pieces or cams (Figure 1.10). These are the components of the lock that actually interact directly with the bolt or latch mechanism which is holding a door or drawer shut.

Remember, it's not a lock's job to hold something *shut*. You can easily prevent someone from, say, accessing a particular room of your house by applying brick and mortar to the doorway. That will surely keep unwanted people out, right? What is the problem with such a solution? The answer, of course, is that such a solid wall of stone isn't the best thing to have if you're also concerned with *allowing authorized people in*. That is what locks attempt to do for us... they assist in giving otherwise robust security *a means of quickly, easily, and reliably opening* when necessary. It is our deadbolts, our padlock shackles, and other similar hardware that actually provide the means by which things *remain shut*. Our locks are mechanisms that simply *trigger the release* of the said deadbolts and shackles at (we hope) the appropriate time.

There are a number of attacks that we will discuss in Chapter Five which focus on ignoring the lock mechanism entirely as one seeks to simply interact directly with the latch or bolt hardware deeper within the door. Many of these attacks focus on weaknesses in the way that the lock core (often, the rear of the plug specifically) interacts with a tailpiece or cam.

NOTE

If you disassemble a lock, pay particular attention to the means by which the turning of the plug translates into turning of other components deeper inside the device. You might just notice a means by which force can be applied that opens a door without ever having to turn the plug at all!

The final stage of fabrication of the plug (usually) is the drilling of pin chambers. These are often drilled from above, all to a uniform depth, and equidistant from one another. That is by no means a hard-and-fast rule, however. We will discuss some unique designs in Chapters Five and Six that vary from this norm. However, one feature that tends to be uniform in almost all locks is the alignment of the pin chambers *from front to rear*. Ideally, these chambers will be drilled in a perfectly straight line... but as we will see in the following chapter, that is, unfortunately a very difficult thing to achieve with utmost precision (Figure 1.11).

There are some additional features that may be added to plugs by certain manufacturers. It is not uncommon for small additional chambers or holes to be fabricated near the front face of the plug. These are subsequently filled with ball bearings or ceramic inserts that can frustrate and impede drilling attacks. Such features are shown in Figure 1.12.

The other large component from which the core of a lock is constructed is the housing. This contains the plug and all other associated smaller elements such as pins and springs. Much as we did with the plug, let's take a look at how the housing is constructed in order to properly understand its function and role within the lock (Figure 1.13).

One of the first components to be milled into a lock's housing is often the large, central bore that will accommodate the plug. It is typically fabricated straight through with an even diameter (see Figure 1.14).

An additional ridge is milled into the housing at the very front of the bore opening, to interface with the lip on the front edge of the lock's plug. Figure 1.15 shows this ridge from both the front and side view.

Pin chambers are then drilled into the housing from the top surface. As with the fabrication of the plug, every attempt is made to ensure that these chambers are uniform and that they align perfectly from front to rear. These chambers appear in Figure 1.16. As with our discussion of the fabrication of a lock's plug, the figure's "front view perspective" on the left side of the diagram now reflects a point approximately 5 mm in from the lock's face.

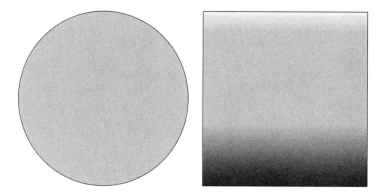

FIGURE 1.13

Much like the plug of a lock, the housing is often manufactured from a raw, solid billet of metal. Harder materials including various grades of steel are more common in fabricating the housing. A pin tumbler lock housing can come in many shapes. Some are pear shaped (as with many European lock cylinders and, to some degree, "key in knob" style cores used around the world), while others are larger, more regular forms such as ovals or circles. In these diagrams, a simple round shape is shown for simplicity. One aspect that is always universal, however, is the round bore that is cut through them in order to accommodate the plug and allow for its rotation.

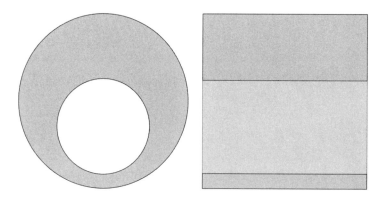

FIGURE 1.14

The plug bore has been milled through the housing. As with our earlier diagrams in Figures 1.5–1.12, the left side of the figure shows the work piece from a frontal perspective, while the right side of the figure gives a side-view perspective, incorporating some cutaway elements to the diagram. Also as before, the left side of the figure will focus on a cross section approximately half a centimeter deep into the lock.

The two main components of the lock are now complete and ready for assembly. The plug is inserted into the housing from front to rear, since the milled lip and ridge prevent it from passing through in any other direction. Upon complete insertion, all the drilled pin chambers of the plug and the housing should line up equally, as seen in Figure 1.17.

The plug is now typically secured by the previously mentioned retaining clip or screw cap. Figure 1.18 shows a retaining clip style of assembly.

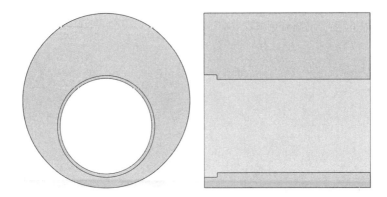

FIGURE 1.15

The ridge milled into the front of the plug bore.

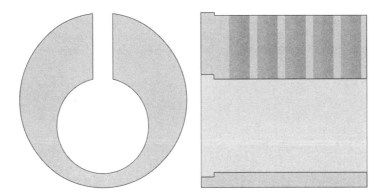

FIGURE 1.16

Pin chambers are drilled vertically into the housing. Often, this step incorporates some milling or flattening of the very top of the housing.

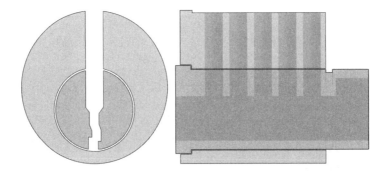

FIGURE 1.17

The plug has been fully inserted, aligning all its pin chambers with those that are found in the housing.

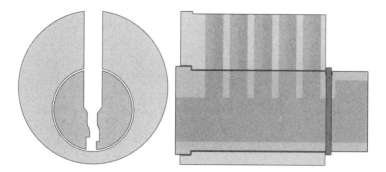

FIGURE 1.18

The plug is held securely by the addition of a retaining clip. It cannot slip back forward and out of the plug, nor can it pass further inward due to the milling of the front surfaces.

The lock is now ready to be pinned. The pins are fabricated in a very rudimentary process by means of milling increasingly tightening cuts into pieces of very thin bar stock. Brass and steel are the most common materials for pins. (Again, the quality of the lock and its overall cost are considerations that dictate, during the design process, what metal is to be used.)

The pins in a lock are almost always of uniform diameter, but will vary in length. Some pins will be almost perfectly cylindrical, save for slight rounded edges at the top and bottom, while others are quite pointed on one end. There are advantages and disadvantages to each design. Occasionally, pins are color-coded during manufacturing in order to denote their size. This can be a benefit in helping a locksmith sort his or her pin kit should it ever become slightly disorganized. However, some also view the coloring of pins as a security risk, since persons could, in theory, peer into a lock from the outside using specialized tools like a locksmith scope or an otoscope from a doctor's office and observe the pin colors, potentially gaining insight into what sizes of pins have been used in the lock.

The first pins to be inserted into a lock during assembly are the key pins. They are so named because they ride against the user's key during normal operation of the lock.

NOTE

You will occasionally hear people refer to these pins as "bottom pins" since they often sit "lower" in the lock than their counterpart components. However, this is a very geographically specific term. It is the norm for locks in North America (and some other parts of the world) to be installed with the pin stacks extending above the plug, but this is by no means necessary. Most locks in Europe, for example, are installed in exactly the opposite way, with pin chambers drilled in what could be called the "bottom" of the plug and the housing. In such lock installations, the key pins actually appear to be *on top* of most other components in the lock core. In truth, it is helpful to not think of the lock with these restrictive terms. Hence, this work will always make reference to key pins and their counterparts, which we will introduce shortly, driver pins. Similarly, when addressing tool placement, which we will do in the next chapter, it is helpful to speak of the "outside" or the "center" of the plug as opposed to terms like "top" and "bottom" that are equally nebulous. Physical security hardware appears in all parts of the world installed in both the "pin up" and "pin down" manner and I invite you to join me in attempting to always adopt neutral terminology when speaking about locks and their components.

In the interest of uniformity throughout this work, however, we will continue to look at locks from the "North American" perspective in diagrams and figures, showing pin chambers that are fabricated in the "top" of the plug and the housing.

The key pins are installed in the lock and pass completely through the drilled chambers of the housing, coming to rest entirely within the plug.

As you are able to see in Figure 1.19, the pins are not all of the same height. The differing sizes of the pins in a lock correspond directly to the different cuts that are seen when observing a key. That will become clearer in moments. Before we discuss how the pins allow a lock to *open*, let's first continue with the assembly of this example lock and demonstrate how some pins keep the lock *closed*.

After the key pins have been installed in the lock, the next phase of assembly involves the insertion of driver pins into each chamber. These will drop partway into the plug, but in each chamber they should protrude out into the housing of the lock, as shown in Figure 1.20.

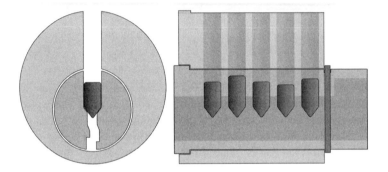

FIGURE 1.19

An assembled lock that has had key pins inserted into each chamber. If you focus your attention exclusively upon the right half of the diagram in Figure 1.19 (the side view), it may not be immediately clear what prevents the pins from "falling further through" the keyway. However, notice on the left side of the diagram (the front-facing view) how the wide pin chambers are milled only halfway into the plug. The rest of the milling in the plug (the keyway) is too narrow to accommodate the pins, preventing them from passing downward any further.

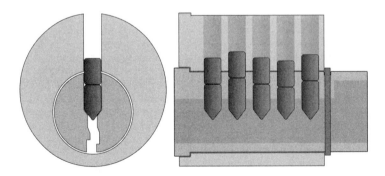

FIGURE 1.20

The lock has had driver pins installed.

Note how, at this particular moment, we have now prevented any means by which the plug can turn. With driver pins sticking through the plug and the housing in each chamber, the plug is effectively immobilized. This is the means by which the components of a pin tumbler lock hold it shut when no key is present.

Much like with key pins, the driver pins are sometimes called by a number of other names... some of which derive from somewhat geographically narrow-minded points of view. You will occasionally hear people refer to these as "top pins," but such a term has obvious limitations in the context of international locks where, as we discussed, the entire apparatus is installed and operates from what we in North America would call an "upside-down" perspective. I have also heard driver pins referred to by other terms, such as "set pins" or even "binding pins." The former term is somewhat obscure and little-used, and the latter term really applies only to the process of manipulating or picking the lock. In all of this text, the term driver pin will be the only one used. You are free to adopt your own nomenclature, but again I will stress the usefulness of this term, which I value for its neutral nature and instant comprehension by parties near and far.

The final phase of assembling the lock comes with the insertion of springs into each pin chamber, finalizing the creation of pin stacks. The whole affair is then topped by some manner of cap or retention material (Figure 1.21).

The lock cylinder is now fully assembled and ready for installation within a deadbolt, a doorknob, a padlock, or any number of other hardware items that could require it.

NOTE

The actual means by which the pin chambers are topped varies a great deal from one manufacturer to the next. Some will use a small plate of metal that either clips or slides into position but which is easily removable at a later time to allow the lock to be serviced and rekeyed with ease. Others will top the lock's chambers with plugs of metal. This process is quick and provides a very robust enclosure for the pin stacks, but makes servicing at a later time a much more involved process. It is often still possible to disassemble and reconfigure such locks, but additional tools (such as a plug follower) and a higher degree of skill are necessary. The noted Locksport enthusiast Schuyler Towne started the "Lock Field Stripping Contest" at the annual DEFCON security convention in the summer of 2007 which pits contestants (both practicing locksmiths and amateur devotees alike) in a race against one another and against a time clock to see who can service such locks the fastest. It's sometimes quite a sight when someone is not careful as pins and springs go flying every which way unexpectedly.

The lock is now totally assembled and ready to be installed in whatever piece of security hardware it is designed to operate. In its current form as we are seeing it in Figure 1.21, this is what would typically be called a lock cylinder or lock core. It would be installed in (and become the crucial component of) a deadbolt, a padlock, a door handle, etc. Terms can get slightly confusing, given that the word "lock" can represent all of these things, depending on the context. It is not improper to refer to the mechanism that holds shut your front door (the entire mechanism) as simply a "lock"; nor is it wrong of merchants with shelves of prepackaged deadbolts to call these wares "locks" in their entirety.

To avoid confusion, this book will always seek to use as specific a term as possible and to reference accompanying diagrams or photographs. In the most general sense, an analysis of the following terms and their definitions may serve to clarify matters somewhat.

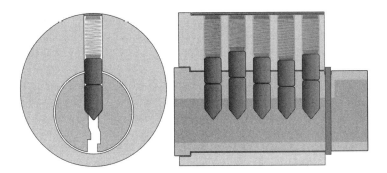

FIGURE 1.21

Springs have been added to each chamber and the housing has been topped with a plate of metal that holds everything in place.

- *Lock*—any hardware device that remains in a fixed position until operated by a user with the appropriate physical token (typically a key) or correct combination.
- *Lock cylinder*—the core component of a physical security hardware product which accepts either a physical token or a combination input and then allows turning or pressing by the user; this turning or pressing actuates a mechanism that enables the encompassing hardware product to open or yield in some manner.
- *Padlock*—a physical security hardware product in which the lock cylinder is enclosed in a force-resistant body and which features a shackle (typically made of metal) that serves to hold shut some other piece of hardware external to the entire unit. (i.e., a hasp, a chain, or adjacent plates of metal) Many padlock shackles are U-shaped and protrude conspicuously from the unit's body, while others are straight or only slightly bent rods that are contained partially or wholly within the lock body. Padlocks may feature a removable lock cylinder, or the operating mechanism may be fully integrated into the body and not easily serviced or replaced.
- *Deadbolt*—a physical security hardware product that contains a lock cylinder, which when operated by the user, interacts with a solid rod or flange mechanism that *does not rely on spring pressure* to maintain its position when at rest. Deadbolts typically secure doors or other rights-of-way and are designed to be robust against most forcing and bypassing attacks.
- *Locking door handle*—not to be confused with a deadbolt, some door knobs and door handles incorporate a lock cylinder as part of their functionality. Typically, however, such door handles attempt to maintain a closed stature by means of spring-loaded latches. These latches are able to be withdrawn by means of turning the door handle. The lock cylinder, if one is present, does not interact directly with the *latch* but instead provides some means (often rudimentary) for preventing the *handle* from turning. Thus, in many instances it is possible to spring open this style of latch without ever interacting with the lock or turning the door handle. It is also quite common for these devices to be of weaker construction overall than deadbolt assemblies, and given a direct application of enough torque upon the handle, they can frequently be broken and forced to turn regardless of the lock cylinder contained within, thus operating the latch and opening the door.

Pin tumbler lock operation

Now that we have seen how pin tumbler locks are constructed and assembled, let us examine how they function. Those who have been following along closely may already begin to understand how the pins and key interact in a typical lock and may already be picturing what is about to be described. Just to keep our terminology straight, let's examine a typical key in further detail, as shown by Figure 1.22.

When a user inserts the proper key into a lock, the key pins ride along the edge of the key's blade (see Figure 1.23). The blade travels into the lock until the key comes to rest either by its tip encountering the rear of the keyway or by the key's shoulder coming to rest on the front face of the lock. Locks that function in this manner are called tip-stopped or shoulder-stopped, respectively.

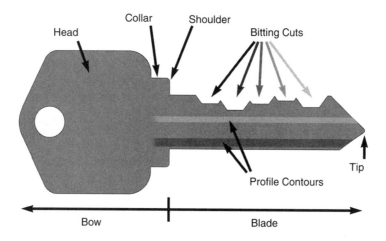

FIGURE 1.22

A key that would operate a typical pin tumbler lock.

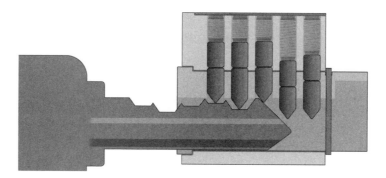

FIGURE 1.23

A key in the process of being inserted into a pin tumbler lock.

Upon complete insertion in the lock, most (or, much more typically, all) of the blade of the key will be within the plug, while the bow of the key remains outside, allowing the user to apply turning pressure in the necessary direction. The bow of the key will typically be comprised almost entirely of the key's head, although in some models of lock (particularly those where the keyway is recessed in some manner, as with certain automobile ignitions), the key will have a distinctly longer collar; this serves to extend the key's head out further from the lock mechanism. The user grips the key by the head; its shape is typically large enough to aid in the manual application of torque as well as being a distinct enough shape and design to help differing manufacturers' products be rapidly identified at a glance.

When the proper key has been fully inserted into a lock, a unique phenomenon can be observed... all of the pin stacks will have been pushed into exactly the right position such that the split between the key pins and driver pins (known as the pin shear line) will be aligned across the edge of the plug, in effect becoming one with the plug's own shear line. When the pin stacks are all in this perfect position, there is nothing obstructing the plug from turning. This alignment is represented in Figure 1.24.

It is a common misconception that pins (particularly the key pins) within a lock can come from the manufacturer in a wide array of varying sizes. In fact, the key pin sizes (and the corresponding depths of the bitting cuts on the blade of the key) only appear in regular, evenly spaced intervals. I have never encountered a manufacturer who utilized more than nine or ten distinct sizes of key pin in this simple design of lock (and thus, their keys only featured nine possible distinct depths of cut). Many manufacturers fabricate their whole line of lock products with as little as five or six possible bitting depths.

These bitting depths can be measured and are frequently described by manufacturers by the use of a bitting code, which locksmiths can use to fabricate new keys even if the original keys are not present. The numbers in a bitting code correspond to how deeply a particular cut should be made into a key at a given position. The larger the number, the deeper the cut. Thus, on a blank key, a "zero cut" would not involve the removal of any metal at all in that position. A "one cut" is just a slight

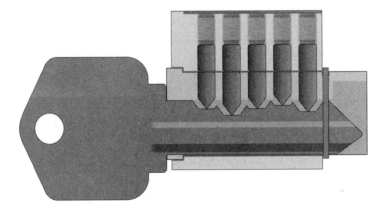

FIGURE 1.24

A key fully inserted into its lock. Notice how all the pin stacks shear lines are at the exact edge of the plug, allowing for its rotation.

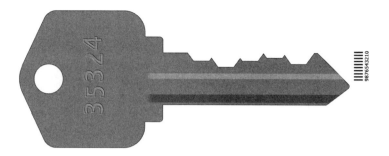

FIGURE 1.25

A typical blade style key shown next to a scale representing possible cut depths. Note the bitting code stamped on to the bow of the key. This is a very common practice.

cut, while a "five cut" would be considerably deeper. On the bitting code of a typical pin tumbler lock like the one we have been considering in these diagrams, the numbers represent the cuts made from the shoulder proceeding towards the tip. Look at our hypothetical key in Figure 1.25.

Notice how clearly one can gain a sense of the regular, even intervals between the cut depths (the vertical depth of the cuts into the blade, not their horizontal spacing apart... which is also even). This key has cuts in all five pin positions, so there are no "zero cuts." Similarly, if one views the small scale shown to the right of Figure 1.25, you will see that there are also no "one cuts" either. The most shallow cut anywhere on this key is in the fourth pin position, where the key is cut to a depth of two. Looking along the blade of the key, proceeding from the shoulder out to the tip, we can see cuts appearing in depths of three, five, three, two, and four. Not coincidentally, those are exactly the same numbers stamped on the bow of the key. This is a very common practice.

Take a look at some of the keys you might have in your possession. How many of them have numbers stamped on the bow? How many appear to be the straight bitting codes shown completely in the clear?

NOTE

While bitting codes can be a boon to locksmiths, they also make acquisition of knowledge concerning a lock's internal construction rapid, if not instantly, possible. The stamping of codes on keys is quite common. Sometimes a blind code is used instead of the bitting code, which corresponds only to an entry in a lookup table or reference book. Such resources are ostensibly only supposed to be possessed by locksmiths, but this type of information has a way of leaking out into the world. Still, being mindful of what is stamped on your keys is a good idea. It is not advisable to let your keys dangle exposed on your belt or lie unguarded in full view. Keep your keys in a private location, away from casual glances, and consider making duplicates (without any markings) of any keys that have clear bitting codes stamped upon them.

When all of the pin stacks in a lock have been pushed to the proper position (when all of the shear lines are aligned with the edge of the plug), the lock can be opened (see Figures 1.26 and 1.27).

While the differences between pin sizes can seem quite small (often the increment between cut depths is one millimeter or less), even a misalignment of this size in a single pin stack can sometimes be enough to prevent the plug from turning. Consider the examples in Figures 1.28 and 1.29: a key

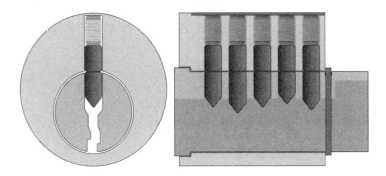

FIGURE 1.26

All pin stacks are at the proper height to align the shear line. No pins are binding and the plug is free to be turned.

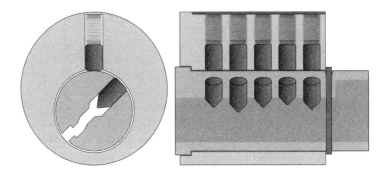

FIGURE 1.27

The plug is being turned. In this particular case, it is being turned in a clockwise direction, from the user's perspective.

with a bitting cut in one position that is a single value too deep, and a key with a bitting cut that is a single value too shallow.

The cut in position number two, the second one inward from the face of the lock (the pin stack which is second from the left in this diagram), is too deep, and the corresponding pin stack is hanging too low. The result is that the driver pin is binding in the shear line, preventing the plug from turning. On this key, the bitting is cut to a code of 36324 as opposed to 35324. That one difference is enough to make the key not function.

In Figure 1.29 we have another example of a nearly perfect (but yet still nonfunctional) key. The cut in position number two, the second one inward from the face of the lock (the pin stack which is second from the left in this diagram), is too shallow, and the corresponding pin stack is lifted too high. The result is that the key pin is binding in the shear line, preventing the plug from turning. On this key, the bitting is cut to a code of 34324 as opposed to 35324. Again, this is a very small deviation from the proper bitting, but it is still enough to interfere with the operation of the lock.

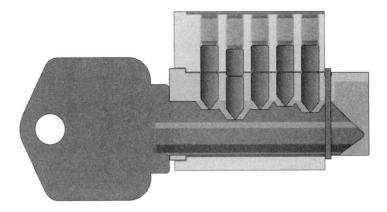

FIGURE 1.28

Here we see a key that has properly aligned nearly all of the pin stacks, save one. The cut in position number two is too deep.

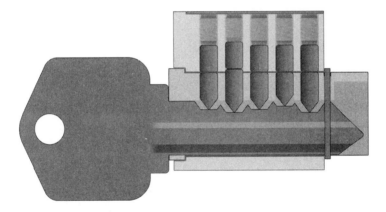

FIGURE 1.29

Here we see a key that has properly aligned nearly all of the pin stacks, save one. The cut in position number two is too shallow.

Speaking of minor variations of a key and how they may or may not affect the operation of a lock, consider for a moment the small points of metal that protrude upward from the blade in between the flat lands of each bitting cut. These are a natural result of the size and shape of the cutting wheel and the distances by which each bitting cut are separated from one another. The resultant "points" that remain in between the cuts on the blade of a key can provide a satisfying series of perceived "clicks" as the blade rides into the keyway (as each pin stack passes across the ridges), but the points themselves are not a crucial element of the lock's easy and successful operation. In theory, one could file or grind down all of those extra pointed segments on the blade of the key (taking care to not disturb the specific depths of each bitting cut on their flat middle section) and such a key would still be functional. It would, however, appear somewhat odd (see Figure 1.30).

Such a key wouldn't produce as many noticeable "clicks" as it did before, but there is no real reason why it would fail to function adequately when being used in a lock under ideal circumstances (see Figure 1.31). The bitting surfaces would still push the pin stacks to the requisite positions and there's even the possibility that this type of key would reduce potential wear and tear on the pins themselves.

Speaking of wear and tear, however, there exists one potential point of difficulty with the prospect of modifying one's keys in this fashion. Most of the materials used in the fabrication of a lock's

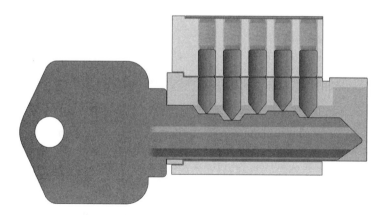

FIGURE 1.30

The same key that we first saw in Figure 1.24, after having its "points" filed down. This leaves a relatively flat, smooth surface across the entire blade edge. Note the lack of any conspicuous rise out by the tip of the blade, as the bitting depth of the last position can be maintained all the way out beyond the tip.

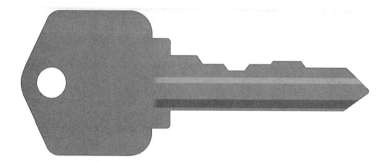

FIGURE 1.31

A key with the sharp points removed from in between the bitting surfaces. This key will still function as far as opening the lock is concerned.

components (particularly the more intricate pieces such as pins and usually even keys) are soft metals, chiefly brass. Over time, through repeated uses, these metals can deform. The tips of pins (particularly key pins) can become worn down, and small pits or valleys can begin to develop on the bitting surfaces of a key.

Many of you have no doubt had a key that stopped working reliably over the years. That is because the effects of wear and tear have reduced the key's ability to accurately line up all of the pin stacks at the shear line uniformly. Conditions such as these are represented in Figure 1.32. When this happens, considerable effort is sometimes required by the user to jiggle or cajole the lock into operating.

There are two things that users often attempt to do when operating a lock with a key that is past its prime: they will jiggle the key up and down or attempt to wiggle it in and out of the lock slightly while attempting to turn the plug. The former technique does not produce a great deal of movement, given that the warding of the keyway greatly limits how much an inserted key can move up or down.

Pulling the key slightly outward, however, often produces better results. Why is this? It has to do with those leftover ridges that are in between the bitting cuts on a freshly made key. Observe the behavior of the pin stacks seen in Figure 1.33 as a key is withdrawn slightly from the plug.

While the removal (by means of filing or grinding) of the pointy ridges in between the bitting cuts on one's key may make operation a bit more smooth (and potentially may reduce how much poking into your thigh that you feel from within your pocket), I do not feel it is always the best course of action to modify your keys in this manner. While slightly rounding off the sharpest edge at the tops of each little ridge might help to reduce the stress on your lock's pins and make for smoother operation, that's about as far as I'd go when it comes to modifying keys for everyday use.

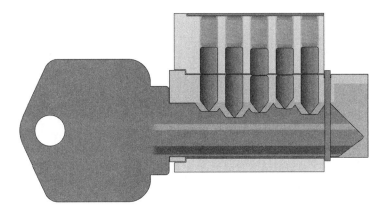

FIGURE 1.32

A key that is deformed through repeated use. Note that the bitting cuts in the third and fourth position from the left have started to slope downward into small "valleys" that cause the third and fourth pin stack in this lock to be positioned slightly too low. The driver pins in those two chambers are ever so slightly caught in the shear line of the plug. Considerable effort would be needed to get the plug to turn in this condition.

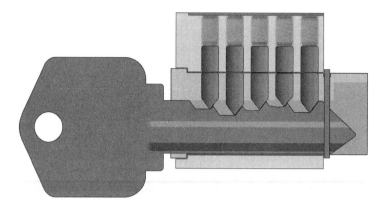

FIGURE 1.33

A malfunctioning key, slightly withdrawn from the lock that a user is attempting to operate. The pointed ridges of metal on the key blade that occur in between the original bitting cuts are capable of providing just enough additional lifting that the two problematic pin stacks are now in a position to better allow for rotation of the plug.

WAFER LOCKS

The second most common style of lock that is encountered in the real world, particularly in business environments, is the wafer lock (see Figure 1.34). These seem to present an interesting puzzle for many training instructors and authors of books. Many wafer locks which come preinstalled in office furniture are so unsophisticated (and, consequently, so trivial to open in most instances) that a number of texts and training classes seem to either skip them entirely or give them just a basic overview treatment, which can be often summarized as, "You just sort of rake them and they pop right open." There are a few manufacturers who produce wafer-based locks of considerable quality that do offer a higher degree of security. The Miwa Company of Japan and the Illinois Lock Company are two such exemplars.

While it is true that most wafer locks are hardly high-security and that they typically pose no significant challenge to anyone attempting covert entry, it is unfair (particularly to those just starting out) to gloss over this topic entirely. These are, after all, the second most common style of lock in use in office buildings, and they are inevitably "protecting" sensitive materials like paperwork, backup media, essential wiring, server racks, and electrical cabinets. For that reason, we will now cover a solid overview of this style of hardware.

Wafer locks are often found in places where a cheap and semieffective means of preventing accidental opening or operating something is necessary. They are typically sourced and implemented by the manufacturers of furniture or other such equipment. For this reason, these preinstalled locks are almost always made *exceedingly* cheaply with low-quality components and *very* loose machining tolerances. And yet, such locks wind up protecting a surprising number of resources that could be considered critical, as seen in Figures 1.35 and 1.36.

FIGURE 1.34

Wafer locks in their most typical form factor.

FIGURE 1.35

A wafer lock on the cover of a surveillance camera.

FIGURE 1.36

A wafer lock on an alarm panel.

Wafer locks are a common sights on access panels (especially those relating to electrical power and circuit breakers) as well as office furniture like desks and filing cabinets. Many automotive locks are wafer locks as well (see Figure 1.37).

Wafer locks are also often employed as electrical switching mechanisms, either completing or breaking a circuit. Sometimes this can be as simple as controlling the lights, thermostat, or exhaust fan in a room where casual passersby shouldn't be able to change the environmental settings. However, equally common is the sight of a wafer lock enabling or disabling an electronic keypad, the override mechanism on a cash register, or (as shown in Figure 1.38) the operating buttons of an elevator.

WARNING

If you need to protect critical areas of your facility, this is *not* a means of achieving that end.

Let's take a closer look at wafer locks to understand how they perform and how they differ from the hardware that we have already examined. The keys of a wafer lock often appear to be quite similar to those of traditional pin tumbler locks. And, if observed directly from their front face, wafer locks can occasionally be hard to identify (see Figure 1.39). After all, like pin tumbler locks, they operate by means of a plug that rotates along a simple axis.

However, an aspect of a wafer lock's construction that differs significantly from a pin tumbler lock is almost immediately apparent when the mechanism is viewed from an off-angle.

FIGURE 1.37

The great bulk of automotive locks are wafer locks as well.

FIGURE 1.38

An elevator using wafer locks to regulate access to certain floors.

FIGURE 1.39

A wafer lock can have the appearance of a pin tumbler lock when viewed from the front. There is a keyway that features on the center of a plug that turns during operation.

The very large tailpiece (known as a cam) that features on the end of the plug can be clearly seen from this angle in Figure 1.40. What *cannot* be seen, however, is any large housing surrounding the plug. Notice in Figure 1.41 how the wafer lock's housing is almost nonexistent. If this were a pin tumbler mechanism, there would have to be a much larger shell containing room for pins, springs, etc.

Wafer lock construction

Wafer locks are constructed and operate in a much simpler and rudimentary manner than pin tumbler locks. Let us now step through the process by which the few components are fabricated and observe how they interact.

> **NOTE**
>
> While the diagrams in Figures 1.42–1.49 will proceed to show how such hardware can be manufactured by drilling and milling, it should be understood that most wafer locks are produced by much cheaper means, such as casting from simple metals or even injection-molding of plastics. Still, to continue the theme established earlier, a step-by-step process will be shown in these diagrams.

It looks quite simplistic, indeed... but once we review the manner in which the plug of a wafer lock is constructed, the functionality should become clear.

While the plug of a wafer lock does incorporate a keyway, there are few similarities with pin tumbler locks beyond that. The milling is far squarer and, as we shall see, the chambers are much thinner and simpler.

FIGURE 1.40

A wafer lock that has been removed from its installation.

FIGURE 1.41

If this were a pin tumbler lock, there would be a larger housing containing pin stacks.

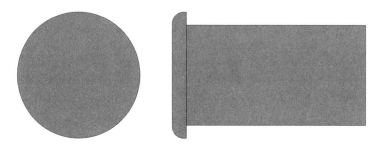

FIGURE 1.42

A wafer lock's housing consists of a simple cylindrical piece, often featuring a lip or collar around the front edge.

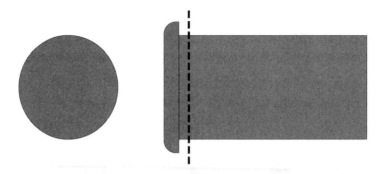

FIGURE 1.43

As with the earlier diagrams in Figures 1.6–1.12 that discussed pin tumbler locks, the cross-section view (appearing on the left side of these figures) will represent a segment of the lock approximately five millimeters inward from the front face.

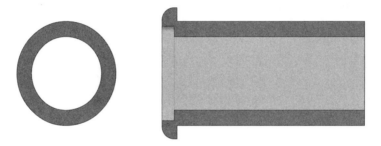

FIGURE 1.44

A wafer lock, like locks seen in the section on the Pin Tumbler design, has a long channel running through the housing to accommodate the plug. An additional milled lip in the front is typical in all models, since plugs are installed from the front and secured in the rear.

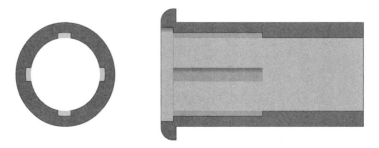

FIGURE 1.45

Channels are created within the walls of the plug, sometimes in just one or two places, but there can be up to four in most typical wafer locks. These channels dictate the positions at which the plug can be held in place and where the key can be removed.

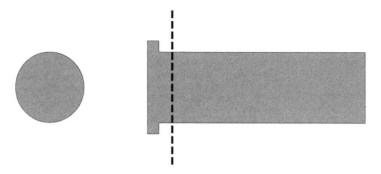

FIGURE 1.46

As with the housing, these diagrams that describe the construction of a wafer lock's plug will incorporate a cross-section view on the left side of the figure. That view will represent an area approximately five millimeters inward from the front face of the lock.

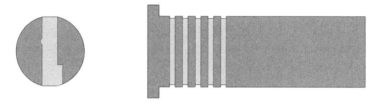

FIGURE 1.47

The thin, square cut chambers in a wafer lock plug.

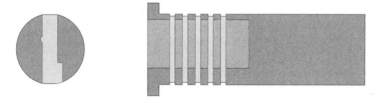

FIGURE 1.48

Even the keyway of a wafer lock tends to be very square and rudimentary.

The plugs milled into a wafer lock do not accommodate rounded components (like the pins of a traditional lock) but instead are fitted only with thin, flat segments of metal... the eponymous wafers.

The means by which a wafer lock's plug is held stationary much of the time, but allowed to rotate easily with the use of a key, come from how the wafers are shaped and installed. Let's first just take a look at a single wafer, installed in the lock, seen in Figure 1.50.

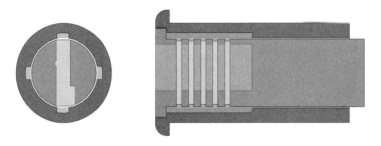

FIGURE 1.49

The plug of a wafer lock inserted into the housing.

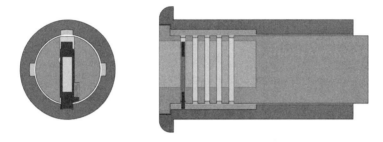

FIGURE 1.50

A wafer has been installed in the first chamber. Spring pressure keeps it pressed to the outer edge of the plug. (From this perspective, one could say that the spring keeps the wafer at a "downward" position.)

When the lock is at rest, the wafer prevents the plug from turning by hanging "down" into the "lower" channel of the housing. Lifting of the wafer makes it clear the lower channel, thus allowing rotation of the plug. However, the lifting cannot be indiscriminate; if raised too far, the wafer's other protruding edge will extend into the "upper" channel, thus blocking movement of the plug.

Wafer lock operation

In order to accommodate keys that have bitting cuts of varying height across the blade, manufacturers produce wafers for their locks that have the central, rectangular hole in differing positions (see Figure 1.51). Thus, the locks can be keyed to various (albeit, rather limited) bitting combinations.

By varying the position of the cut within the wafer, it varies the degree to which the blade of a key will lift the piece of metal. Hence, keys can have a series of discrete cuts. As with pin tumbler locks, however, the possibilities for variation are mechanically quite diverse, but in practice it is rare for wafer locks to have more than half a dozen potential bitting depths on the blade of the key. A fully assembled wafer lock is shown in Figure 1.52. Note the lack of considerable variation in the positions of the key cuts within the wafers themselves.

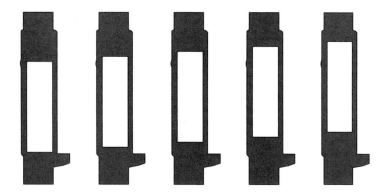

FIGURE 1.51

Various wafers that could be installed in a wafer lock to allow bitting.

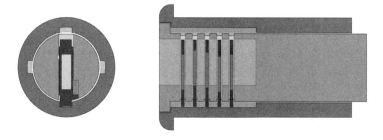

FIGURE 1.52

A wafer lock, fully assembled. Notice the varied positions of the key cuts within the five wafers contained in the plug.

I have said that it is slightly beyond the scope of this work to examine in great detail the tail-pieces or cams on the rear of plugs. Wafer locks tend to be simple enough for us to continue in this vein. The only significant and notable feature that sometimes appears on their tail side is a rotation-limiting bit. Unlike pin tumbler locks—which almost always allow for plug rotation in either direction, limited only by the possible positions of movement of the bolt or release latch or whatever mechanism the lock is operating—a great number of wafer locks incorporate features that limit which direction and how far the plug can rotate regardless of whether the lock is installed or whether the tail piece is contacting anything. This small bumper bit and cam washer system is shown in Figures 1.53–1.55.

One last consideration regarding wafer locks has to do with the manner in which they can be serviced. The bulk of wafer locks on the market fall into one of two categories: locks that cannot easily be disassembled and serviced, and locks whose tail pieces can be unscrewed, which then allows the plug to fall forward out of the housing.

FIGURE 1.53

The rear side of a wafer lock, showing the plug rotation limiter.

FIGURE 1.54

The rear side of a wafer lock, highlighting the notched plug limiting washer.

FIGURE 1.55

The rear side of a wafer lock, highlighting the plug limiting bit on the housing.

NOTE

You should be aware (particularly if you perform any covert entry work during pen testing jobs where time is of the essence and you are concerned about leaving behind detectable or noticeable signs after the fact) that there is a lesser-known type of wafer lock that is not serviced by the removal of a rear screw.

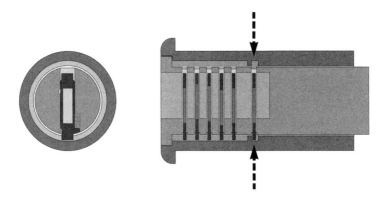

FIGURE 1.56

A wafer lock featuring a "control wafer" deep within the plug. Notice that the forward-perspective cutaway diagram (on the left side of this figure) focuses at a much deeper point than normal: the position of the control wafer.

Believe it or not, occasionally a manufacturer will design a wafer lock that can easily be field stripped and even rekeyed. On rekeyable wafer locks, there is an additional wafer at the far rear position within the plug. While most wafers in a lock are equidistant from one another, often times this special "control wafer" is separated by a greater than normal distance from the rest of the wafer pack (see Figure 1.56). Most users' keys will never reach deep enough into the lock to contact this wafer and it will tend to never be pushed out of its default position, even when the lock is operating.

On such a rekeyable wafer lock, the tailpiece does not screw or fasten directly to the plug, but simply aligns and snaps together by means of a square or hexagonal hole. If the control wafer is lifted (by means of a specialized key that not only acts upon the regular wafer pack, but which is also long enough to reach this last, deepest wafer), then the entire plug is free to slide outward and be removed from the housing. It is then possible to select a different wafer plug and use a similar control key to install it.

I do not know of this feature being used necessarily with great frequency. However, it has some very real implications in the field of covert entry... namely, if you're not careful, you can start out trying to quietly and quickly open, say, a desk drawer and wind up instead with half the lock popping out into your hands or rolling across the floor. The desk can be unlocked if you reach into the large hole that has just appeared, but now you have the problem of the ejected plug with which to contend. Such a matter is easily resolved, however, and with some dedicated pressure in the right spot (lifting the control wafer just the right amount), you can slip the plug back in and it should lock into its original position.

Better wafer locks

Not *all* wafer locks are this rudimentary. Most (indeed, I would say almost all) wafer locks offer little in the way of security; however, there are a few standouts which we have encountered that truly break from this trend. Shane Lawson pointed out to me that during his time in Japan, he often encountered wafer locks protecting homes and offices. Produced by the Miwa company there in the Land of the Rising Sun, they are anything but weak or cheap. Also impressive, due the complexity of wafers and the sheer number installed, is the Duo lock produced by the Illinois Lock Company (see Figure 1.57). I have also observed elevator control locks featuring an atypically large number of wafers (see Figure 1.58).

FIGURE 1.57

Two pairs of wafers (left) and the entire wafer pack (right) in a Duo lock. This is not your average wafer lock at all.

Courtesy of datagram

FIGURE 1.58

A wafer lock produced by the American Lock company which I found being used as a control switch in a Dover elevator cab. While it doesn't have quite as many wafers as the Duo lock shown in Figure 1.57, it is still impressive compared to an "average" wafer lock.

SUMMARY

This chapter has exposed you to the inner components of the most typical styles of locks in use today. By seeing how the pieces of pin tumbler locks and wafer locks are fabricated, you are better suited to understand how and where imperfections can develop during manufacturing.

It is these small flaws, which we will discuss in the next chapter, that make picking possible.

The basics of picking: Exploiting weaknesses

2

INFORMATION IN THIS CHAPTER

- Exploiting weaknesses in locks
- Picking with a lifting technique
- Picking with a raking technique
- Using jiggler tools

Nearly all mechanical locks have weaknesses that make them susceptible to picking attacks. This chapter will examine the types of flaws that are commonly found in the locks people rely on day in and day out. Various techniques for exploiting these flaws will then be revealed.

EXPLOITING WEAKNESSES IN LOCKS

We have discussed the manner in which the most typical locks used in our world are assembled and how they function under normal conditions. It is essential to understand, however, that "normal" conditions are often anything but. There are a number of ways that locks can fail to operate as their designers expected. Small imperfections in the manufacturing process, unanticipated interactions between adjacent components, and even simply too much space into which unauthorized tools can be inserted... all of these factors can cause a lock to be easily picked or bypassed.

Manufacturing imperfections

Companies in the lock industry are similar to other enterprises in the realm of manufacturing. They seek to bring a product to the marketplace that consumers will purchase, and they wish to do so in a way that yields the maximum potential profit. There are primarily two ways of doing this: offer high-quality goods that can command a substantial price tag and make production as economical as possible to reduce costs. These aims are often somewhat incompatible, and a great many companies (particularly companies who are in the business of manufacturing a wide array of goods, including hardware that is not directly related to security needs) tend to focus on the second principle. By reducing overhead and supply expenses as much as possible on their factory floor, their entire line of products can be fabricated for less money and yield a higher rate of return. Unfortunately, most typical cost-saving measures that can be implemented by manufacturers of hardware goods tend to compromise the efficacy of consumer items like locks and security products.

The two key ways in which costs can be saved during the lock manufacturing process pertain to the quality of materials used and the methods by which they are fabricated into the necessary components.

Practical Lock Picking. DOI: 10.1016/B978-1-59749-611-7.00002-7

Choice of materials

The question of what materials should be used for various components of a lock is not as straightforward as it may seem. There are of course the most basic factors such as supply cost (stainless steel vs. brass can be quite a distinct line on a company spreadsheet) but the decision to use a specific material also has ramifications that are felt through the entire fabrication process and even the final product's life cycle.

The harder a metal is, the more resistance it will demonstrate during machining. Cutting the varied angles and depths necessary to create a keyway down the middle of a lock's plug, for example, will require considerably less force if brass is being used as opposed to harder materials. Using a material that can be molded or cast as opposed to cut will also change how easily and how quickly a component can be produced. Of course, all of these same considerations will also affect the quality of the resultant parts. Pitting, scratching, and other blemishes can result on parts that are produced from lower-cost materials or by means of less-intensive processes.

Cutting and drilling

Even when milling and drilling is a part of a lock's production, the choices that the manufacturer makes with considerations of cost in mind can affect the quality and security of the final product. For example, the vertical chambers of a traditional pin tumbler lock (that are separately drilled into both the plug and the housing in order to accommodate the pin stacks) are often produced by means of a work piece advancing along an assembly line, being held temporarily in a clamp, and then being subjected to five brief penetrations with a drill bit. Either a single bit is rapidly advanced and inserted by means of numerically controlled equipment or a large drill jig equipped with an array of multiple drill bits held in close proximity to one another completes this task. If a company elects to not form their pin tumblers by a casting method, they are often manufactured by advancing a piece of rod stock through a milling machine as a blade rapidly cuts concentric rings of decreasing size, as if turning a piece of fine woodwork on a lathe.

In all of these circumstances, the instruments used in drilling and cutting into the metal will wear out. Any time spent bringing production to a halt in order to perform maintenance and replace parts is a hindrance to profit. Similarly, the replacement tool components also contribute to overall cost. Many companies seeking to maximize revenue will push their manufacturing equipment beyond its ideal limit perhaps replacing drill bits only after they have become very unreliable or running machines at a very fast pace while allowing for some slightly looser tolerances in the final shape and size of the finished pieces.

Such cost-cutting methods may not yield results that are very detrimental if a company is producing hinges or shovels or any one of a thousand other consumer items that we see on the shelves of our local hardware store. When is the last time you squatted down by a box of carriage bolts and meticulously picked out half a dozen that you feel have no blemishes or marred edges? You're not shopping for eggs, after all. However, these sorts of small imperfections can have a *very* real impact on the usefulness and efficacy of a product like a lock. Blemishes and pitting on the pins, or slightly off-center or misshapen milling of rounded parts and rounded holes... all of these very minor issues (some of which are barely visible to the naked eye if you inspect a lock) can add up to serious security weaknesses.

Mechanical imperfections lead to security weaknesses

Let us consider some of the most common ways in which mechanical imperfections can present themselves in typical locks and thus come to understand how they can be exploited by lockpickers.

Picture the components of a pin tumbler lock, in particular the plug. Figure 2.1 shows us a top-down view of the plug on the left side, next to the whole assembled mechanism.

In a world with no mechanical imperfection and utterly perfect materials used in all instances, the pin chambers would be aligned perfectly. In such an ideal world, all the pins would be fabricated to exactly the same diameter, and the plug channel would not allow for anything other than perfect rotation down the precise center axis.

As shown in Figure 2.2, in this idealized (and, in practice, unattainable) lock, any attempt made to rotate the plug without a key present would cause the driver pins to bind in the shear line... and they would do so with a force that was perfectly and evenly distributed across all the pin stacks.

We do not live in a perfect world, however. At some point, a computer-drafted diagram must be sent down to a machine shop and actually produced using real materials, not just ones and zeroes. When that happens, and when the manufacturing company starts deciding just how and where they want to try to cut costs, these tiny imperfections start to crop up. In the real world, when a lock finally rolls off the assembly line, its components look much more like those seen in Figure 2.3.

Although the best manufacturers attempt to fine-tune their equipment and produce parts without flaws, some subtle blemishes will always be there, even if they are not easily detectable with the naked eye. Most locks, if you look closely, will exhibit at least a few signs of such imperfection. Many products, in fact, will be *glaringly* deficient in their quality control. Figures 2.4 and 2.5 are photographs of the plug and pins, respectively, of a non-name brand, off-the-shelf lock. These photos were taken without the lock ever having been used so much as a single time; nothing seen here represents wear and tear but is simply a representation of the product as it came from the manufacturer.

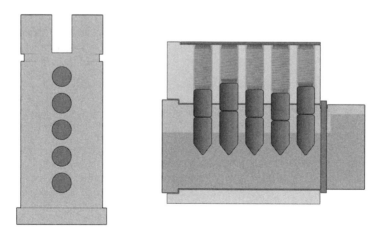

FIGURE 2.1

Imagine a disassembled pin tumbler lock from a top-down perspective of the plug.

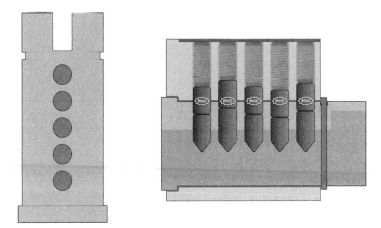

FIGURE 2.2

In a perfect world, all driver pins would bind with exactly the same force.

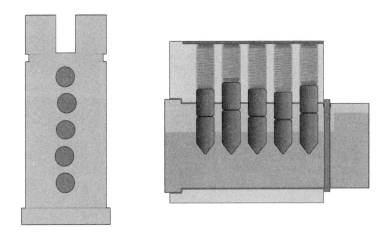

FIGURE 2.3

A lock in the real world. Notice (in the top-down view on the left side of this diagram) the slightly misaligned and misshapen pin chambers. This is what happens to some degree in all mechanical locks.

All of these imperfections cause the following critical situation to arise: when rotational force is applied to the plug of a lock, the mechanisms designed to prevent turning (pins, wafers, etc.) do *not* all experience the same degree of force. Most of the time, the force is borne by very little of the lock's internal mechanisms. In many cases, a single pin stack (whichever pin stack is the *most* misaligned and closest to the wall of the housing in whichever direction the plug is being turned) will bind, while the other pins simply sit in their chambers without making any significant contact with any surfaces at the shear line.

FIGURE 2.4

Close-up view of a plug from a typical off-brand lock. The considerable imperfection of the pin chambers (in both alignment and finishing around the edges) is the result of manufacturing only; the lock has never been used.

Courtesy of Austin Appel

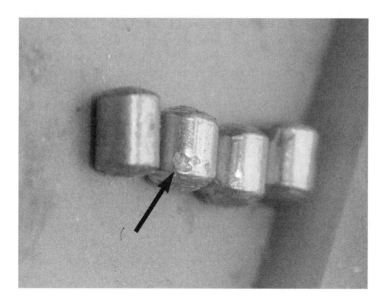

FIGURE 2.5

Close-up view of the pins from the same unused padlock. The deep scars and other blemishes on the pins are not the result of abuse in the field. The pins came that way from the factory.

Courtesy of Austin Appel

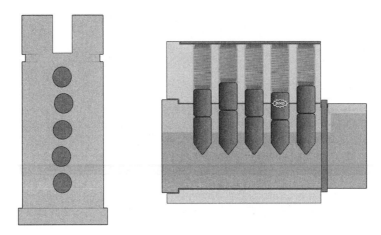

FIGURE 2.6

An attempt made to rotate the plug of a lock, causing one pin stack to bind.

Figure 2.6 attempts to show the effect of attempted clockwise rotation (from the perspective of someone facing the front of the lock) of the plug. The fourth pin stack chamber in the plug happens to be the most substantially misaligned in a way that favors the right side; thus, the driver pin in that chamber (provided the driver pins were manufactured to rather uniform sizes) will be the first one to generate binding force. Attempting to turn the plug in an alternate direction could potentially have an exact opposite effect, or something entirely different could take place. Since these mechanical imperfections are not just the product of alignment but also have to do with the shape and size of pins, chambers, and other components… the manner in which the pins bind varies with every lock.

A series of half a dozen locks produced one after the other on an assembly line, all by the same manufacturer, will exhibit different behaviors. The one constant that can usually be counted upon is for a lock to have a specific binding *order*. That is, the mechanical flaws inside of a lock tend to remain relatively static (although wear and tear can change things somewhat) and one person's picking experience of a lock will likely be similar to what is felt by the next person attempting to pick the same lock. We will speak more about binding order in this next section, "Picking with a Lifting Technique."

PICKING WITH A LIFTING TECHNIQUE

Consider what is happening mechanically with the binding pin stack of a lock when rotation of the plug is attempted without a key. Figure 2.7 shows a more detailed view from the forward-facing perspective.

When rotational force is applied to the plug, a very small degree of movement (often almost imperceptible to the naked eye) will take place. The plug will turn, perhaps a fraction of a degree, and the driver pin of the binding pin stack will be pressed against the walls of the pin chamber in both the plug and the housing.

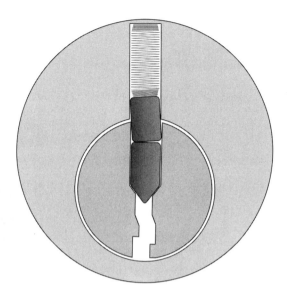

FIGURE 2.7

A binding pin stack, viewed from a forward-facing perspective. Clockwise pressure is being applied to the plug.

While the plug can no longer move any further, there is still room for a different type of additional movement within the lock. The pin stack is still free to move up and down within its chamber. Granted, the pressure that is being applied to the lock will cause friction against the driver pin as it binds in the shear line. However, if a proper pushing force is applied to the pin stack (and if the torsional force being applied to the plug is soft enough, thus lightening the friction experienced by the pins), the stack will begin to move vertically, as shown in Figure 2.8.

If this motion continues, notice what will eventually happen. As shown in Figure 2.9, enough vertical motion on the part of the pin stack will *inevitably* cause it to finally reach its proper operating height—the height to which it would have been raised had the proper key been inserted into the lock by an authorized user—and at such a time, *this pin stack will no longer be binding.*

When this moment is reached, a number of things will happen simultaneously. Firstly, the plug will manage to rotate... not enough to open the lock (not nearly enough so, perhaps not even enough to be observed easily with the naked eye from an exterior perspective), but it will happen. This rotation will cease when the lock begins to bind on yet another pin stack. (It will tend to begin binding again on whatever the *next* most misaligned pin stack is in that direction.) However, another critical occurrence will have also taken place in this moment. Look closely in Figure 2.9 and you will see how the plug, now that it has rotated ever so slightly, will have "captured" the driver pin. The driver pin is now held up in the housing, just barely, by coming to rest on the protruding lip at the top of the plug's pin chamber. Even if lifting pressure is no longer applied to that pin stack, the driver pin will not slip back down into the keyway (as long as some rotational force is still being applied to the plug).

In this condition, that particular pin stack has been set. The overall process of applying tension, lifting, and clicking into position is called setting a pin, and it is the basis of all pin tumbler lockpicking.

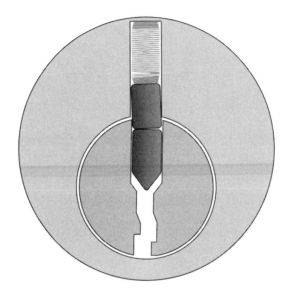

FIGURE 2.8

A binding pin stack that is being lifted by means of force applied from below.

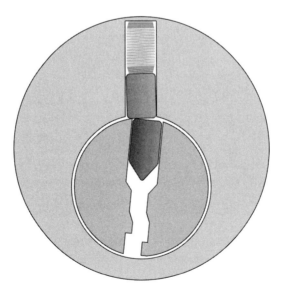

FIGURE 2.9

After substantial lifting, this pin stack is no longer binding.

A lockpicker would now be free to set the next binding pin in the lock, and the next one, subsequently removing each one (individually) from the equation until there are *no remaining pin stacks binding* and the plug is free to turn. The series of diagrams and photographs in Figures 2.10–2.27 illustrates this process.

When picking a lock, the first step is the application of tension (by means of rotational force upon the plug) with a tension tool.

NOTE

Tension tools are known by a variety of other names. Perhaps the second most popular term for this piece of picking equipment is the name "tension wrench." I myself have used this phrasing in the past, as have virtually all of my associates and friends at one time or another. The use of the word "wrench" anywhere in reference to this tool, however, probably does more harm than good...especially as far as new learners are concerned. Not only does it invite an even *further* muddling of terms (occasionally you'll hear someone get particularly mixed up and say "torque wrench," especially if they make a pastime of automotive repair) but it also gives some indication that the tool is supposed to aid in the application of considerable force to the lock. Nothing could be further from the truth. A tension tool should be applied as *gently as possible* when lockpicking is attempted. For this reason, I discourage people from getting into the habit of using the word "torque" or calling this item a "wrench" or "spanner" or anything so forceful-sounding. A good friend and noted locksport enthusiast pointed out that "torsion tool" or "turning tool" are perhaps better names, given the nature of the force being applied (Kiczko Walter, oral communication). I would support that definition from a purely technical standpoint, but I feel that a great degree of growing and evolving of language among lockpickers will be necessary before that specific phrasing receives the widespread acceptance that it deserves. For now, "tension tool" or just "tensioner" are the terms I tend to use, and that is the terminology that will appear in this text.

FIGURE 2.10

An "edge of the plug" tension tool inserted into a lock.

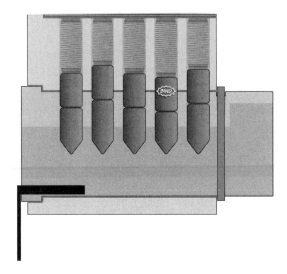

FIGURE 2.11

With tension applied to the plug, a driver pin (in this case, the one in position number four) begins binding.

Figure 2.10 shows a tension tool inserted into the plug of a lock in what is perhaps the most typical manner, at least for lockpickers in North America. Our keyways tend to be somewhat wider and offer more room in which to work than some of the locks one might encounter in Europe. Consequently, these "edge of the plug" tensioners are the most popular and appear most frequently in pick kits sold and used in North America. (Other styles of tension tool will be discussed later in this chapter.)

When gentle pressure is applied to the handle of this tool, it will cause a rotational force upon the plug. This will, consequently, cause a binding force within the lock as one of the driver pins gets caught in the shear line (Figure 2.11).

The other tool that is used in this process is, quite obviously, a pick tool. These come in a wide variety of sizes and shapes and are available with a whole host of different handles and ergonomic grips, but they vary far less in function than they do in form.

NOTE

Some might argue that tension tools, since they are part of a "lockpick set," are also "pick tools" in the broadest sense of the word. This book will reserve the term "pick" and use it exclusively to refer to the implements that apply pressure to pins or other retaining elements within a lock and manipulate them into position. Tensioners are no less essential to the process of picking open a lock (indeed, many of us feel that they are the *most essential* components of the equation, particularly as far as one's skill and finesse are concerned), but they will always be designated by that name or as "tension tools" in the text of this book.

As we shall see, the bulk of all pick tools are either lifting picks or raking picks. We will discuss these terms and techniques in greater detail to clarify things further.

The lifting pick tool is aligned with the bottom of a desired pin stack and simply pressed upward. Some lockpickers will raise the entire pick vertically, while others will attempt to move the handle (outside of the lock) downward, thus pivoting the shaft of the pick on the bottom of the keyway and causing its tip to move upward. Neither technique is particularly "right" nor "wrong" and each has advantages and disadvantages.

NOTE

You will see this line of reasoning *a lot* when it comes to lockpicking. If a technique works for you, by all means use it. Often you will find that many "simple" techniques are the most effective tactics when facing cheaper, weaker locks but that the tighter spaces or better engineering of higher quality locks make such techniques less effective on other occasions. That doesn't mean that one way is "better" than another... but rather that it is more or less useful in certain situations. Perhaps the healthiest thing one can do is always try to keep an open mind and never get *so accustomed* to a single technique that it becomes a habit one is incapable of breaking.

In general, the "rocking" of a pick can make lifting pin stacks easier and more controlled, but it is not always possible to do in tight spots. Also if an "edge of the plug tensioner" (like the one shown in Figures 2.10 and 2.12) is being used, rocking the pick downward can interfere with the clean and even application of sustained pressure on the plug. It can knock the tensioner out of its resting place or otherwise complicate matters.

FIGURE 2.12

A lock that now has both a tension tool and a pick tool inserted.

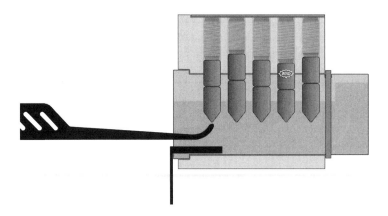

FIGURE 2.13

Tension is being applied, and a hook pick is approaching the first pin stack, which will then be lifted upward.

Figure 2.13 shows a lifting pick (in the next fifteen diagrams, a basic hook-shaped pick of medium-reaching depth is represented) approaching the first pin stack.

Since this pin stack is not binding, there will be little resistance felt when the pick is pressed up into the stack. The lifting will be inhibited only by the very slight (but still noticeable) pressure of the spring at the top of the stack.

NOTE

As mentioned before in Chapter 1, terms like "up" and "down" or "top" and "bottom" can be a bit problematic with respect to how locks are installed and operated around the world. This text will continue to address locks from a North American perspective, although whenever possible, generic terms that apply universally will be used.

Figures 2.14 and 2.15 show the hook pick lifting the first pin stack. This has no effect on the situation. The lock is not affected by any manipulation of the first pin stack because binding force is being felt elsewhere in the lock. One can lift and release the first pin stack (in this instance) multiple times and it will continually drop back down (both the driver pin and the key pin together) to the default position.

The same is true for the second pin stack (as seen in Figure 2.16) and the third (shown in Figure 2.17).

It is not until lifting force is applied to the fourth pin stack (since this is where the binding pin is located) that things get interesting (see Figure 2.18). Almost immediately (to a trained lockpicker) it will be evident that something different is afoot. A greater resistance will be felt, and the pin stack will not be as easy to lift upward (see Figure 2.19).

It should be obvious when a certain significant point is reached during the lifting of a binding pin stack. If all goes well, the driver pin will fully clear the chamber, the shear line of the pin stack will be aligned with the plug's edge, and there should be a noticeable "click" that can be felt and/or heard (see Figure 2.20). Don't expect the earth to shake, of course… but it can often be felt quite substantially. The resulting slight movement of the plug may also be noticed.

NOTE

Given that the handle of one's tension tool extends outward along the radius of rotation, this tool can often be a better indicator of any movement the plug has experienced. The longer the handle of your tension tool, the more magnified and pronounced its movement will be at the farthest tip. Movement on the order of just a degree or two might not even be noticed up in the middle of the keyway, but if a tension tool is five inches or more in length, its farthest tip may be seen to move an eighth or a quarter of an inch or more. Now, I don't recommend that you go out and obtain the longest tension tool you can find (this would not only be difficult to fit into a typical lockpick case but could also be cumbersome in the process of picking), but it is often a good idea to apply your tension pressure with a fingertip placed as far out to the edge of the tension tool as possible. This allows you to better control the pressure you are applying and also puts you in the best possible position to observe or feel any such movement in the plug when it takes place.

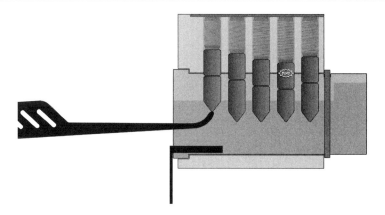

FIGURE 2.14

Lifting the first pin stack. No binding tension is felt and there is virtually no resistance to the lifting force.

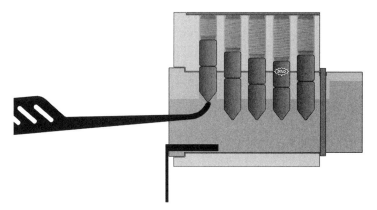

FIGURE 2.15

Further lifting of the first pin stack. It has now been "overlifted" at this time, meaning the shear line has been passed and now the key pin is protruding up into the housing. Still, however, the stack is not binding.

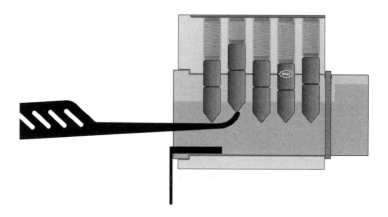

FIGURE 2.16

Lifting the second pin stack has a similar effect to the first. Nothing happens.

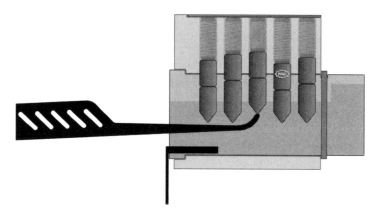

FIGURE 2.17

Lifting the third pin stack has no effect. It drops right back down when released.

Once you feel that first "click" you are well on your way.

When lifting pressure is removed from this pin stack, one should not expect the key pin to remain raised. True, there is no spring pressure being applied to it (via the driver pin which would normally be pushing down upon it) but there is nothing else keeping it "lifted" either. It is free to flop around in any direction in its chamber within the plug. Again, if the lock were installed with the pin stacks below the keyway (as in many European installations), the key pin would not appear to "move" even after the pick ceased putting pressure upon it, but that would also just be a function of gravity. Here in North America, gravity will typically play a role in the key pin falling back toward the middle of the keyway. The important thing to remember, regardless of the orientation of the lock, is that this casual up or down movement of the key pin within its chamber has no effect on the lock at this time.

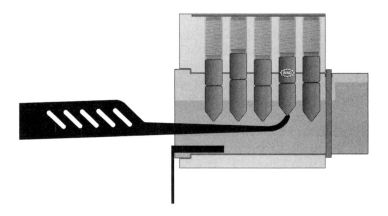

FIGURE 2.18

When lifting pressure is applied to the fourth pin stack (where the driver pin is binding), the stack must be lifted with additional and deliberate pressure.

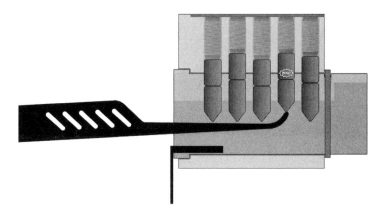

FIGURE 2.19

The fourth pin stack has been lifted even higher. There is the same feeling of resistance from the binding driver pin.

It is now time to seek out the *next* binding pin stack and apply lifting pressure again, in order to set another pin. As the plug will have rotated slightly (even if you couldn't visually observe this with ease), some other pin in a different chamber will now be binding. As with the first pin stack to bind, you cannot easily predict where this next pin will be located. You will have to simply continue the process of lifting individual pin stacks and seeing which one feels the "tightest" and offers the most resistance.

As the picking process continues, Figure 2.21 shows us that the next pin stack to bind is in bitting position number three. Perhaps the lockpicker finds it right away, or perhaps some searching is involved, as shown in Figure 2.22.

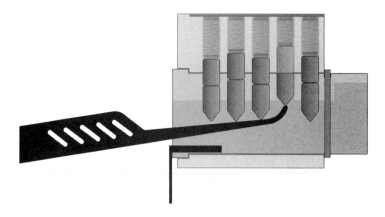

FIGURE 2.20

The pin stack in the fourth chamber has been set. The driver pin is represented in a faded color to indicate that it is no longer in play.

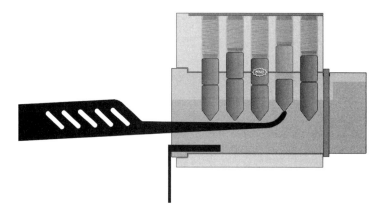

FIGURE 2.21

The lifting of the key pin in the fourth chamber is easing off. The key pin is dropping back to its default position at the bottom of its chamber; this is normal. Binding pressure is now being felt by the driver pin in the third chamber, and it is up to the lockpicker to hunt around and determine the location of this newly binding pin.

When this latest binding pin is located, however, the process of lifting and setting is the same as was seen before (see Figures 2.23 and 2.24). Gentle, upward pressure is applied with the pick while care is taken to not press too hard with the tensioner. Of course, one doesn't want to ease up *too* much on the tension tool, since that would result in a full release of any pin stacks that have been set already.

Ultimately, if all goes well, there will come a time when there remains only one pin stack which has yet to be set. At this time, that one final driver pin is all that is preventing the plug from turning.

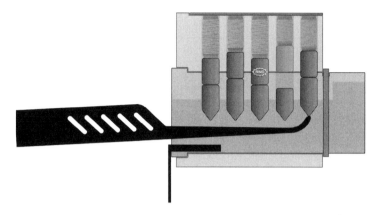

FIGURE 2.22

The third pin stack is now binding, but the lockpicker moves on to test the fifth pin stack at the rear of the lock. No luck is had.

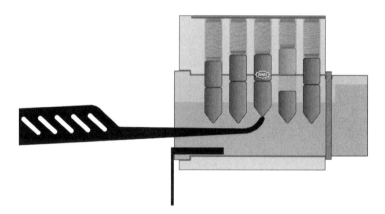

FIGURE 2.23

Upward lifting begins on pin stack number three, which is currently binding.

Figure 2.25 shows this situation. Lifting proceeds in the same manner as with all of the previous pin stacks. The driver pin will set just like all of the others, as shown in Figure 2.26.

When the final driver pin has been clicked into position, nothing is holding the plug stationary any more. It should almost immediately begin to rotate (see Figure 2.27). (Some picking experts refer to this as the point at which the plug "breaks over.") Rotation should happen immediately since the tension tool is still applying rotational pressure to the plug.

The tension tool alone is often strong enough to provide the turning force necessary to completely rotate the plug and operate the lock, thus opening it. (That's assuming, of course, that you have turned in the proper direction!) It should be understood, however, that even tensioners are delicate tools used for finesse purposes more than anything else. Any lock which requires considerable effort

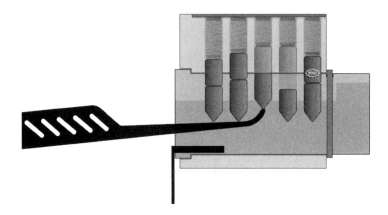

FIGURE 2.24

The driver in pin stack three has now been set. Pin stack five is now binding.

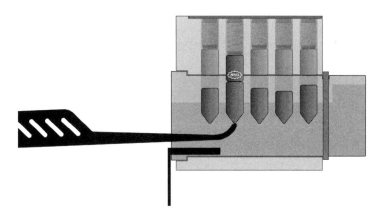

FIGURE 2.25

The hook pick is in position, preparing to lift the only pin stack which is still binding.

to operate even with the proper key will need equally substantial force when a lockpicker attempts to rotate a plug that has begun to turn freely. Having a thicker, more robust tension tool in your kit (even if it's not your favorite one to use) is a good idea. At a pinch, a flat head screwdriver or any other such tool can help to encourage a plug to turn. One sometimes encounters stiffness like this on deadbolt locks.

The problem of too much tension

One of the biggest mistakes that people make when they are first learning to pick locks pertains to proper control of the tension tool. I have seen more complicated and counterproductive ways of gripping a lock and positioning one's fingers than I can count or care to remember. As always,

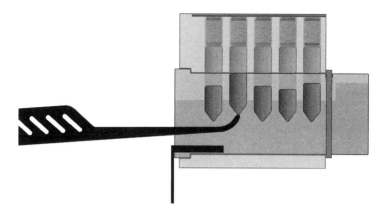

FIGURE 2.26

The last remaining driver pin has been set. The plug can now turn.

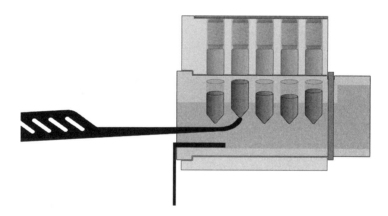

FIGURE 2.27

The plug has begun to "break over" and rotate. The key pin from stack number two is still lifted quite high at this time. It does not matter, however, since there is no space for the key pin to move. It has reached the edge of the plug and is now facing the flat wall of the plug channel within the housing.

I stand by my axiom that if something works for you, it's not wrong per se. However, more often than not, oddball ways of holding a lock or applying tension tend to do little beyond making life difficult.

First, let us discuss positioning of one's finger (or fingers) upon the tension tool. While there is nothing inherently wrong with having more than one finger on the tensioner, it's rarely called for. . . and is often a sign that you may be applying too much force. Also, it's a good idea if your contact with the tensioner is geared towards applying a "pushing" force against it in some manner, not attempting to "pull" upon it with a hooked finger, as seen in Figure 2.28.

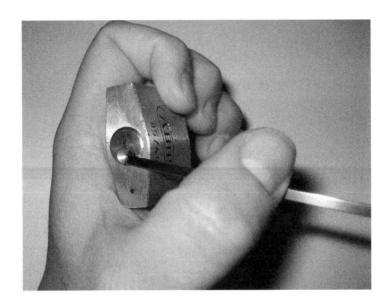

FIGURE 2.28

Attempting to apply clockwise rotational force to the plug by hooking the tension tool with one's thumb and pulling it "downward" and toward you. This method of using the tensioner is not recommended.

Placing a single finger, often the index finger, on the tension tool and pressing downward is often the best course of action. Even here, however, there is some room for varied techniques. I highly recommend that people attempt to localize the tip of their finger and apply pressure further out towards the end of the tension tool.

Compare the photos in Figure 2.29 (a finger position that I do not find very effective) and Figure 2.30 (the finger position that I use when picking) to see the distinction.

The other common problem that users can encounter when applying tension is the mistake of using far too much force. This is perhaps the most common stumbling block that impedes the progress of those who are starting to learn lockpicking. I cannot stress enough just how *little* tension is required when you are picking a lock.

TIP

If you are starting to learn lockpicking and it isn't going well, the odds are overwhelming that the problem has to do with your use of the tension tool... specifically, too much pressure being applied to it.

My dear friend Babak Javadi likes to explain the matter to new lockpickers by asking them to consider a typical membrane keyboard, like those found on modern laptops. "Imagine the amount of pressure you'd need to use to push a key on such a keyboard," he will tell the crowd gathered around him as he gives an introductory lecture. "You want to use about *half* of that much pressure on the tension tool... perhaps even less than that," he will say, often to the students' amazement (Javadi Babak, oral communication). This is a very good analogy.

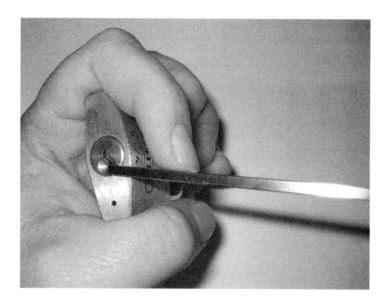

FIGURE 2.29

Applying pushing pressure (which is good) at a position very close to the head of the tension tool (which isn't all that good).

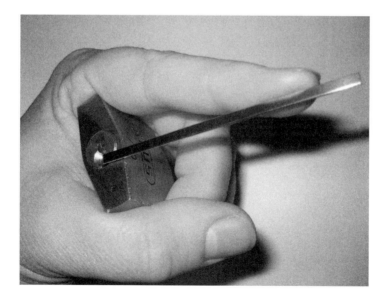

FIGURE 2.30

Applying pushing pressure at a position much further along down toward the tail end of the tension tool. This allows for maximum control and tactile feedback.

Perhaps you don't have a lot of experience with laptop keyboards, however. Maybe you still type everything on a vintage IBM model M keyboard (talk about physical security hardware... if you own one, you can simply bludgeon intruders into submission should anyone break into your office and it will *still* function just fine afterwards) and thus have no concept of the soft pressure that we encourage. In that case, a simple yet effective way for you to gauge how hard you should (or shouldn't) be pressing is to look at whether or not you're losing color in the tip of your finger.

Compare the photographs in Figures 2.31 and 2.32. The first shows proper pressure being applied to the tension tool. The user's fingertip shows a similar flesh-tone to the rest of the hand. In the second photo, however, too much pressure is being used. The fingertip displays a notable lack of color and a considerable "dent" where the tension tool is resisting.

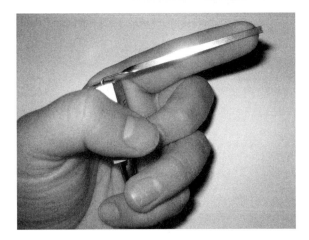

FIGURE 2.31

Proper pressure with a tension tool.

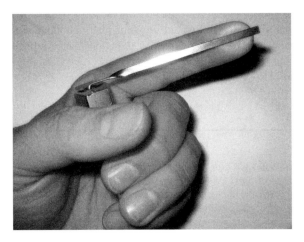

FIGURE 2.32

Too much pressure on the tension tool. Notice the whitening of the user's fingertip.

The peril of overlifting

One other significant problem that is common for individuals who are just starting out with lock-picking pertains to too much pressure when lifting the binding pin stack. If a pin stack is raised too much, as in Figure 2.33, then not only will the driver pin be out of the plug, but the key pin will be as well, at least partially. If the key pin becomes stuck in the shear line (and thus begins to be held by the friction of binding force, as seen in Figures 2.34 and 2.35), there is no easy way to bring it back down and out of the way. The only course of action is to release all pressure on the tension tool and allow *all* pin stacks, including ones you may have already set, to spring back down into their original default positions.

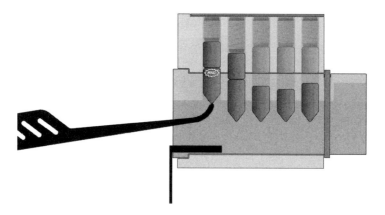

FIGURE 2.33

Three pin stacks have been set, but the lifting of this fourth stack has gone too far.

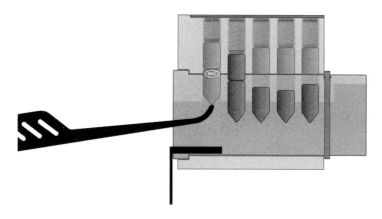

FIGURE 2.34

Now, the key pin in the first chamber is binding in the shear line.

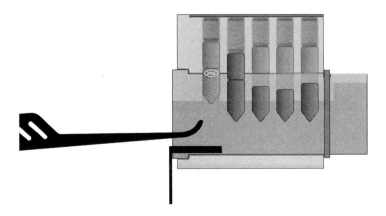

FIGURE 2.35

Even if the pick is moved away, that stack will refuse to drop back down now.

PICKING WITH A RAKING TECHNIQUE

Not all of the tools in a typical lockpick kit are specifically designed for the lifting technique. If you've already seen items of lockpicking equipment, you know that only some of the tools in a set will tend to be hook-shaped picks. A number of the items will have tips that are either wavy or feature a series of angled points. These are known as rake picks and they are used in a somewhat different manner than what we have already seen in the first lockpicking walkthrough illustrated in Figures 2.11–2.27.

Rake picks are operated in a somewhat similar manner to lifting picks. That is to say, slight rotational pressure is applied to the plug with a tension tool and the pick is inserted vertically in the keyway much like we have already seen in Figure 2.12. Figure 2.36 shows a side-view diagram of the beginning of the raking process.

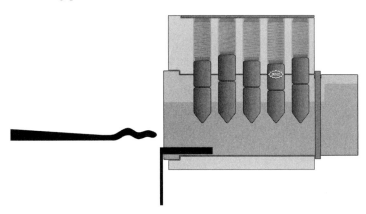

FIGURE 2.36

With tension applied (and thus, a pin stack binding), a rake pick is moved toward the keyway.

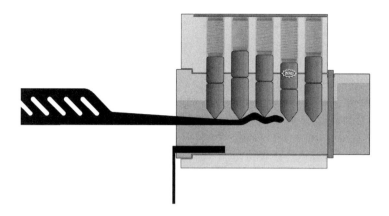

FIGURE 2.37

The tips of rake picks are large enough that they can contact multiple pin stacks (or wafers) at the same time.

Rake picks are typically designed so that their working surfaces are wide enough to contact multiple pin stacks simultaneously, as seen in Figure 2.37. They are used by scrubbing back and forth, in and out of the lock, so that the pick jostles the pins into a wide variety of positions.

The size of the tips on a rake pick, coupled with the rapid movement that characterizes their usage, often results in the setting of multiple pins stacks in very rapid succession. On occasion, the speed with which this is accomplished can be astonishing... with the lock popping open so suddenly as to take a person by surprise.

There is quite a bit of variation possible in the use of a rake pick. While an in/out movement is the primary way in which such a tool is operated, many lockpickers will vary the angle at which the tool is held (in terms of its pitch upward or downward, that is... the "blade" of the pick is always kept as close as possible to the vertical alignment of the keyway in which it is operating) and the overall height at which it is moving within the keyway. Observe the series of diagrams in Figures 2.38–2.41, which depict the process of rapidly setting pins via raking, to see the multitude of differing positions at which the rake pick is held at various times.

I do not wish to give the impression from this latest series of diagrams in Figures 2.36–2.41 that the holding and working of a rake pick at these varied angles and heights is a consciously deliberate decision. One should usually make the effort to attempt adequate variety with the pick's movements, but it is rarely a matter of saying to oneself, "Alright, in this pass I'm going to hold the pick very low at a downward angle...now in the next pass I'll try the same angle a bit higher...and now I'll vary my angle to be a bit flatter..." etc. No, the movement of a rake pick in and out of the plug tends to be so rapid as to preclude such specific orchestration of one's movements.

As long as you do not stick to just a single, unwavering movement of the rake, you will increase your chances for success. The same can be said of your work with the tension tool. While fluctuation and variation of your pressure upon the tensioner is not a normal part of lifting picking, it is quite common during the raking of a lock.

I regret that there is not a more formalized, step-by-step process to this style of opening a lock. It is rather easily understood, but much harder to convey instructions to someone who is attempting

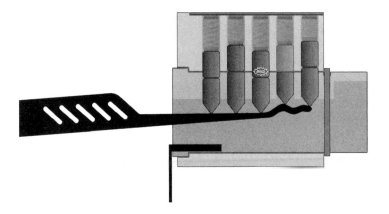

FIGURE 2.38

A rake pick, lifted high and angled upward, has set the first binding pin in a lock.

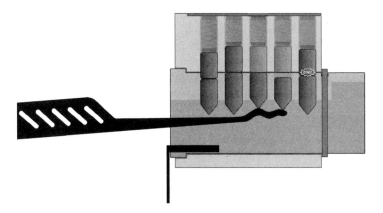

FIGURE 2.39

The same rake pick, slightly withdrawn, has set the second binding pin in the lock.

it. Unlike the precise science of lifting picking (which could be said to be like baking... follow these steps in a specific order and you usually get a predictable, successful result), raking is more of an art (like cooking... you use your best judgment and experience gained in the past to whip up something that you hope goes over well for all involved).

There is also a popular technique for opening locks that I tend to informally label with the term hybrid picking. This is the alternating use of both a rake and a hook pick without easing off of the tension when switching between tools. Simply put, a few passes with a rake might set most (but not all) of the pins in a lock. If you keep maintaining gentle pressure with the tension tool (and thus keep the pins which have been set already from falling back into the plug) while you switch to the hook, it may be then possible to "finish off" any remaining pin stacks that require a little bit of additional lifting.

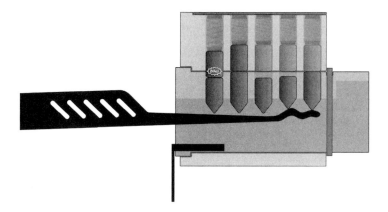

FIGURE 2.40

The rake pick proceeds deeper in the lock and sets a third pin... this time it is being held at a slightly flatter angle. Notice that it is routine to make repeated contact with key pins in chambers where the driver has already been set. This is totally natural and not a problem, those key pins will jostle slightly in their own chambers but that will have no effect on the opening of the lock.

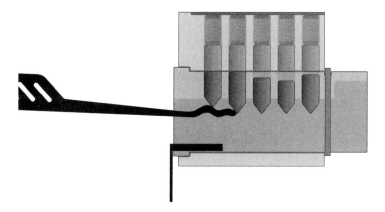

FIGURE 2.41

The rake pick is being withdrawn while at the same time its handle is being lifted upward. The tip, at this slightly downward-facing angle, manages to set the last two remaining pins in almost the same moment. At this time, the plug would now turn and the lock could be opened.

The half diamond pick

There is one other style of picking tool that is a common sight in most lockpick kits, and it deserves a brief mention here. Called a half diamond, this is a terrific item (see Figure 2.42). Praised for its versatility, I consider it to be an indispensable addition to anyone's tool set because of the multitude of ways it can be used and also its ability to perform specialized tasks like no other equipment you're likely to have with you at any given time.

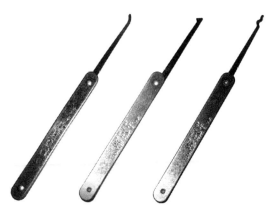

FIGURE 2.42

The three most popular styles of lockpick tools. On the left is a lifting hook. On the right is a rake. (This particular one is called a "Snake" rake. For a more detailed breakdown of picking tools and their names, see the Appendix: *Guide to Tools and Toolkits.*) Between these two tools is a half diamond.

People often ask me if the half diamond is a lifting pick tool or a raking pick tool. A simple "yes" is always my succinct response. A popular story one encounters frequently is, "Imagine if a hook and a rake could have a child… this offspring would be a half diamond pick." That analogy is quite apt, given that a half diamond can be used to lift individual pin stacks delicately or it can be scrubbed back and forth quickly. Its efficacy is not always likely to be quite as decent as a specially tailored pick tool (a dedicated hook will have greater reach and can focus more precisely on a specific pin chamber, and the multiple ripples of a dedicated rake will more easily make contact with multiple pin stacks at once than the head of a half diamond pick), but the fact that it can be used both ways almost simultaneously is a huge advantage in terms of speed and simplicity.

For some of my friends, the half diamond is the first thing they reach for when approaching a new lock for the first time. After all, as my number one picking axiom states, "Why make things harder than they have to be?" If a lock can be easily opened with a few raking passes and then a little additional lifting in one or two remaining chambers (the "hybrid" style I described earlier), it may not be necessary to fumble with more than one tool, swapping between a hook and a rake. Sometimes, a half diamond pick can handle all of these motions adequately.

Another highly useful feature of the half diamond pick is the fact that its very front tip has a downward-angled face. This can be incredibly useful if one is working in an exceedingly tight keyway and wants to "shovel" the pin stacks in order to get them moving upward. By aligning the half diamond tool at the proper position and then inserting it straight into the lock (see Figure 2.43), the leading edge can slip beneath the key pins, letting them ride up on the front face of the pick.

The half diamond pick is often quite forgiving of abuse and stress, since its tip tends to be thicker and more robust than hooks or rakes which tend to be comprised of more intricately fashioned material, particularly at their functional end. When attempting to lift individual pin stacks with a half diamond, it is helpful to try to localize its point directly beneath the key pin in question (see Figure 2.44) but, again, an imperfect aim is likely to not cause much trouble if you are using this very adaptable tool.

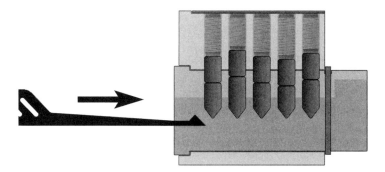

FIGURE 2.43

Inserting a half diamond pick straight into a lock can often help the pin stacks move upward as they ride along the angled leading edge of the tool. This can be especially effective when you don't have a great deal of room in the keyway for vertical pick movement.

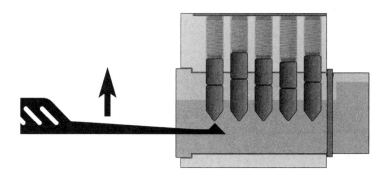

FIGURE 2.44

Lifting a single pin stack with a half diamond pick.

There is one more, very unique, way in which a half diamond tool can be used by a lockpicker. Even if you do not come to enjoy *picking* with a half diamond, this additional technique alone is reason enough to keep the tool in your kit at all times. The half diamond is uniquely suited to *exploring* locks, helping you gather information in places where you cannot use your eyes to observe, and must instead rely on what you can learn simply with your hands.

Often, the half diamond tool will be the only pick in someone's tool case that has a long, flat surface along one side all the way out to the tip. Rakes and hooks do not offer such a surface. Such a long, continuous plane can be used to help you in discerning things such as how many pin stacks a lock contains… quite a useful piece of information if you're tackling a piece of hardware that you have not encountered before. Over time, you will come to know many manufacturers and be relatively able to predict just what sort of features are within a lock simply by seeing its brand and model. Most Master Lock padlocks feature four pin stacks, most Kwikset and Schlage residential door locks incorporate five. In industrial settings, six-pin locks are seen more frequently, but five-pin locks are still common there, as well.

However, there are plenty of no-name locks on the market, and even well-recognized manufacturers are developing new designs all the time. If you wish to learn just how many pin stacks are in a given lock, grab your half diamond tool and insert it into the keyway *upside-down*, with the pointed tip facing away from the key pins. With the pick far away from the pin stacks (keep it at the "bottom" of the keyway if possible), insert it until you feel an obstruction at the rear of the plug (the tailpiece or cam or a blocking plate will be what you are striking with the tip of your pick). Now, lift the half diamond upwards, attempting to raise all of the pin stacks evenly and at the same time, as shown in Figure 2.45.

When you have all the pins raised as high as possible (much of your pick tool will now be riding against the top of the keyway), slowly begin to withdraw it from the lock, as shown in Figure 2.46. Make sure it is traveling completely horizontally. If there is a slight wiggle or clicking as you begin to move it, that may be a sign that the tip of the tool (deep within the keyway) is encountering a small lip or uneven milling around the rear of the plug. This is typical. Continue removing the half diamond while maintaining solid "upward" pressure against the top of the keyway and you should soon feel the pick moving along a smooth, flat path.

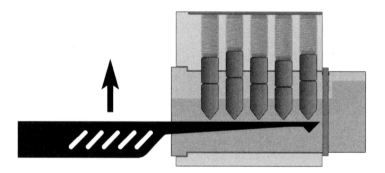

FIGURE 2.45

Using an inverted half diamond pick to lift all the pin stacks of a lock simultaneously.

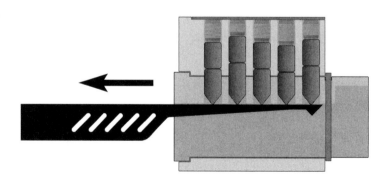

FIGURE 2.46

Removing the inverted half diamond pick along a smooth, flat path.

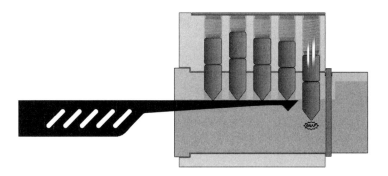

FIGURE 2.47

As the half diamond is slowly retracted, pin stacks will begin springing back down into their default position. This will produce an audible "snap" when they strike the bottom of their pin chambers.

As the pick tool's tip begins passing the pin chambers while it is being removed from the plug, the pin stacks that had been pushed up will come snapping back downward due to the pent up spring pressure above them (see Figure 2.47). You can clearly hear (and sometimes feel) this snap effect. Count the snaps, and you will have determined how many pin stacks the lock contains.

A half diamond tool can be used to squeeze into unconventional spots, triggering release catches or popping small components out of position just long enough to allow a lock to be attacked in a nontraditional manner. It can even be inserted with its "broad" side towards the pins and rocked slightly to act as a dimple pick if one is not available. (We will cover dimple locks in Chapter 6.) All told, the half diamond could be thought of as the least specialized and yet potentially the most useful pick in your toolkit.

Tension tools

There are a few items which aren't "picks" per se but which are indispensable to have with you in a pick kit. As we first saw in Figure 2.10, tension tools are a part of all lockpicking efforts. Tension tools come in a number of different styles and shapes, and it is a good idea to have a healthy assortment of them available when you are picking locks.

For the most part, tensioners can be classified as either "standard," "flat," or "specialized," but of course a number of other names exist. Let's take a look at the two main categories first: standard and flat (see Figure 2.48).

In its simplest form, a tension tool will often be nothing more than a short, thin strip of metal that has had a small segment of its length (typically ½ inch or 1½ centimeters or so) bent at a right angle. This is the most common tensioner that is seen in pick kits in North America as well as many other places around the world. Often, terms such as "head" and "handle" will be used to refer to the short bent segment and the longer straight section, respectively, but they are not separate pieces of metal. It is very common for tensioners to have additional bends or twists incorporated into their handle. See Figure 2.49 for such examples.

In contrast with the "standard" style of the tensioner, another popular and often-seen design is the "flat" tensioner. Many times you will see this referred to as a "Euro" tensioner, because of the

FIGURE 2.48

A "standard" tensioner (on the left) next to a "flat" style tensioner (on the right).

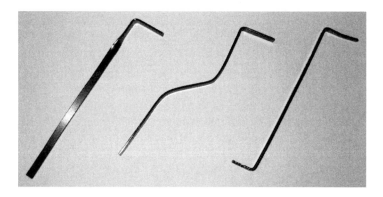

FIGURE 2.49

Variations on the "standard" tensioner. On the far left is a tensioner that features a twisted handle. In the middle is a tensioner with a scalloped shaft (known as a tulip handle) which makes it easier to apply tension to a lock that is located in a recessed cavity or up against a wide door jamb. On the right of this photo is a tensioner that has been bent at both ends, making a double-ended tool. If you look closely at this last tool, you may notice that the "short" end has been augmented with notched teeth that can grab a keyway more tightly. Also, the "larger" head of this tool has been curved slightly, which also helps it to grab more firmly within a keyway. In spite of their modifications, these three tools would all still be referred to as "standard" tensioners.

popularity of tighter keyways in Europe and thus the increased use of flat tensioners when picking those locks. Occasionally, the terms "edge of the plug" and "center of the plug" will be substituted for "standard" and "flat," respectively. Such terms refer to where in the plug the tools are inserted, as you will soon see. (As always, I'll point out here that I *greatly* prefer these terms over any designations that are region-specific. Some people will make reference to "top of the keyway" and "bottom of the keyway" but, for reasons that I have discussed before in Chapter 1, I try to break people out of the habit of using those sorts of names.) Much like standard tensioners, flat tensioners can have additional features such as gripping teeth, double-sided ends for extra size options, and so forth.

FIGURE 2.50

A standard tension tool that has been inserted in the keyway at the edge of the plug. (On most North American locks, this would be called the "bottom" of the keyway.)

Each style of tension tool has its own unique advantages and disadvantages. The primary difference between standard and flat style tension tools is where and how they are inserted into a lock's keyway. Standard tension tools are traditionally used by inserting the head into the keyway at the edge of the plug, away from the pin stacks (see Figure 2.50).

Let us take a closer look (in all three dimensions) at exactly how the head of a standard tension tool fits into the lock when it has been inserted in this fashion. Figure 2.51 shows both a front-facing and side-view perspective, indicating how far into the plug the head of the tensioner is likely to reach.

As you may notice, having a tool inserted into a lock like this can present a couple of problems. First and foremost is the fact that the tensioner is occupying a significant portion of the available space in the keyway, thus limiting how much free room remains for someone to insert and operate a lockpick (see Figure 2.52).

Another problem that can arise when attempting to pick a lock while using a standard tension tool placed at the edge of the plug pertains to how most keyways are milled in locks today. Recall from Chapter 1 that in most cases, the keyway is cut straight through the bottom of the lock's plug, leaving the entire bottom of the plug wide open. Now, this is not usually a problem during normal operation. Indeed, most users never notice this, since the warding works together with the key profile to keep the blade of the key "raised" ever so slightly while it is being inserted into the lock. Contrary to what you may believe, the blade of the key rarely rubs significantly against the walls of the housing inside of the plug chamber.

A tension tool, however, does not incorporate any special features to keep it "elevated" within the keyway. As pressure is applied and the tool nestles down into a snug position within the keyway, the

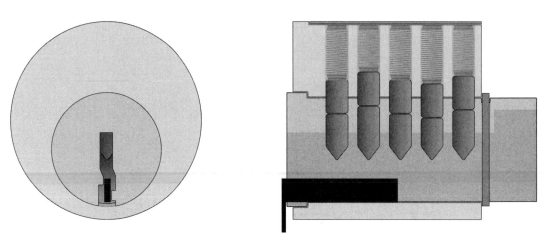

FIGURE 2.51

This diagram demonstrates where a typical "standard" tension tool's head fits within the keyway of a typical pin tumbler lock.

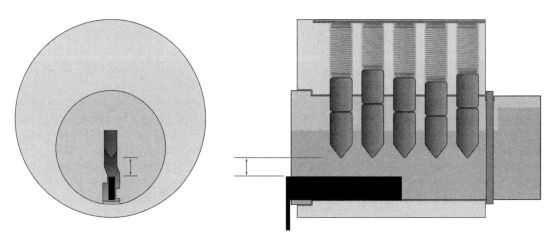

FIGURE 2.52

Notice how the available work space is diminished once the tension tool has been inserted into the keyway.

tensioner head may stick through the bottom of the keyway, rubbing up against the plug channel and causing friction with the lock housing (see Figure 2.53).

To overcome these two common difficulties that sometimes arise when standard tensioners are employed, some lockpickers prefer (and, indeed, some situations all but require) flat style tensioners. These are tension tools that consist of a single, unbent flat piece of metal which is cut or stamped

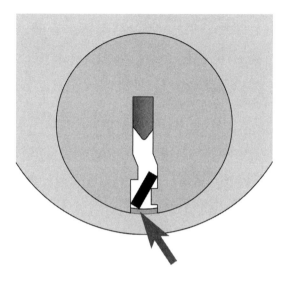

FIGURE 2.53

A forward-facing perspective of lock after tension has been applied. In this instance, the head of the tension tool (also shown here in a forward-facing cross-section view) has nestled downward and angled slightly, causing it to bind and drag somewhat against the housing. This is a common problem and can affect the precision control of tension upon the plug, as well as how easily the lock can be picked.

into a specific shape. Unlike standard tensioners, which are often inserted in the keyway at the edge of the plug (opposite the pin stacks), flat tensioners are most commonly inserted into the keyway at the center of the plug, often nestling right up against the first pin stack. Indeed, that is a common concern of the designers who fabricate and sell flat tension tools... the head needs to be short enough to not protrude too far, thus rubbing against the first pin stack. Some flat tensioners (like the one seen in Figure 2.48) feature an extra lip or shoulder that regulates how far they can be inserted into a keyway. Figure 2.54 shows a flat style tension tool in a lock.

As you can see from the pair of perspectives in Figure 2.55, this particular tensioner offers far greater room within the keyway for someone to maneuver a lockpick and attempt either lifting or raking.

It may seem at first glance that for these reasons, flat style tension tools are far superior to the "standard" variety that is so popular in North America. There is one more important consideration, however. The flat tension tools make far less contact, overall, with the plug than their standard counterparts. That means that the grip a flat tensioner has on the plug will tend to be more precarious. (It is precisely for this reason that small teeth or grooves are such a popular feature on the head of most flat tension tools.)

It is possible to reduce the loose, wiggly feel of a flat tensioner by fabricating it in such a way that it is wide enough to easily contact both sides of the keyway when it has been inserted (see Figure 2.56).

The trade-off that manufacturers of tools must consider is one of interoperability versus a snug fit. If a flat tension tool is tailored to the exact width of a specific manufacturer's keyway, it will have a wonderful grip on their locks, but it may be imperfect (or, indeed, totally unusable) in locks

FIGURE 2.54

A flat style tension tool, inserted into a keyway at the center of the plug.

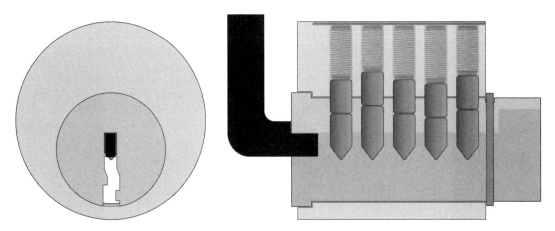

FIGURE 2.55

This flat tension tool leaves much more free space in the keyway, allowing for more freedom of movement with a picking tool.

of another brand. A flat style tensioner that is quite thin, on the other hand, will surely slip with ease into nearly all keyways… but keeping it steady long enough to successfully pick the lock can then become a challenge. It may not surprise you to learn that many skilled lockpickers wind up picking and choosing a healthy variety of tensioners, often from a wide range of suppliers, and including them in their pick kits.

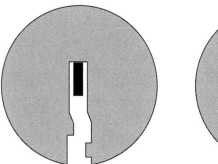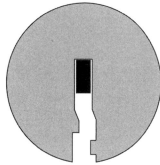

FIGURE 2.56

Two possible sizes of head on a flat tension tool. The one on the left is narrower and will potentially fit in more locks, but it will not have nearly as stable a grip on the keyway as the wider-headed tensioner shown on the right of this diagram.

TIP

When I was visiting some of my friends in the Netherlands, I attended a meeting of their local chapter of The Open Organisation Of Lockpickers. I overheard a conversation in which one member was asked hypothetically if he could "have only ten, or perhaps a dozen, tools in his pick kit...what would they be?" His response was that he would choose his favorite hook pick (one known as a Gonzo), a sturdy half diamond, a Bogotá rake, and then fill the rest of his allotted space with as wide a variety of tensioners as he could obtain (Weyers Jos 2008, oral communication, 26th March).

As my Dutch friends are fond of saying, think of the *tensioner* as the tool that actually picks the lock. Yes, the hook or the rake will surely help a great deal, by manipulating the pins, but it is your finesse and precision with the tensioner that makes the most difference. And if you can't get a good, controlled grip on the plug with a tensioner that is comfortable to use, almost everything else you try to do will not matter.

We have yet to discuss the third category of tension tool... that of "specialized" tensioners. These are, for lack of a better term, tension tools that do not adequately fit into either of the first two categories.

There are a variety of items that can be called "specialized" tensioners in the sense that they are designed to be used in just a single brand or model of lock. Two that come to mind are the "long finger" tensioner that is used when picking the old Schlage Everest lock and a tensioner that features "gripper fingers" that is used when attempting to overcome Small Format Interchangeable Core locks. (Both of these tools are produced and sold by Peterson International, by the way.)

There are tensioners that mount or fasten to the face of a lock and then can be calibrated to apply a specific degree of tension to the plug without the user having to hold them at all. (Sometimes called "dial tensioners," these might make an interesting addition to a professional locksmith's kit, but I have never seen one used by penetration testers.)

Just about the only kind of "specialized" tension tool that you are likely encounter in a typical lockpick tool set or use with any frequency in the field is known as a "wishbone" tensioner, sometimes also called a "tweezer" tensioner.

NOTE

I am not as happy with the use of the term "tweezer" because it could be seen by some as some sort of indication that the tool is used by somehow pinching together the two paired arms. This, plus the fact that *actual* tweezers are often part of a locksmith's tool kit since they are used in servicing and re-pinning locks, makes me much happier with the name "wishbone" in reference to this type of tensioner.

Two models of this style of tensioner can be seen in the photo in Figure 2.57.

There are two specific situations when wishbone tensioners can sometimes be helpful. One pertains to pin tumbler locks, the other to wafer locks. Let us first consider the former. Some pin tumbler locks are *very* small. Luggage locks, briefcase locks, and other such mechanisms often have exceedingly tiny keyways. The keyways can be so small, in fact, that once a traditional tension tool has been inserted (either a standard tool at the edge of the plug or a flat tensioner at the center of the plug), there remains essentially *no* additional room for the insertion of picks (see Figure 2.58).

A wishbone tensioner can solve this problem (see Figure 2.59).

The other way by which a wishbone tensioner can prove useful pertains to certain styles of wafer lock. We did not discuss this in the section on wafer locks in Chapter 1, but some such locks are what are known as "double sided wafer locks" in which some of the wafers protrude out from one side of the plug, while others protrude in exactly the opposite direction (see Figure 2.60).

The most typical place that one can encounter double-sided wafer locks is in automotive equipment. Most car doors and vehicle ignitions are double-sided wafer locks. The photo in Figure 2.61 shows a plug from such a lock removed from its housing.

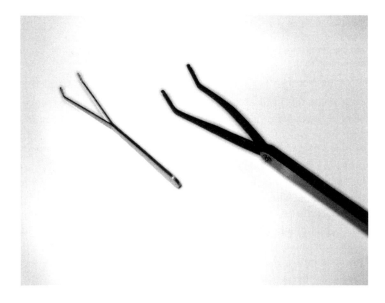

FIGURE 2.57

A small wishbone tensioner (often used for picking small pin tumbler locks) and a large, specialized wishbone tensioner (designed to aid in the opening of automotive locks).

FIGURE 2.58

Once the tension tool has been inserted into this lock that features an exceedingly tiny keyway, there remains essentially no additional room for picks to be inserted and moved about.

FIGURE 2.59

A wishbone tensioner, inserted into the same lock seen above, leaves over twice as much room in the keyway for picks to be inserted and moved with ease.

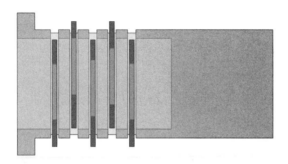

FIGURE 2.60

The plug of a double-sided wafer lock, in which some wafers must be pushed upward and others pressed downward in order to allow the plug to rotate freely.

FIGURE 2.61

The plug from a double-sided automotive wafer lock.

These locks are commonly attacked with raking, much like single-sided wafer locks, but since pressure must often be applied at both the top and bottom of the keyway (often times alternating back and forth between both spots), a traditional tension tool can sometimes get in the way. Whether it's a standard tensioner on one side of the keyway or a flat tensioner at the other side of the keyway, ultimately there often comes a point when a rake needs to move right up against the tension tool's head.

The very small footprint of a wishbone tensioner, however, often allows someone to maintain even turning pressure upon the plug of a double-sided wafer lock, as seen in Figure 2.62.

FIGURE 2.62

A wishbone tensioner being used in a double-sided automotive wafer lock.

It is perhaps appropriate that we have wrapped around again to the topic of wafer locks, since I would like to close this chapter with a mention of one last piece of equipment that can be of great use to you if you have it in your toolkit. I am speaking of jigglers.

Jiggler tools

Let me be frank... I absolutely *love* the set of jiggler tools that I have in the pick kit that accompanies me just about everywhere. I find plenty of uses for them and consider them to be absolutely the most effective way of rapidly opening many of the locks I encounter on pen testing jobs, while making my actions seem the least obvious to those around me.

Much like many of the tools in a lockpicker's kit, jigglers are known by a number of other names. They are often called "wafer lock jigglers," "wafer jigglers," "wafer rakes," or even "wafer picks" due to the fact that they are designed to be used almost exclusively in wafer locks. Still, I find the insertion of the term "wafer" into the name a bit redundant and also potentially confusing, as it invites the misapplied term "rake" or even "pick" as seen at the end of the aforementioned list. Sometimes, jigglers are called "repo keys" or "tryout keys," although this is also a misnomer. Products by those names do exist, but they are rather different in design and function.

Tryout keys (a.k.a "dealer keys" or "repo man's keys") are often made by the manufacturers of automobiles, or are at least designed and fabricated according to the standards for production of actual automotive keys. They tend to have the look and feel of actual automotive keys (see Figure 2.63).

Tryout keys are used by car dealers (and also by automobile repossession agents) when the exact, original key to a vehicle is unavailable. Cars and trucks of the same make will often have door and ignition locks that are all vastly similar to one another. It may surprise the owner of a Ford vehicle to

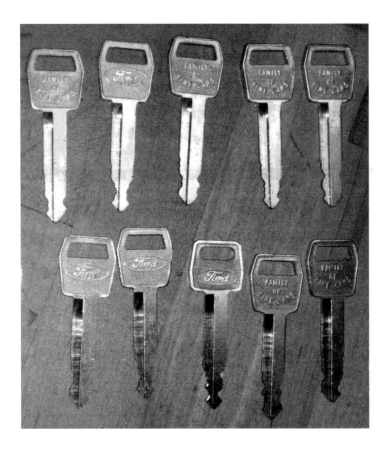

FIGURE 2.63

A series of auto dealer tryout keys.

Courtesy of Ed Roskelly

learn that at least one of only a dozen keys on a large "tryout key ring" will most likely open their car's doors and allow the ignition to start. I drive a GMC truck; in the past, I have successfully used other individuals' car keys (they were also the owners of vehicles made by General Motors) to open my truck's door and even start the ignition. You may have noticed this phenomenon in the past, particularly when a car key has become worn down with age and has a curved appearance on its bitting surfaces. Tryout keys exploit the similarities shared by many automotive locks and work on the principle of "just keep trying them; with luck one is bound to eventually work." Jigglers are not exactly tryout keys, they are something else... and used in rather different ways.

WARNING

Just because jigglers are not explicitly the same thing as tryout keys, sometimes the law will treat them as such. We have yet to discuss many of the finer points of law with regard to lockpicking (in any event, much of that topic is beyond the scope of this book), but it should be understood that *many* state criminal statutes have special categories of crimes that pertain exclusively to automotive property and auto theft. It is in these statutes, which are often written broadly and with stiff penalties, that devices such as "tryout keys" or "repo keys" are regulated. While jigglers are not the same thing, they have a similar enough appearance and function that I could see an over-zealous prosecutor's office attempting to base charges around possession of them in some circumstances. As with all matters pertaining to the subtleties of law, consult with an attorney who is well-versed in the specifics where you live and work.

Actual jiggler tools are far simpler than tryout keys. They are manufactured from thin, flat, stamped pieces of metal and exhibit a very wide array of curves and shapes on the surface of their "blades," as seen in Figure 2.64.

A jiggler can be thought of (more or less) as a rake and a tensioner all in a single piece of material. They are used in somewhat similar ways to rakes—scrubbing back and forth while being held at various angles—but an even greater degree of vertical up/down motion is customary. Hence, the name "jigglers," since they can be moved directly up into a wafer pack or down away from one without pulling in or out of the lock. Tension is applied to a lock during such a tactic not by means of a separate tool, but by attempting to turn the jiggler in its entirety, like a key.

Using jigglers can be a bit of a tricky prospect, but hopefully the following tips and advice will help you. First of all, there is the matter of selecting which jiggler you wish to use (these items are almost always sold as a package set on a key ring or clasp). My advice is to attempt to approximate the shape and style of whatever key you are attempting to "replace" with the jiggler. Is it flat on one side, symmetrical, wide, narrow, etc.? See Figure 2.65 for more advice in this vein.

In practice, the usage of jigglers is as abstract and hard to describe as the act of raking. I can give you a basic idea of some of the motions that you might employ, but the actual performance of this task is as much an art as it is a science. Once inserted in the lock, jigglers can be moved vertically—that is, held flat while being pushed to the bottom of the keyway (Figure 2.66) or the top of the keyway (Figure 2.67)—and they can be worked at varying angles—that is, the tip can be pointed upwards (Figure 2.68) or downwards (Figure 2.69)—all while the tool is being moved to various positions deep in or somewhat pulled out of the lock. Continually attempt to turn the plug, either clockwise (Figure 2.70) or counter clockwise (Figure 2.71) and, hopefully, the plug will eventually turn (Figure 2.72).

Try them out and it just might astound you. . . jiggler tools are an amazing addition to any lockpick kit.

FIGURE 2.64

A typical set of jigglers.

FIGURE 2.65

Choosing the right jiggler tool for the job is often a matter of seeing which one most closely approximates the key for the lock you are attempting to open. On the left of this series of photos, I have highlighted two jigglers that are flat on one side. If I were attempting to open a filing cabinet or desk drawer, I'd start with those. The middle photo shows jigglers that closely approximate most double-sided wafer keys seen in the automotive world (the two on the right half of that highlighted group of four work wonders on GM vehicles, for example). The final photo on the far right shows jigglers that are very vague and which might need a lot of in/out motion to strike all the necessary wafers within a lock. If all else fails, I'd be adventurous and try those.

FIGURE 2.66

Working a jiggler downward into the bottom of the keyway.

FIGURE 2.67

Working a jiggler upward into the top of the keyway.

FIGURE 2.68

Angling a jiggler with its tip pointed upward.

FIGURE 2.69

Angling a jiggler with its tip pointed downward.

FIGURE 2.70

Attempting to rotate clockwise while working with a jiggler.

FIGURE 2.71

Attempting to rotate counter-clockwise while working with a jiggler.

FIGURE 2.72

Success with a wafer jiggler.

SUMMARY

This overview has introduced you to essentially all of the basic tools and techniques for lockpicking, as far as the most typical locks are concerned. Even though there is no shortage of styles and designs for lockpicking tools (as you can see in this book's Appendix: *Guide to Tools and Toolkits*), the actual techniques used to manipulate a lock are fairly uniform and universal. Lifting, raking, and jiggling are the predominant styles of attack that you will use... regardless of what tools you happen to have in your kit. Do not be intimidated by the huge selection of equipment you might see in someone else's collection. (And do not be overly willing to part with your money and invest in a massive "fifty piece" or larger tool set right out of the gate.) Remember that, in general, there are hooks, rakes, and a few other small helper tools. Much of what you see in a typical locksmithing catalog are just variations within these categories. In Chapter 3, we will walk through a series of exercises and lessons that you can use when becoming familiar with these tools in your own hands as you develop your skill.

Beginner training: How to get very good, very fast

INFORMATION IN THIS CHAPTER

- A word on equipment
- The basics of field stripping
- Starter exercises
- Learning exercises
- Challenging yourself further
- Using rakes and jigglers
- Wafer lock exercises
- Extra hints

If you want to become a highly skilled lockpicker, there is nothing that can take the place of dedicated, consistent practice. However, few things can be more frustrating than trying to jump directly into this field by ordering a set of tools from the internet and buying an armload of locks at your local hardware store. If you simply dive right in, you might pop one or two locks (perhaps out of sheer luck), but you are likely to encounter significant frustration much of the time. This book seeks to *ease* you into this field gradually, in a way that is both satisfying and understandable. The lessons in this chapter should go a *long* way towards making your first exposure to lockpicking both rewarding and successful.

A WORD ON EQUIPMENT

There are a number of vendors, both online and at security conferences, who offer items of lock equipment which are designated as some form of training aids. Some of the most popular items are: cutaway locks, weakened locks, and progressive locks. While I can understand the rationale behind each of these products, for the most part I find a lot of them less than desirable, particularly as far as return-on-investment is concerned. Each does serve a function, but in many cases you're likely better off saving your money and obtaining a very small selection of one specific type of training aid.

Cutaway locks

Cutaway locks are very popular sales items offered by most outfits that sell lockpicking supplies. A cutaway is a lock that has had material milled away (either by the manufacturer or by an after-market third party) in such a way as to reveal the inner workings of the lock and make them visually

Practical Lock Picking. DOI: 10.1016/B978-1-59749-611-7.00003-9

FIGURE 3.1

A hand-made cutaway that shows the inner workings of a basic pin tumbler lock.

Courtesy of datagram

observable, often from a side view angle. A typical cutaway lock can be seen in Figure 3.1. Additionally, I have seen a number of locks that are manufactured—in whole or in part—out of Plexiglas or some other see-through resin. Some people will refer to these to as "cutaway" locks, although that would not be a proper term in this case. Still, the effect is similar... the construction allows someone to observe the lock's operation, including elements which would never be visible under normal circumstances. One such pseudocutaway lock can be seen in Figure 3.2. Many of these locks are designed for sales and marketing purposes in order to showcase specific functions of a lock to customers.

While these sorts of products can be useful teaching aids if one is attempting to educate others regarding how *locks* work, in my view they are of limited use when it comes to learning how *picking* works... or, more specifically, how to *become skilled* in the discipline of lockpicking.

The reasons for such a limitation are manifold. Cutaway locks often do not "perform" exactly like their real-world counterparts. The manner in which pin stacks will tend to bind during pressure from the tension tool is harder to predict and make repeatable. Often, the plug of a cutaway can only be rotated in one direction, but not the other, out of concern that pins will come spilling out if they are not properly held captive by the lock's housing. Also, with large segments of the keyway occasionally missing, one wouldn't truly learn the real-world feel of how a tensioner tool might fit or how it would have to share space with a lockpick. Plastic see-through locks solve some of these problems, but often cause others. Such locks are far less robust than their all-metal counterparts, and carelessness or overzealous effort on the part of a novice who is still learning can result in deformation

FIGURE 3.2

A pseudocutaway, see-through lock made by installing a factory plug from a pin tumbler lock into a housing fabricated out of Plexiglas.

of material, not to mention scratches on internal surfaces that will render much of the "see through" experience diminished.

Perhaps the overall reason why such locks are not the most effective training aids is the fact that lockpicking is not a visual process by any real means. Yes, direct viewing of the lock can have its place (as we will see on occasion in this chapter), but the great bulk of what one must observe during the process of lockpicking are subtle hints that are *felt* and *heard* as opposed to *seen*. The best training aids, in my opinion, are ones that allow someone to feel a lock with their own two hands and have it offer up the same sensation and feedback as would be experienced in the real world. To that end, I often support the adoption of progressively pinned locks more than anything else when someone is beginning to learn lockpicking.

Progressively pinned locks

My favorite training aid in the field of lockpicking is a set of progressively pinned locks. Sometimes referred to in sales catalogs by nicknames like "a lockpicking school in a box," these are an array of locks (all of which are typically keyed alike) that pose a slowly increasing challenge to the user in the form of additional pin stacks. Frequently, these progressive training aids are sold as a "kit" and feature multiple, distinct locks which are all separate from one another, bearing labels that designate which lock is which. The progressive locks that I use when conducting training courses, shown in Figure 3.3, are of this style.

While such locks are often the easiest means for a new learner to begin immediately attempting their introduction to picking, recently a different style of progressive training lock has entered the market and has gained significant popularity, particularly among intermediate lockpickers who are seeking to augment their skills. Known as a drilled and tapped cylinder, this is a lock that can be very easily and very rapidly reconfigured without the need for specialized tools or locksmithing skills.

FIGURE 3.3

A set of progressively pined locks, all keyed alike, starting with a single pin stack and containing up to six pin stacks.

A drilled and tapped cylinder—these training aids are also known by other names; one online vendor designates their product simply as an "Ultimate Practice Lock"—is created by milling and drilling additional material away from the top of the housing on a pin tumbler lock. By tapping threads into the tops of the pin chambers, the pins and springs of a pin stack can be retained with small screw caps, as opposed to a top plate or retention cap as was shown in Figure 1.21. All that is needed to quickly service and reconfigure this lock is a small screwdriver or Allen key, depending on what screw caps are used. A drilled and tapped practice lock can be seen in Figure 3.4.

There are advantages and disadvantages to each of these two styles of progressive training aid. A full kit will be easier for an *absolute beginner* to use, without any needed configuration. It also lends itself well to any training exercises wherein someone wants to switch between various difficulties of lock repeatedly and in rapid succession. A drilled and tapped practice lock, on the

FIGURE 3.4

Drilled and tapped practice locks being serviced and re-pinned.

other hand, is sometimes less expensive and usually takes up less space among one's collection of supplies. Additionally, this latter type of practice lock, provided it comes with a collection of extra pins and springs (this is often the case), can be reconfigured to a wider range of difficulties than a simple set of multiple progressive locks.

Ultimately, either progressive lock option is very well suited for the exercises and lessons described in this chapter. Your own budget, space requirements, and level of comfort with lock-smithing skills can dictate what you choose to obtain. If you are particularly adventurous, you can even create your own progressively pinned practice locks. In the upcoming section concerning Field Stripping, we will cover the details of that process, as well.

The importance of a vice

While this can seriously introduce added bulk and weight to any assortment of lockpicking supplies that you begin to assemble, I strongly recommend obtaining a decent vice. It is absolutely possible to pick all sorts of locks (from padlocks to door locks to everything in between) simply by holding them in your hands, but many people find that having a stable platform with which to hold their work pieces does wonders, particularly as novices spend time getting a very comfortable feel for their tools in their hands. Using a vice can also give a much more realistic experience if you are practicing as a penetration tester.

NOTE

Heavy-duty vices used in wood and metal work are not necessary; a simple hobby vice that either clamps on to the edge of a table or sits on top of a table (either with a heavy weighted base or a vacuum attachment) is sufficient. Some individuals speak very highly of vices that feature a ball joint of some kind, allowing for articulation in a wide range of directions.

THE BASICS OF FIELD STRIPPING

If you want to create your own progressively pinned locks as training aids, or if you wish to be able to service and reconfigure many of the locks that you may encounter when searching for new and interesting challenges, you will need to know some basic locksmithing skills. This section could never hope to go into full detail concerning the multitude of facts and details regarding the assembly and installation of locks. Detailed knowledge in categories such as manufacturer-specific criteria, compatibility of tailpieces, interoperability with door and latch hardware, and even a working grasp of various properties of metals can only come from the experience of working professionally in the locksmith trade for years.

However, one rather elementary locksmithing skill that can be learned even by beginners and applied with great effect while learning to pick locks is known as field stripping. Instrumental to the process of rekeying, field stripping is the means by which a lock cylinder can be disassembled with all the parts preserved so that they can be inspected, serviced, and reassembled in either the same or a new configuration. All that is needed are some steady hands and a very simple tool known as a plug follower.

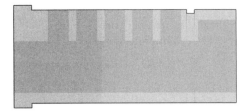

FIGURE 3.5

At a pinch, a wooden dowel can work fine as a plug follower, provided that it is as close as possible in diameter to the plug of the lock you are servicing.

Plug followers can be purchased and obtained through locksmithing catalogs in a wide variety of sizes and materials, but in a sense they often tend to be little more than solid cylinders with a diameter that is very similar to the plug of the lock being serviced. At a pinch, a wooden dowel (or even a raw stick of hot glue) from a craft supply store can work just as well as proper plug follower, as long its size matches up with the relevant plug, as seen in Figure 3.5.

As you know from the material in the first two chapters, the plug of a pin tumbler lock will not effectively move at all if the pin stacks are not set at the shear line. Thus, the first step in field stripping a lock is ensuring you have the means of freeing the plug and allowing such movement. Having the correct operating key is a big help. If you do not have this key, it is necessary to either pick or bump or shim the lock open. (We have already covered picking in Chapter 2. We will discuss the other techniques in Chapter 5.)

Also necessary is the removal of the retaining clip or screw cap from the rear of the plug. If this hardware remains in place, it is not possible to slide the plug outward toward the front face of the lock (which is typically the only direction in which it can ever be ejected). Some people find it easiest to remove such hardware (especially the clip style retaining mechanisms, if they are particularly tight) before the pins have been set, since forcing the plug to remain stationary can assist in this process.

Regardless of the order in which it is achieved, the plug must be made free to move rotationally as well as laterally in the plug, as shown in Figure 3.6. Rotate the plug slightly (this guarantees that the raised driver pins will not become mixed into any other chambers or in any way fall back into the plug) as shown in Figure 3.7 and bring your plug follower tool up against its tail surface as shown in Figure 3.8.

Taking care to keep the open ends of the pin chambers in the plug facing upward, push the follower tool into the housing, as shown in Figure 3.9, thus forcing the plug completely out of the front face of the lock.

If all goes well, you will then be left with two distinct components, both of which will contain pins: an ejected plug, still containing the key pins (see Figure 3.10), and a lock housing with the driver pins and springs still in their original chambers (see Figure 3.11).

The use of a plug follower allows the lock to be re-pinned to a different key bitting and the plug to be reinserted without ever having to displace the driver pins. However, if you do ever need to fully service a lock (for instance, when creating your own set of progressive locks using store-bought products), the plug follower can be removed at this point, allowing the driver pins to spring free, as in Figure 3.12.

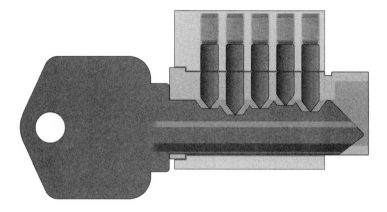

FIGURE 3.6

With the tail clip removed and the operating key in place, this plug is now able to move both rotationally and laterally in the plug.

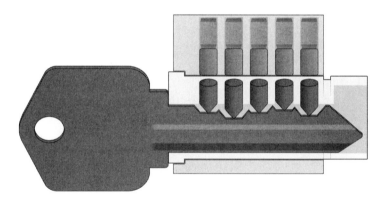

FIGURE 3.7

Rotating the plug slightly will keep the driver pins up and out of the way.

To reassemble a lock, simply reverse this process. Slowly inserting a plug follower into a pin tumbler housing as springs and drivers are placed in their chambers (a small pair of tweezers and/or a small channel cut into the front face of the follower tool is often helpful in this part of the process) will prepare it to accept a plug that has all its key pins in place. With a plug fully inserted, the key can be removed (take care to not accidentally start backing the plug out as you do this), thus locking the whole affair together (as the driver pins will then begin to bind). The plug can now safely and easily have its retaining clip or screw cap reapplied to the tail side.

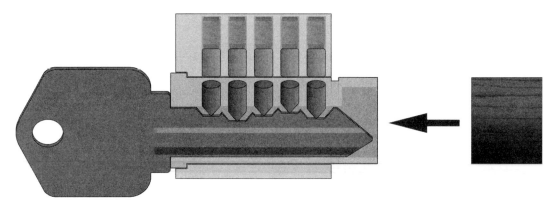

FIGURE 3.8

Bring your plug follower tool up against the tail side of the plug that is about to be removed from the lock housing.

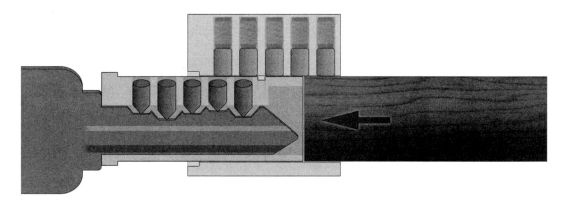

FIGURE 3.9

Push the plug out of the housing using the follower tool. The driver pins will remain in their lifted positions the whole time.

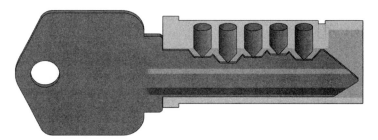

FIGURE 3.10

An ejected plug containing the lock's key pins. Take care not to let the chambers face downward (do not let it roll if you lay it on a tabletop), as those pins will easily slip out.

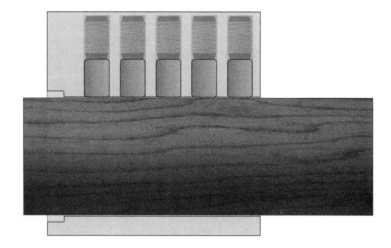

FIGURE 3.11

A pin tumbler lock's bare housing after having ejected the plug. As long as the follower tool is kept in place, the driver pins and stack springs will remain in their chambers.

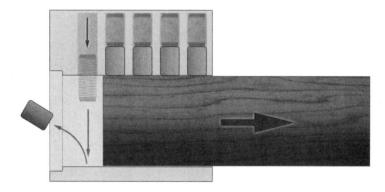

FIGURE 3.12

If you do seek to fully disassemble the lock, simply remove the follower tool and the driver pins will eject out one at a time. Take care, because they will tend to shoot out significantly as the stack springs are under pressure. Be careful not to lose these small components as they spring free.

STARTER EXERCISES

You may use the field-stripping skills described in the preceding section to build your own progressively pinned practice locks, or you can avail yourself of the training supplies that are commercially available. Once you have such suitable locks and a stable mounting surface (like a hobby vice), try the following exercises as a way of familiarizing yourself with your tools and the overall feeling of the lock, particularly the internal components that you can't visually observe directly.

Lockpicking is all about *feel*. . . the only way you're going to "see" what's going on inside the lock is with your hands.

Inserting and moving the pick

Begin by trying to become aware at least at a basic level and establishing an awareness of how deep (or shallow, depending on your perspective) you should ever insert a lockpick into the plug. Take a short hook pick tool (I recommend that you start with this tool for these introduction exercises as well as your first few attempts at picking; a full index of tools is available in the Appendix: *Guide to Tools and Toolkits*) and slowly insert it as deeply as you can within the keyway. As shown in Figure 3.13, do not concern yourself with reaching toward (or even contacting) the key pins. You are interested only in how far the pick tool can move before either reaching an obstruction or emerging out of the tail side of the plug.

Seeing just how deeply you can insert a pick tool will give you some notion of the working space that you have within the keyway. Remember, even the *deepest* pin stack will not be quite this far back from the front face of the lock. Some people will chose to make a small temporary mark on the shaft of their pick tool, a reminder that signifies "The pick *never* needs to go any deeper than this point."

Next, try positioning the pick at various depths within the plug and see how high you can comfortably lift it in the direction of the pin stacks. You may be able to observe that at certain positions you are rather limited in your lifting range (Figure 3.14) while other times you can reach *very* far up beyond the keyway (Figure 3.15). You are feeling the pin chambers and the flat spaces between them. Bear in mind, you should never concern yourself with lifting the pins *beyond* the "top height" that you can reach in-between pin stacks (the height felt in Figure 3.14), since a normal operating key in a typical pin tumbler lock would never need (or indeed, be able to) lift up beyond the height of the keyway.

Find the very first pin stack at the frontmost position within the plug. While it is possible to visually detect when the tip of your lockpick finds the first pin stack directly, recall that I am a big supporter of trying to distinguish and discern things by touch alone. It's never too soon to develop this skill.

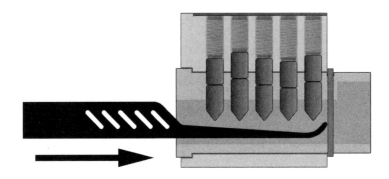

FIGURE 3.13

Insert a lockpick into the keyway as deeply as possible. When it strikes an obstruction and cannot proceed further, note how much of it has entered the lock.

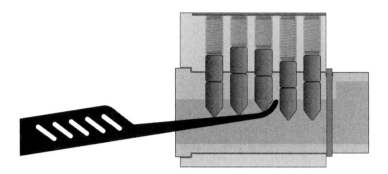

FIGURE 3.14

Try moving the tip of your pick tool in the direction of the pin stacks. You will feel some obstruction at points where you are in-between pins and you strike the "top" surface of the keyway. This is an important "height" since you should rarely, if ever, have cause to push the pick tool beyond that level.

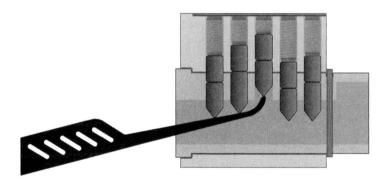

FIGURE 3.15

A pick lifting up on a pin stack and pushing it well beyond the height normally required during picking.

By whatever means you choose, bring the tip of your lockpick right up against the first key pin. Experiment with ways of pushing on the pin stack. The two primary ways of pressing on the pin stacks of a lock during picking are what I call raising and rocking. As with most aspects of lock-picking, as I am often wont to note, it's always a trade-off and both techniques have their own pros and cons.

When pin stacks are moved by the technique I refer to as raising, the pick tool is held relatively horizontal (in alignment with the plug and keyway) the whole time and is lifted "vertically" in its entirety toward the driver pins. As seen in Figure 3.16, the tool's handle is moved upward, and this lifts the pin stack.

Compare that technique with what I call "rocking" the tool. Instead of keeping everything perfectly horizontal, in this method, the handle of the lockpick is moved "downward" while the shaft of the tool rests upon the bottom of the keyway and pivots, as seen in Figure 3.17. Thus, the tip of the pick tool moves upward, and this lifts the pin stack.

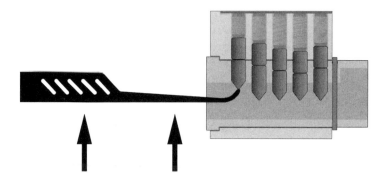

FIGURE 3.16

The method of pushing on pin stacks that I refer to as "raising."

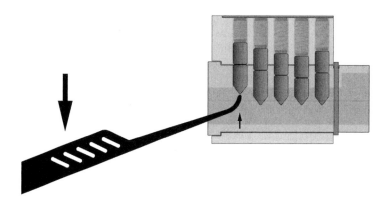

FIGURE 3.17

The method of pushing on pin stacks that I refer to as "rocking."

Which method is better? Well, that's largely a function of what type of keyway is in the lock that you are picking, but the overall concern (as is so often the case) is what works best for you. It is possible to summarize the relevant merits of both techniques by saying that raising can often be performed more easily in very tight keyways that have a lot of warding which complicates pick movement, but rocking is often easier to control and allows for more nuanced articulation of the pin stacks, particularly in locks where pin movement is sticky, tight, or otherwise less than ideal.

Experiment with both of these techniques and feel how your pick tool fits comfortably in your hand (again, whatever seems to work best for you is fine... some people will hold a lockpick like a pencil, others like a chopstick, and still others will grip it with their whole fist and perhaps extend one finger down along the shaft to better feel the subtle tactile clues that a lock will offer when being probed and picked. See Figure 3.18 for examples of each of these distinct styles of holding a lockpick.)

FIGURE 3.18

Three different styles of holding a lockpick. Neither is "superior" to the others in any keyway. All that matters is what is most comfortable for you and which gives you the best articulation and tactile feedback.

Feeling the spring

The time has come when you will want to begin working with a progressively pinned training lock. Start out with just a basic "Progressive Number One"... that is to say, a lock that contains only a single pin stack in the first chamber, as shown in Figure 3.19.

A tension tool is not needed for this exercise; use only a short hook lockpick. Using the pushing techniques described in the previous section and shown in Figures 3.16 and 3.17, and holding a short hook pick using any of the styles shown in Figure 3.18 (or any other grip you find most comfortable), lift this pin stack as shown in Figure 3.20.

Feel the pin stack move up and down. Can you feel the resistance of the spring that is part of this assembly? No matter the angle at which the lock is held, the resistance you feel should remain consistent. Remove the pick, reinsert it, find that first pin stack, and feel the resistance of the spring again.

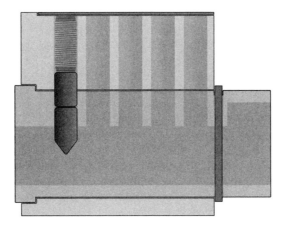

FIGURE 3.19

The first lock in any progressively pinned set of training locks should contain only a single pin stack, located in the first pinning chamber (the one closest to the front face of the lock).

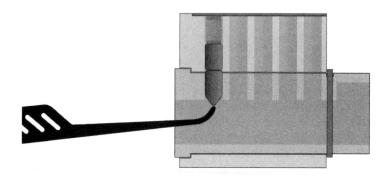

FIGURE 3.20

Lifting the only pinned chamber in the first lock of a progressive set. No tension tool is being used, all one needs to hold is a hook pick.

Setting a single pin stack

Remove your lockpick tool from this Progressive Number One lock. Insert a tension tool into the keyway and apply tension to the plug in either direction you desire. Use any tensioner you like, in whatever manner you choose... but, as described earlier and shown in Figures 2.28, 2.29, and 2.30, the nature of your grip and application of pressure on the tension tool will have a *significant* impact on how successful your picking attempts are likely to be. Do your very best to apply very light pressure to the plug. Because you are currently working with a lock that has only one pin stack, there can be no doubt as to where the binding driver pin in the lock is currently located. It is in the first chamber... that is the only possible chamber, since this is the only pin stack present (see Figure 3.21).

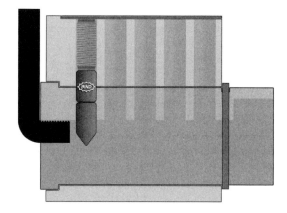

FIGURE 3.21

With tension applied to the first lock in a progressive kit, there is no confusion as to where the binding driver pin is located.

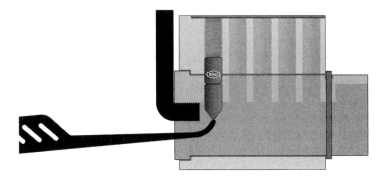

FIGURE 3.22

Pushing on the only binding pin stack within this first progressive lock.

By whatever method you choose, push this binding pin stack (see Figure 3.22) until the driver pin sets at the shear line. Since no other pins are present in the lock, the plug will completely turn at this time. While it may not seem impressive, given that such a lock with only a single pin stack puts up little resistance, do not discount the reality of what has happened just now... some of you may have just picked your first lock!

LEARNING EXERCISES

With the fundamentals now laid down for holding and operating your tools, and with an in-depth understanding of how locks function and how picking works, it is now time for you to try a series of exercises that should help to develop your abilities as a lockpicker. No one can become a master at any intricate skill overnight, but I am confident that if you follow some of these suggested exercises, you'll achieve greater success in a shorter period of time than you otherwise might using other training techniques.

Slow down, lighten up

Start with the same progressive lock from the previous exercise. If it is still "picked", turn it back to the center position and let the driver pin drop back into the plug, locking it in place. Pick the lock again, this time more slowly. Really try to control very deliberately how you lift the pin stack. Once it is picked, reset it again. Pick the lock again, trying to deliberately apply less pressure to the tension tool. Reset the lock, and now pick the lock yet again, this time conscientiously using *even less pressure on the tension tool*. Each time, you may start out thinking to yourself, "I was already using a ridiculously light pressure on the tensioner... there's *no way* that this can work this time." Still, I all but guarantee that each time you lighten up on your tension pressure, it will actually feel much *easier* to move the pins and to allow the "click" moment to happen as the driver pin sets at the shear line.

What you really want to feel is the distinction between a nonbinding pin stack (which will offer some degree of resistance, due to the presence of the spring within the pin stack) and a binding pin stack (which should offer considerably more resistance when you lift it while attempting to set the driver pin). Alternate between attempting to lift the pin stack with no tension tool at all in the lock and applying tension as you lift the pin stack.

NOTE

Learning to distinguish between a binding and a nonbinding pin stack is perhaps the most essential aspect of becoming a skillful lockpicker. Really take the time to alternate between different styles of holding your tools, applying tension, and pressing upon the pin stack when working with this first progressively pinned lock. By becoming adept at distinguishing between the feel of a binding and a nonbinding pin stack, you will be much more successful in your attempts to identify the binding pin amid a whole series of pin stacks.

Two pin stacks

Once you feel confident with your ability to discern some of the tactile feedback that a lock can offer you, switch to the second lock in your progressively pinned kit. Shown in Figure 3.23, this is a lock with two functional pin stacks.

This will be the first lock where you can truly attempt to observe and recognize when you have successfully set one driver pin, but not yet fully unlocked a lock. Apply very light tension to the lock (in the manner you trained yourself to do in the last exercise) and try to push upon either of the two pin stacks. Can you distinguish which one offers almost completely no resistance? Now, an important consideration... if you push properly on the binding pin stack, can you observe the behavior of the lock (particularly the plug) when this first pin out of two becomes set at the shear line?

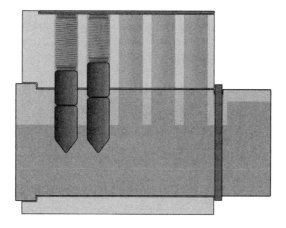

FIGURE 3.23

The second lock in a progressively pinned training kit.

There is a very real chance that you'll be able to feel and/or hear a slight click within the lock. While many of us in the physical security community are quick to point out that lockpicking isn't a visual art, I will mention here that it may indeed even be possible to look at the face of the lock and observe this moment when one pin has set due to slight rotation of the plug. Some people will even choose to make a marker line on the front of their lock (as shown in Figure 3.24) and thus be able to more clearly see when movement has occurred (as shown in Figure 3.25). While this may not be necessary at this early stage of the learning process, it can still be slightly helpful to some people... and it most certainly can be used to great effect later on when we discuss circumventing pick-resistant pins in Chapter 4.

Attempt to pick this second progressive lock (which shouldn't be too difficult, given that it has only two pins) a few times. Try to observe (either visually or manually) the moment the first pin is set and the plug clicks slightly into position. Try turning in the opposite direction as you make some of your attempts. Does the same pin set each time? Or does the binding order reverse? This will become an interesting question as you move on to three and four pin stacks in a lock, etc.

Right here would perhaps be the best place to mention a couple of points about the picking process that are occasionally points of confusion for persons just starting out, as they begin really learning how to set pins. Sometimes, there exists some confusion with respect to the key pin (the "bottom" pin in the stack) and its movement and position within the plug during picking. Some novice pickers can be seen peering deeply into the keyway of a lock upon which they are working, and are sometimes heard to remark with disappointment that they feel they have set a pin, but it's not

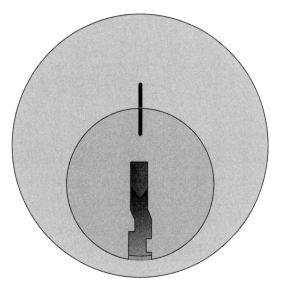

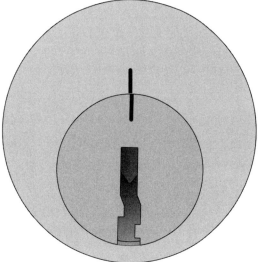

FIGURE 3.24

A marker line drawn on the front face of a lock, showing the default alignment of the plug within the housing when it is at rest.

FIGURE 3.25

After a pin has been set and the plug rotates slightly, the marker line may be able to help you observe this subtle movement.

"staying" up. What they are often observing is the key pin, which is now free to move around in its channel within the plug. This is totally normal. (This was referenced in Chapter 2 and such freedom of movement was even shown specifically in Figure 2.21.) Do not assume that you are not properly setting driver pins simply because you are still seeing the tips of pins hanging in a very low position. It is not necessary (or, indeed, desirable) to keep the entire pin stack (including the key pin) completely static. One does not push the head of the tension tool deeper into the lock, either, in an effort to catch or trap such pins and prevent their continued movement.

In the vein of our exercise for "discerning types of pressure" where I asked you to attempt to distinguish between normal spring force and a binding pin stack, we could add a third category... can you discern when you are pushing on a pin that has *no* pressure acting upon it from the opposite side? When no springs, no binding, nothing at all can be felt... you are almost certainly just feeling a key pin that is floating free within its chamber and you have likely set the driver pin in that position.

Three pin stacks

Have you been able to feel the clicking of the first driver pin you can set while working with the second lock in your progressive training kit? Have you observed a slight rotation of the plug, or heard an audible click when this took place? If you are confident that you were able to discern these subtle cues, you may be ready to move on to a lock that features three pin stacks. Either obtain the third lock in your progressive training set, or if you are working with a drilled-and-tapped practice lock or using field-stripping techniques to build up a lock as you go, reconfigure your existing lock to include three pin stacks, as shown in Figure 3.26.

Continue attempting to pick as you did in the previous exercise that featured the two-pin lock. Can you hunt around and feel for the binding pin stack, then press until you feel the driver pin set at the shear line? Can you distinguish the specific order in which the pins are binding? Does that binding order seem consistent, provided you continue applying tension in a uniform direction? Try applying your tension in the opposite direction... how does this affect the binding order?

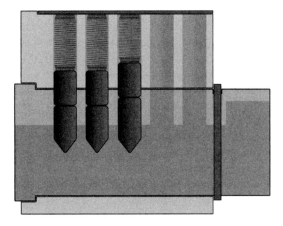

FIGURE 3.26

The third lock in a progressively pinned training kit.

If you are not self-conscious about it, I *highly* recommend that you try to pick with your eyes closed, particularly once you reach this point in your learning process. This can really encourage you to pay attention with your ears and your hands and help you to not rely exclusively on visual evidence, which should become less and less instrumental to the process.

Some people report a significant increase in difficulty between levels three and four of a progressively pin set of practice locks. However, fear not... it isn't necessary to immediately jump right up to the next level. If you are enjoying yourself and you feel you are learning a lot with a Progressive Number Three type of lock, you can continue challenging yourself and developing your skills with this piece alone for a bit longer. In addition to attempting to pick in both directions, try attempting to pick with various styles of tension tool. Center of the plug, edge of the plug, and even wishbone tools can all be used and they will perform in their own unique ways. Try both the raising as well as the rocking methods of pushing the pick into the pin stacks. You may have already settled into a happy routine, featuring the particular tools and techniques that you like the most... but expanding your level of comfort with a wide range of tactics is a very good thing. And it's far easier to achieve such comfort (and to feel satisfaction as opposed to frustration) when working with an easy-to-medium-level lock such as one that features only three pin stacks.

You can vary the situation a bit and keep the challenges interesting even within this single lock, by field stripping it (or by removing the top retaining screw caps, if you are using a drilled-and-tapped lock) and re-pinning it in a different order. Remember, even simply switching the driver pins around can sometimes have an effect on the binding order and the ease with which a lock can be manipulated. True, the inconsistencies in the drilling of the pin chambers often contribute much more to the specifics of binding order, but do not discount the pins. Changing around the existing components within a three-pin lock can offer additional challenges if you feel you aren't quite up to the difficulty of a lock featuring four working pin stacks.

WARNING

If you opt to re-pin your number three lock as advised here, or *any* of your locks for that matter, you should bear in mind that this can remove your ability to operate a practice lock with its original key, should it have come with one. Now, this may not make life difficult with a three-pin or even a four-pin lock, but if you suddenly have no way of easily unlocking a Progressive Number Five or Number Six, you will have a hard time field stripping it again should you wish to remove pins, reconfigure the lock, etc. Of course, a drilled-and-tapped cylinder will not offer such an obstacle, because the tops of its pin chambers can always be removed and all pin stacks can be dumped out at any time.

Four pin stacks and beyond

Once you begin applying these same techniques to locks with four and five pin stacks, you are essentially picking real-world locks at that point. Many common padlocks feature only four pin stacks (like the progressive lock shown in Figure 3.27) and will offer similar levels of resistance to you. The bulk of door locks in North America (especially in residential settings and smaller offices) are five-pin locks.

It is entirely possible at this point for you to visit your local hardware store and seek to acquire additional practice locks. I will offer the following three tips of guidance to you when it comes to acquiring new practice locks:

TIPS

1. Spend Wisely—Don't go crazy right off the bat, buying a dozen or more locks at the hardware store. You may have just wound up with virtually twelve of the same thing. Now, it is true, that sometimes two instances of the exact same make and model lock will perform differently due to variations in their machining. However, in general, it's best to try for some healthy variety of brands, styles, and materials in your locks when you're learning.

2. Security Pins—Occasionally, even cheap locks at local hardware stores will feature some antipick driver pins (or, more than likely, they will occasionally feature one single security pin somewhere). We have yet to discuss the picking of such pins, but we will cover that in the next chapter.

3. Too Cheap Can Be Unhelpful—Some people who experienced considerable trouble picking a four-pin and five-pin lock when working with their progressive training materials may try to minimize the level of difficulty at the hardware store level by obtaining the absolutely cheapest locks they can find. After all, given that picking is made possible by imperfections that arise within a lock due to cost-savings during manufacturing... it is logical to assume that the cheaper the lock is, the more flaws it will offer, and thus the easier it will be to pick. This is *not* always the case. Granted, cheap locks will almost always feature many minor blemishes and imperfections. However, *very* cheap locks will sometimes come from the factories with *very* bad quality controls. In such extreme instances, the locks may not adequately "behave" properly, for lack of a better term. There may be so much wiggle and flop of the plug within the housing that discerning where and how to tension the lock becomes an indelicate, if not impossible, task. There may be so much imperfection among the shape of the pins and their lack of a tight fit within their chambers that the lock can be set in almost any order and with tremendous ease. While these incredibly cheap locks might be of some use to an individual who is practicing raking techniques, they are usually frustrating, more than anything else, to someone who is seeking to lift individual pin stacks with precision. I'd stay away (at least at first) from locks that feature *no* brand name or significant markings and which perhaps cost less than five US Dollars. This is not to say that such sloppy locks aren't an interesting challenge for an established lockpicker (after all, trying to drive fast down a slick or debris-filled road might be a challenge for a racecar driver, and this could bring them more in touch with the intricacies of their particular hobby), but I do recommend that people who are initially working their way up to four-pin and five-pin locks try to stick to middle-of-the-road quality products when browsing store shelves.

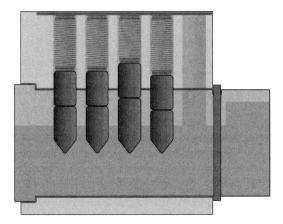

FIGURE 3.27

The fourth lock in a progressively pinned training kit.

CHALLENGING YOURSELF FURTHER

So, perhaps you believe that you've exhausted the possibilities for challenging yourself using progressive training locks and the basic materials that you can buy at the store. Well actually, there are still a number of things you can do with this introductory equipment. By using the field-stripping skills described earlier in this chapter, or simply by unscrewing the tops of a drilled-and-tapped practice lock, you can reconfigure some of the chambers and pin stacks to the following, more advanced, styles.

Deep reach practice

Take a look at the keys on your key ring. I'm willing to bet that few, if any, of them feature an entirely "downward stair" pattern of bitting cuts that grow increasingly low as you look out along the blade, moving away from the shoulder. Almost always there is some point within a lock where you must push "up" (from a North American perspective) on a deeper pin while taking care to not overlift additional pin stacks closer to the face of the lock.

You can pin your locks specifically in ways which allow you to practice this skill. Begin with a simple approach, using a lock with only two working pin stacks. Ensure that the frontmost key pin (the one closest to the outer face of the lock) is longer (thus representing a deeper cut on the key blade at that position) than the key pin in the chamber behind it (see Figure 3.28).

Use this lock to examine whether or not you have any difficulty reaching far enough with your hook to work on the rearmost pin without disturbing the pin stack that is closer to the front face of the lock (see Figure 3.29).

Experiment with moving this pair of pin stacks deeper within the lock. Install them in the third and fourth chambers, or perhaps even the fourth and fifth! Can you still reach adequately and

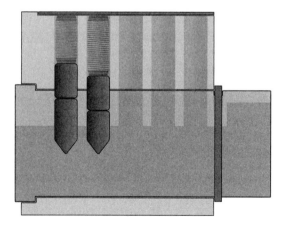

FIGURE 3.28

A "deep reach" practice lock, equipped with a longer key pin in the first chamber.

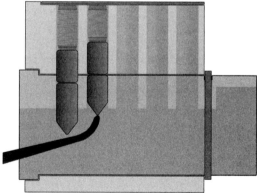

FIGURE 3.29

Reaching carefully with a pick in order to push on a shorter key pin, buried more deeply within the lock than a much longer key pin that is located in the first stack.

appropriately within the lock? Can you pick it in a repeatable and reliable fashion? Experiment with different types of tension tools here, too. Using a standard tensioner at the edge of the plug may not leave you enough room in the keyway to make this reach from such an extreme angle. A flat style tensioner, inserted at the middle of the plug, might become necessary.

You can begin to attempt this manner of deep reach picking on locks that contain increasing numbers of functional pin stacks. By alternating between long and short key pins (with shorter ones located one chamber deeper than each long one, as seen in Figure 3.30), you can begin to offer yourself some *serious* challenges, often beyond even what you might ever find on typical store shelves. This is because of a consideration with which professional locksmiths must address on a regular basis: something known as a lock's Maximum Adjacent Cut Specification, or MACS.

Manufacturers of locks do not just codify the *depths* of the possible bitting cuts with scalar, numerical values. Other factors exist regarding pin size and pin order with which a locksmith must contend. One such issue pertains to the sizes of key pins which can be placed side by side in a lock. Two *exceedingly* different-length pins cannot usually occupy chambers directly next to each other. This is because cuts on the blade of a key must be made at specific, gently sloping angles. Consider the blade of the average key we have been discussing in this book's illustrations, first appearing in Figure 1.22. Think about how the pin stacks ride against the key as it enters the lock, as shown in Figure 3.31. What if the cuts on the blade of a key were made at very sharp, more "vertical" angles? How easily could the key depicted in Figure 3.32 enter the lock? It would be much harder to move the blade along the key pins.

There is nothing in particular about the key in Figure 3.32 that would make it unsuited to rotate the plug of this lock; it would raise all of the pin stacks to their requisite heights, after all. But it would probably be quite an ordeal to get this key inserted into (not to mention subsequently removed from) the keyway. The bitting cuts on the blade of a key need to be at a shallow enough angle to provide the gentle slope necessary to allow for easy movement of the pin stacks.

If a very long key pin (say, a number eight bitting size) were installed in a lock right next to a very small pin (perhaps a number two pin), one of the two outcomes would be likely. Either the

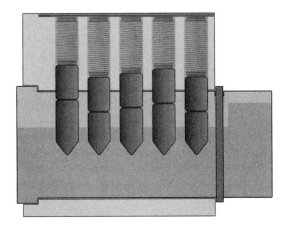

FIGURE 3.30

A practice lock that has been keyed in a repeating "high/low" pattern in order to offer an additional challenge.

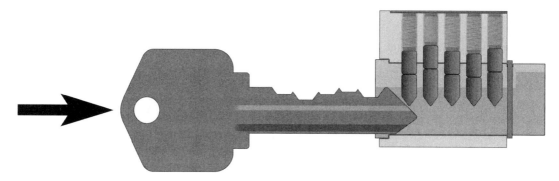

FIGURE 3.31

A typical key being inserted into a lock. The key experiences little difficulty as it travels through the keyway.

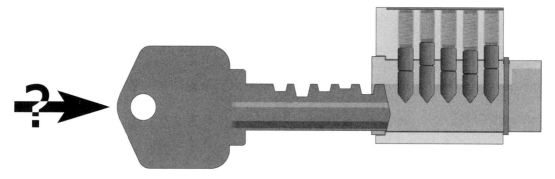

FIGURE 3.32

A highly atypical key featuring bitting cuts that are much steeper and more vertical on their sides. How easily could a key like this be inserted into the lock?

bitting cuts on the blade of the key would have to be made exceedingly sharp and vertical, similar to what is seen in Figure 3.32, or the "deep" cut of a number eight value would have a collateral effect on the adjacent cut positions. A bitting cut at depth number eight (if made with a traditional, wide, and gently angled cutting wheel) would "spill over" to a large degree, preventing that same cutting wheel from creating a proper number two cut depth at the next position.

Because of considerations like MACS that affect products in the real world, it is even possible for you to create practice locks that *exceed* the level of difficulty (as far as bitting codes are concerned) that you would find in the real world.

Blindly mix and match

There's no substitute for the element of surprise. If you have pinned and assembled a lock yourself, you will have a pretty good idea of what components are inside even after you can no longer see them. Field stripping and reconfiguring your practice locks are indeed a fine way to offer yourself some additional challenges, but for maximum effect you might consider asking a friend or associate to play the role of the pseudo-locksmith for you. Put them in charge of reconfiguring the lock, then simply giving it back to you. You are now able to begin inspecting it and attacking it, blind to what specific components are inside. A great many possible games and challenges can be possible like this.

One such game is similar to a training activity that some of my associates in the physical security world and I enjoy at the firing range. It works by having an associate load the magazine of an automatic pistol or rifle, inserting a dummy round of ammunition somewhere in the stack of traditionally bullets. When this magazine is subsequently used, at some point during your shooting the dummy round will be encountered and the gun will fail to fire. As a shooter you then react accordingly, clearing the malfunction and reengaging the target as quickly and efficiently as possible, and one's behavior under such a scenario can be evaluated and assessed. The fact that you, the shooter, did not load the magazine adds greatly to the realism and usefulness of this exercise, since you cannot predict when (if ever) such an inconsistency in the performance of the hardware will happen.

Consider having your friend do something odd to one pin stack of the lock when they are assembling it. If you can spare a spring, cut one down to a smaller size (as seen in Figure 3.33).

Even though it might look quite strange (and could eliminate your ability to use a key in the lock until the next time you field strip and reconfigure it yet again), consider having someone use a driver pin in place of a key pin in one chamber (as seen in Figure 3.34).

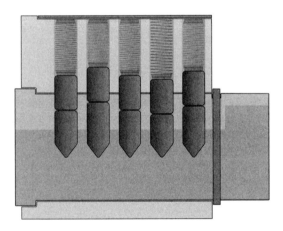

FIGURE 3.33

A practice lock that features a spring in one chamber which is different from all the others. The spring in chamber number four has been cut slightly, thus offering slightly less resistance when pressed upon.

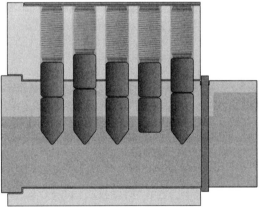

FIGURE 3.34

A practice lock that features a key pin in one chamber which is different from all the others. In the fourth chamber, a driver pin is being used as a pseudo key pin. This might not function properly (note how it cannot drop completely into the pin chamber due to its distinct shape) but can make for an unexpected fun feature within a lock.

Reaching into such a lock and being asked to simply "inspect" each chamber with one's pick tool to try and find which pin stack is not like the others can offer a unique challenge and help someone develop the all-important skill of "seeing with their hands", which is essential to the process of lockpicking.

Of course, beyond these particular diversionary games, it is entirely possible to get a lot of good practice from simply asking your friends and associates to re-pin functional locks for you in order to introduce a plenty of variety representing all the different orders of bitting and binding that you may face with locks in the real world.

USING RAKES AND JIGGLERS

It is hard to spend considerable time describing how to use rake picks and jiggler tools. The method is so random and success can happen so suddenly as a result of a number of small, perfectly timed coincidences. Still, I can try to offer a few points of advice with respect to the use of these items:

1. Speed—When either raking or jiggling, fast movement is the key. Remember, these are not techniques that require finesse; they are designed to catch multiple pins or multiple wafers in the right place at the right time.
2. Variation—It's never easy to predict the exact right position for one's rakes or jiggler tools. The only way you're likely to get lucky when attempting to attack a lock in this manner is by introducing a lot of variety into the use of your tools. Hold the rake perfectly horizontal, then angle it slightly downward, and also slightly upward... all the while moving in and out of the lock rapidly. You can even keep the rake relatively horizontal but vary the overall "height" at which it is being positioned in the keyway. Using some degree of varying pressure on your tension tool is also often a helpful tactic if you aren't experiencing much luck.
3. Light Tension—Due to the feverish, often violent, movements that are associated with raking and jiggling, it is sometimes very easy to slip into the bad habit of applying too much pressure on the tension tool. No matter how clenched your muscles are in one hand, as it rapidly moves your raking tool back and forth, keep your other hand relaxed and do everything in your power to apply gentle, subtle tension to the plug.

Techniques of tool movement

Rakes and jiggler tools can be operated in a number of ways. They can be held almost perfectly horizontal and moved directly along the bottom surface of the key pins in a lock, as depicted in Figure 3.35. This same motion (a direct in-out movement perfectly parallel to the pins) can be

FIGURE 3.35

Straight in–out, lateral movement of a rake pick, held horizontally and moved directly along the key pins.

FIGURE 3.36

Angled in–out, lateral movement of a rake pick, held at a slightly off-angle but moved directly along the key pins.

performed with the rake held at varying angles, as depicted in Figure 3.36. Jiggler tools, on the other hand, are often used with a much greater focus on "vertical" movements accompanying any in-out motion. A series of punctuated up and down motions can force the pins or wafers to move dramatically... as you hope to catch most or all of them close to the shear line at the same time. This motion (shown in Figure 3.37) is less commonly done with a *rake pick*, but it can still be attempted if the need arises... particularly with wafer locks. Of course, there are also tools like the famous Bogotá picks (which will be discussed further in the Appendix: *Guide to Tools and Toolkits*) and they can indeed be used in this fashion to great effect. The last style of typical rake and jiggler usage could be called the "elliptical" movement. Like a piston connected to a crankshaft, the tip of your rake or jiggler tool is worked in and out of the lock while the handle is moved in large, curved arcs. This results in relatively straight in-out movement of the tool's working surface, but with the additional virtue of many small fluctuations on the angle of attack at which the tip is being held. The elliptical style of movement is depicted in Figure 3.38.

As with all other aspects of lockpicking, go with whatever works for you (and doesn't result in lock damage or some other epic fail in the process) and you'll be fine. Practice until you're comfortable and confident with any tools and techniques... even ones of your own design.

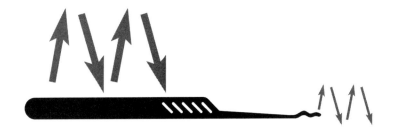

FIGURE 3.37

Jagged vertical movements with a rake pick. This technique is actually much more commonly used with a lifter tool or jiggler as opposed to a pick, but in a wafer lock this might be effective with a rake pick if for some reason in–out motion is having no effect.

FIGURE 3.38

Elliptical movement with a rake pick. The handle is worked in wide, repeated arcs as the tool is moved in and out of the lock, providing a series of nicely varied movements on the part of the rake or jiggler tip.

WAFER LOCK EXERCISES

In spite of the fact that they are of a much simpler design, some people experience difficulty when picking wafer locks for the first time. Since they are not attacked with conventional lifting (which is what all of the exercises here have focused upon up until this point in the chapter), it may be hard to imagine just where to start with the raking and jiggling attacks that are necessary.

Progressive wafer locks

I am not aware of any training supply outfit that sells progressively assembled wafer lock sets. You will occasionally see a few for sale at a conference, but most vendors do not produce them in large quantity. This is due to the fact that just about *anyone* can create their own such kit with ease, quite quickly, for almost no cost. Obtain three or four wafer locks from a hardware store (check in aisles that stock window locks, hinges, and hardware for sliding glass doors) that prominently feature a screw on their tail side.

These locks will usually be able to completely slide apart when that screw is removed. This will expose the wafers and allow you to easily yank out any that you wish to remove. Use a pair of needle-nose pliers to pull (or even a flat-head screwdriver to push) the unneeded wafer(s) out of the plug, then reassemble it. Trust me, you do *not* need to start with a *single*-wafer lock. Even attempting a two-wafer lock will seem trivial. (That is not to say that such locks don't exist in the real world... they *do*!)

Wafer locks of this variety often cost five dollars or less. You can create a whole progressive set, if you really want to, for less than the cost of a set of pick tools.

Tensioning wafer locks

Some people have difficulty adapting to the oddly square keyways on wafer locks. Since anything inserted into such a lock can inevitably stick clear *through* the wafers within the plug, it is possible that the longer head of a standard tension tool will disturb the process somewhat. Don't be afraid to experiment with a flat tensioner or even a wishbone style tool. If you are still having trouble when just starting out, try applying tension to the plug by pressing manually on the tail cam (as shown in

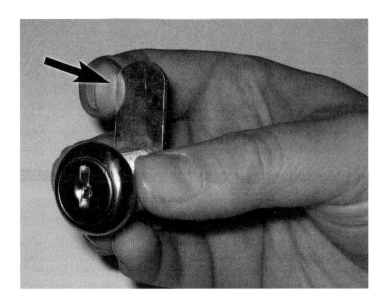

FIGURE 3.39

Applying tension to a wafer lock by pressing with one's finger directly upon the tail cam instead of using a tension tool. This isn't something you can do in the real world (since the tail piece is essentially always hidden from easy access), but this technique can help you become more comfortable with raking and jiggling a wafer lock when you are just starting out.

Figure 3.39) as opposed to using a tension tool at all. Once you become comfortable with raking by this method, you can try working with a proper tensioner instead.

Trust me, it will get easy. If you are having a lot of trouble with wafer locks at first, you're overthinking it. Relax, vary your angle of attack and your tension, and it will all fall into place.

EXTRA HINTS

If you try to walk through the exercises suggested in this chapter, I guarantee you will be amazed at how quickly you will start to see results. As you experiment with more and more real-world locks, the following advice may serve you well and help you to overcome minor confusing issues that crop up.

Which way to turn

A common inquiry when people are in my classroom trainings and public lectures is, "Which direction should I turn the plug?" When you are attempting to pick any practice locks, they will almost always be able to turn in either direction. Of course, the binding order will typically vary... not to mention that in one direction you will be unlocking, while turning in the other direction will entail relocking. Still, since this book is geared primarily towards penetration testers, we will assume that you are most interested in discerning how to unlock items that you encounter in a secured state during auditing and assessment jobs.

Unlock direction for pin tumbler locks

This is actually quite a simple topic, most of the time. Padlocks (as seen in Figure 3.40) whether large or small or expensive or cheap, will tend to open if the plug turns clockwise. On particularly basic padlocks (like the Master Number 3 padlock), it is often possible to turn the plug in *either* direction and still release the shackle.

For doorknobs that feature integrated pin tumbler cylinders (these are known as key-in-knob locks and one can be seen in Figure 3.41), the reverse is almost always true. Turning the plug counterclockwise is the default direction to unlock these models. Of course there are occasional variations to this standard, but they are quite rare.

Just about the only time life gets complicated pertains to deadbolts. The rules here are not quite as consistent and regular as those described earlier, but I will give you the best advice that I can. To make an educated guess as to which direction it will be necessary to turn a deadbolt in order to unlock a door, it is important to understand some very basic features of how dead latch mechanisms interact, how the bolt is thrown, and why this makes various doors work differently from what you might expect.

Deadbolt locks consist of a bolt mechanism that is acted upon by a cam within the door. The cam is integrated in some fashion to the plug of the deadbolt's lock, often by means of a tailpiece, but sometimes (particularly on European lock cylinders) the cam is integrated directly into the plug and not easily removed. The actual bolt mechanism tends to be mounted slightly above the lock

FIGURE 3.40

Padlocks... always try turning the plug clockwise if you want to open them.

FIGURE 3.41

Locking doorknobs. . . always try turning the plug counterclockwise if you want to open them.

(and here, the term applies without much worry of geographical bias, since no matter what direction the lock is *mounted* in its fitting, the bolt does almost always tend to be installed in the door in a position that is vertically "above" the plug and cam components of the lock).

When the plug is turned, the cam will often tend to interact with the bolt upon its "bottom" surface. Observe the diagrams in Figures 3.42–3.44 to better understand this relationship. The crux of what must be understood is that to cause movement of a deadbolt, you typically will want to get the *top of the plug* moving in the desired unlock direction. In the hypothetical deadbolt in these diagrams (mounted in a door such that the bolt protrudes out the left side when you look at the door externally), you want the bolt to move to the *right* during unlocking. Thus, to get the *top of the plug* moving in a rightward direction, that would entail trying to rotate the plug clockwise. If this door were reversed (with hinges on the left side as you approach it and thus with the locking bolt protruding outward and into a door jamb on the right side), then you would be best served by attempting to turn the plug counterclockwise. . . thus making the top of the plug (and, by association, the bolt itself) move to the left.

Of course, if you pick a lock in the wrong direction, it's rarely the end of the world. Simply flip the plug back up to its default position and try picking in the other direction. There are even specialized tools called plug spinners that are designed to introduce a rapid rotating movement to the plug (usually by means of discharging a spring that has been placed under pressure) in the desired direction. Thus, if you have picked a lock in the "wrong" direction (either by mistake or because it was simply easier that way due to the binding order), a plug spinner can help you attempt to still flip the plug the other way and thus open the lock without the need to re-pick the cylinder a second time.

FIGURE 3.42

A deadbolt installed in a door, with the locking bolt protruding out from the left side.

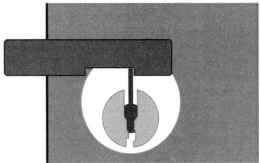

FIGURE 3.43

This pseudocutaway view attempts to show the relationship between the plug and the locking bolt, by means of a cam on the rear of the plug.

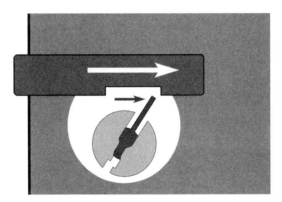

FIGURE 3.44

In this particular deadbolt, turning the plug clockwise (from the perspective of someone outside the door) would retract the bolt and unlock the door.

Unlock direction for wafer locks

Worrying about which direction to turn a wafer lock is rarely an issue. These devices are typically so simple to pick that it's faster to just try one direction and if that doesn't help you, try the reverse.

Plugs stuck upside-down

The last tip I will give you before closing this especially long chapter pertains to a situation in which you may occasionally find yourself. If you pick a lock and turn the plug a full one hundred and eighty degrees, occasionally it will become stuck in this position. Do not panic. Figure 3.45 should give you a good idea of what may have happened.

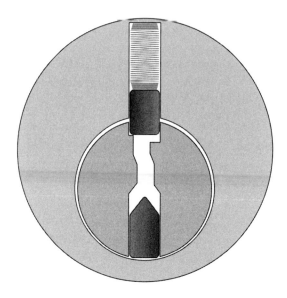

FIGURE 3.45

A plug that has become "stuck" in an "upside down" position is often being held that way by one or more driver pins which have slipped into the underside of the keyway.

Some keyways are cut wide enough at their base to allow the driver pins in a lock to fall out of the housing slightly and slip into the plug at its underside if it has been turned completely around. This would normally not take place during routine operation of the lock because the metal blade of the key would be occupying this space in the keyway... plus the fact that many locks never require a full one hundred and eighty degree rotation in order to lock or unlock.

In any case, if you do accidentally get stuck in this fashion, simply insert a tool with a perfectly flat surface (the underside of a half-diamond pick will work well) up against the driver pins and try to lift them all simultaneously, not unlike the technique described in Figure 2.45. That diagram depicts the lifting of entire pin stacks, so as to release them and count them by hearing them fall. In this case, you're just attempting to free the plug from the intrusion of driver pins alone. You may not have to lift nearly as far. Figure 3.46 demonstrates the motion you're going after. If you lift the right amount, as shown in Figure 3.47, the plug should become free and be able to turn again. Use a tension tool or even just the pick that you have currently inserted to rotate it back in the proper direction.

SUMMARY

This chapter discussed an overview of the basic types of equipment that are particularly helpful when starting out with a study of lockpicking and presented information on the process by which this equipment can be serviced and reconfigured. Getting either a good set of progressively pinned locks or a drilled-and-tapped training lock will allow for a wide range of learning exercises.

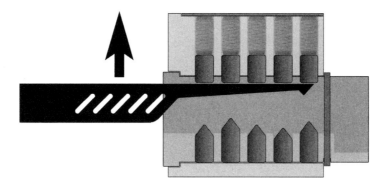

FIGURE 3.46

Use the flat side of a half-diamond pick if the plug becomes trapped in an "upside down" position.

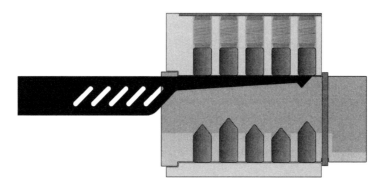

FIGURE 3.47

With the tool lifting the driver pins, they are freed from the plug and it can again rotate normally. Flip it back to the proper position.

With an adequate plan of action, such as the steps for learning highlighted here, much of the initial difficulty that some people experience can hopefully be avoided. A number of extra challenges can be had with typical locks if they are reconfigured to test a lockpicker's dexterity and breadth of techniques.

Inexpensive, preinstalled wafer locks and their exceedingly simplistic design provide a different type of challenge to lockpickers, but they are quite easy to attack once their construction is understood. This knowledge of the means by which locks can be exploited, along with the overview of a few additional tips and tricks at the end of the chapter should have you quite prepared to tackle any number of small obstacles that you encounter during penetration tests or even just casual, hobbyist picking sessions.

Advanced training: Learning some additional skills

INFORMATION IN THIS CHAPTER

- Pick-resistant pins
- Specialized picking techniques
- Specialized picking tools
- Practice exercises
- Real-world locks that offer greater challenges

Some manufacturers add features to their locks that are designed to make them more resistant to picking attacks. The degree to which these companies are successful in this effort depends largely on how much money they are willing to spend on design, manufacturing, and assembly. A number of interesting modifications to the components of a lock can make it "pick resistant," sometimes significantly so. Still, by and large the market for consumer grade lock products is driven by cost more than by form and function. Even locks that are described as somehow "more secure" on their packaging can often be overcome with some dedicated effort. All that is needed is patience, and a fundamental understanding of what is actually taking place inside of the device at a mechanical level.

PICK-RESISTANT PINS

Recall from Chapter 1 that most conventional pin tumbler locks feature key pins that are either cylindrical or slightly tapered to a point on their leading tip along with driver pins that are almost entirely cylindrical and uniform in size (see Figure 4.1).

Perhaps the simplest and most common means for making a traditional pin tumbler lock more resistant to picking attempts is the inclusion of pick-resistant pins (also known as "security pins") when the lock is being assembled. By changing the milled shape of some of the pins within a lock (particularly, the driver pins), it is possible to frustrate the normal methods of pin movement associated with lockpicking. This is a particularly popular option for companies with established production lines and a number of models of lock already on the market, as it does not require a major overhaul of their existing factory machining and equipment assembly processes. All large parts of the lock (housing, plug, tail piece, mounting hardware) remain exactly the same... it is only slightly different pins that are inserted into some (or very occasionally all) of the chambers.

Practical Lock Picking. DOI: 10.1016/B978-1-59749-611-7.00004-0

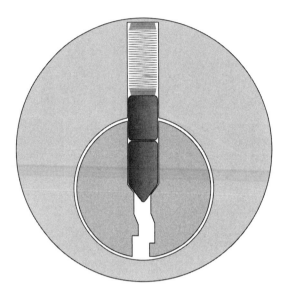

FIGURE 4.1

A conventional lock (the like of which we have already examined in this book) viewed from a front-facing perspective.

Pins with lips

The most popular type of pick-resistant pin is known as a spool pin, so named because it has the appearance of a spool of thread or wire (see Figure 4.2). These types of driver pins can be produced with relative ease by the same machines and processes that fabricate traditional, cylindrical driver pins. Another virtue of spool pins that appeals to many companies who produce locks is their symmetry... there is no way of accidentally installing a spool pin in a lock "upside down" and diminishing its efficacy. Thus, factories that incorporate large-scale automation can more easily use this type of security pin in their production lines as opposed to some other types of pick-resistant pins, which we will discuss shortly.

In Chapter 2, you learned about the process by which lockpicking is performed. It is likely that you can already predict the manner in which a driver pin of this design can frustrate such attempts. When tension is applied to the plug, if this particular pin stack happens to be the one that will bear the brunt of the binding force, it will not simply become trapped against the walls of the pin chamber by its vertical edges. Instead, the spool shape will allow the plug to rotate much further than expected (as seen in Figure 4.3). If lifting pressure is then applied to the binding pin stack, it will not easily "click" into position at the shear line. Instead, the particularly significant angle of the spool pin will cause its protruding lip to catch on the edge of the housing, potentially preventing any additional movement (see Figure 4.4).

Pick-resistant pins come in plenty of other varieties beyond the simple spool style. Another popular design is the mushroom driver pin (see Figure 4.5).

This style of driver pin will have a larger surface area upon which its edge can contact (and thus drag along) the walls of a pin chamber during the binding process. This will offer greater

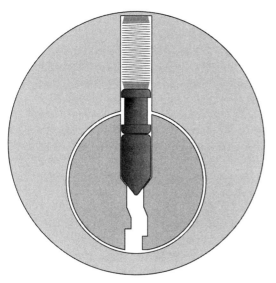

FIGURE 4.2

A lock featuring a pick-resistant spool driver pin, as viewed from a front-facing perspective.

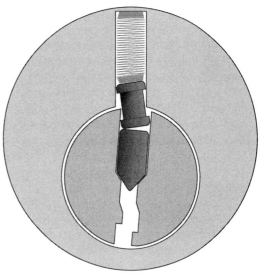

FIGURE 4.3

With tension applied to the plug, a spool type driver pin will allow for significantly greater rotation than a conventional, cylindrical driver pin would.

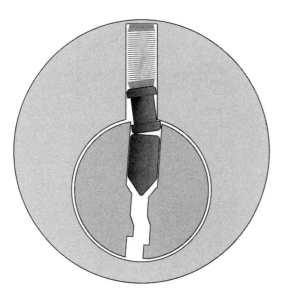

FIGURE 4.4

If a spool pin is binding, the pin stack can be pushed slightly toward the shear line, but it will ultimately get held up when the edge of the spool catches the lip of the lock's housing. It is much harder to push the pin to the proper position at this point.

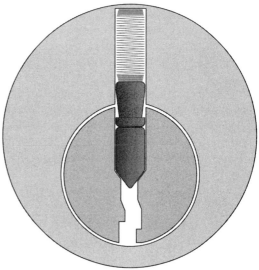

FIGURE 4.5

A lock featuring a pick-resistant mushroom driver pin, as viewed from a front-facing perspective.

friction and thus present slightly more challenge to an individual attempting to push upon that particular binding pin stack. The reason this style of driver pin hasn't seen quite as much market penetration as the simple spool (in my opinion) likely has less to do with the slightly more involved process of milling but instead pertains to the fact that a mushroom driver pin can only be installed in one direction in order to be fully effective. Thus, certain fully automated assembly lines (that feed driver pins from large supply bins) would likely be incapable of reliably inserting these pins in the correct manner.

The spool and mushroom varieties of pick-resistant driver pin are the most popular in a general sense, but they are by no means the full extent of such pins in use today. Some manufacturers have developed their own custom designs that are truly a sight to behold. For example, the TrioVing company (the leading vendor of locks in Norway) uses a hybridized "double mushroom spool pin" (this is simply my term) in every single chamber of even their least expensive pin tumbler locks. Figure 4.6 shows the shape of these unique driver pins. These pins offer a particular advantage to those assembling and configuring a lock. Conventional spool pins, as we have seen, allow for significant rotation of the plug even when the pin stacks are all at rest.

Imagine a simple pin tumbler lock in which *all* the driver pins are conventional spool pins. With no key in the lock, there would still be significant "wiggle" in the plug. It could, in essence, oscillate to the left or right by 10° or more, similar to what is represented in Figure 4.1. Not only would this allow someone inspecting the lock to almost instantly realize the internal makeup of the pin stacks, but it can also potentially complicate the use of the proper key. Attempts to insert or remove the blade of a key in the keyway of a lock will only be successful if the pins can traverse up and down

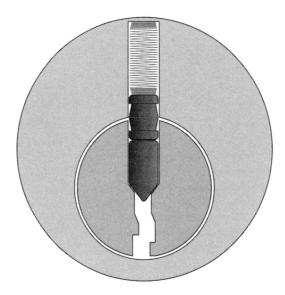

FIGURE 4.6

A lock containing a driver pin of the "double mushroom spool" variety used extensively by the TrioVing company of Norway.

with ease, allowing the bitting ridges of the blade to pass the stacks smoothly. If the pins cannot move up and down, the key will jam and be unable to move further in (or out, for that matter... this is why a key cannot be removed from a lock when the plug is turned, by the way).

The TrioVing design is unique because these driver pins can be installed in all of the chambers without causing the lock to experience this potentially problematic "wiggle" effect in its plug. These pins are also monsters to pick without serious practice. I have taken TrioVing locks and prepared progressive training sets with them in the past. I can only reliably and routinely pick open such a lock with three pin stacks, and even then it becomes quite difficult. Traditional TrioVing locks have six or seven pin stacks. They are quite formidable. (We learned, though, they *can* be bumped! We will discuss the bump key attack in Chapter 5. I offer my heartfelt thanks to John-Andre Bjørkhaug for discovering the perfect TrioVing bump key and sharing it with me!)

Pins with serrations

Not all pick-resistant pins rely on large, protruding lips at their edges in order to frustrate conventional lockpicking attempts. Some pins are milled with numerous small cuts, known as serrations, across most or all of their surface (see Figure 4.7). Such serrated pins naturally have a much greater degree of friction against the walls of the pin chambers and therefore are harder to push into the necessary positions at the shear line. It is very common for someone to over-lift pin stacks that feature serrated pins. Since these serrations can cause an increase in pin friction no matter where they are located, sometimes lock manufacturers will even engineer their *key pins* in this manner. The line of products from American Lock often features serrated key pins, for example.

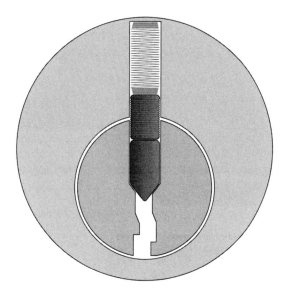

FIGURE 4.7

A lock featuring a pick-resistant serrated driver pin, as viewed from a front-facing perspective.

Coordinated pick-resistant components

Some manufacturers who wish to significantly hamper lockpicking will go to ever greater lengths when it comes to modifying the pins than the designs we have just now examined. The noted Dutch locksmith and revered security researcher Han Fey wrote an article[1] showcasing some of the incredible pick-resistant features found in the products of locks produced by the Swedish company ASSA. Han described in great detail what he refers to as "sneaky pins" that jam and bind in a variety of very frustrating ways. This is due, in part, to the fact that the pin chambers of the plug incorporate what is known as "counter milling" near the shear line. These extra lips provide even more ways for the pins to catch, jam, and refuse to move unless a proper key is being used. See Figure 4.8 for greater detail concerning just how "sneaky" some pins can be, and where counter-milling appears in some locks.

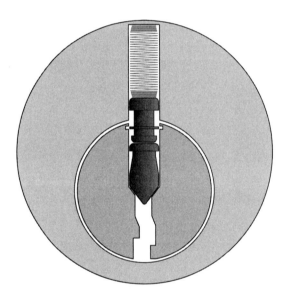

FIGURE 4.8

A lock featuring highly pick-resistant driver pins and key pins, as viewed from a front-facing perspective. Note the counter-milling that has been performed within the plug near the "top" of the pin chambers, just next to the shear line. The key pin, a style sometimes known as a torpedo pin, is designed to frustrate attempts at impressioning.

SPECIALIZED PICKING TECHNIQUES

Despite their intimidating appearance, it is often possible to still pick open locks that feature these sorts of specialized pins. While I'll admit that it is unlikely that the ASSA design shown in the last example could be defeated regularly and repeatedly by anyone other than a handful of the world's top lockpickers, such pins are not nearly as common as simple spool drivers. With some understanding, patience, and—above all—practice... you, too, can tackle and overcome locks that feature typical pick-resistant pins.

Counter-rotation

The critical aspect of picking locks that feature spool pins (as well as the various pins of a related design, like mushroom drivers, multispool drivers, and combined designs such as the TrioVing pins) has to do with what lockpickers often call counter-rotation. In order to help a pin stack move beyond the point where these features would normally "trap" it on a lip or edge, the plug must be allowed to rotate slightly in the direction *opposite* to the way it is being picked. The diagrams in Figures 4.9–4.13 will help to explain this concept further.

When starting out with the process of trying to attack (or even just trying to learn more about) pick-resistant pins, some lockpickers will draw a marker line on the front face of their lock, across the plug and the housing, so that they can more accurately visualize any small rotation that takes place. In this hypothetical example, we will look at a lock featuring a spool pin (see Figure 4.9).

When pressure is applied to the plug and this pin stack binds, there will be very significant rotation visible. The two marks will likely become completely separated, and the plug may turn as much as 10° (see Figure 4.10).

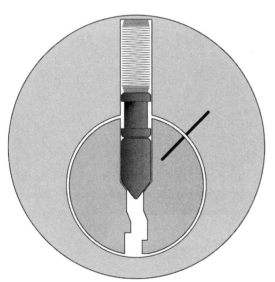 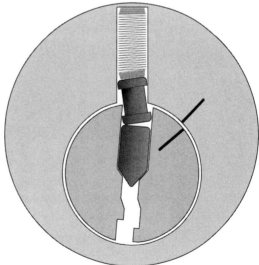

FIGURE 4.9

Some people will place a marker line across the front face of a lock when they're learning to tackle pick-resistant pins. Observe how the two segments of this line change position in relation to one another across the diagrams in Figures 4.9–4.13.

FIGURE 4.10

Binding a spool pin is almost immediately noticeable. The plug will rotate *significantly* more than you're used to. Notice the marker line's significant offset.

When you attempt to put pressure on a binding pin stack featuring a spool pin, something unique will happen. As the pins move in their chamber, it will begin to affect the rotation that was initially observed in Figure 4.9 with respect to the plug. In Figure 4.11, the pin stack has been pushed "upward" to the point that the lip of the spool pin is now catching on the lock housing. However, examine the marker lines. Compare Figures 4.10 and 4.11... it's *very* subtle, but there is a slight difference.

This "counter-rotation" can be observed more plainly when additional lifting force is applied to this binding pin stack. If a lockpicker can subtly ease off the pressure on the tension tool, then the attempts to move the pin stacks will cause the plug to continue its counter-rotation. As seen in Figures 4.12 and 4.13, continued attempts to push the pin stack further into position will result in the plug continuing to move in a counterclockwise direction.

There is no special trick to picking locks that feature these sorts of pins. All that is needed is significant discipline with respect to usage of the tension tool. Make certain that you're applying the absolutely least amount of tension pressure possible on the plug, and begin the process of hunting for binding pin stacks and setting them. You will almost surely come to recognize when you've hit a spooled surface, due to the almost comically over-the-top "clunk" noise and significant rotation of the plug that can be observed. (Recall Figure 4.10 and the extreme degree to which the plug will tend to turn... rotation of as much as 10° or more is commonly seen.)

When that happens to you, press up slightly harder on that pin stack. (Take care to *not* allow yourself to apply any extra pressure on the tension tool at that time!) Does the plug seem to respond to this pressure? Do you observe any counter-rotation? Even if you have left one pin stack, tried

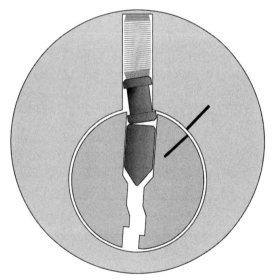

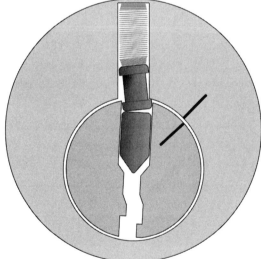

FIGURE 4.11

Pushing this binding pin stack will not just move the pins, it will actually begin to cause the plug to rotate back in a counterclockwise direction, ever so slightly.

FIGURE 4.12

Lifting pressure is being applied to the pin stack. This pressure coming from the "bottom" of the spool pin causes it to shift position slightly and, by association, causes the plug to counter-rotate.

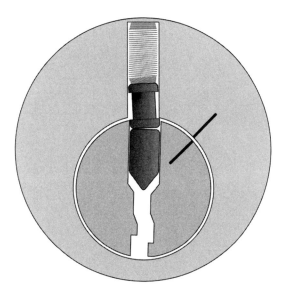

FIGURE 4.13

Can you see this counter-rotation that the plug is making through these past three diagrams? If the shifts have been too subtle, compare this image with Figure 4.10. Note the difference in the positions of the marker lines.

other pins, and then come back to it... that counter-rotation should still be slightly evident somewhere. Push the pin stack further, and hopefully it will click into what feels like a "set" position for the second time. Now you may have finally reached the proper shear line. (Or you may have just hit a *second* spool lip, if you are working with a particularly sneaky lock.) Keep in mind, this counter-rotation may "un-set" some other pin stacks that you have already picked. Go back and hunt around further to see if this is the case.

SPECIALIZED PICKING TOOLS

There are a number of "specialized" lockpick tools which some people claim can help you a great deal, particularly if you are contending with a lock that is hard to pick.

Featherweight tension tools

Attacking spool pins and other such pick-resistant hardware is delicate work. Applying too much tensioning pressure to the plug will cause the pins to become hopelessly jammed up at their edges and prevent any chance of you observing the critical counter-rotation that is essential to the process.

To that end, a number of vendors who design and sell lockpicking equipment offer tension tools that purport to be more useful than conventional tensioners during this process. Perhaps the most popular of these items is the "feather touch" or "featherweight" tensioner shown in Figure 4.14. This tool is sold by a number of popular retailers of locksmith supplies. I do not understand its enduring

FIGURE 4.14

A so-called "featherweight" tension tool. This tool has such limited purpose and performs its function with such mediocrity that I cannot recommend that anyone invest in one.

popularity, beyond the fact that it may seem appealing to novice pickers. Indeed, I am forced to admit that I was taken in by the marketing hype of this particular product and could have been heard recommending it to others at one time in the past. (It may have even made its way into some of the very first training kits I put together for use at conferences.)

Instead of adding a featherweight tension tool to your kit, consider performing the exercises listed in the upcoming section using a typical tension tool (either in the center of the plug or at the edge of the plug) made of very stiff material. I know some people who have even hardened the metal in some of their lockpick tools using tempering techniques such as heating and quenching the metal. In the end, using stiff tools and becoming very in tune with the feedback the lock is giving you is likely to serve you far better than attempting to acquire tools that have great flexibility (and, thus, offer you greatly diminished tactile feedback).

TIPS

If my logic here is not enough to convince you, consider the fact that most "typical" tension tools (made simply out of bent metal) cost approximately a dollar apiece... even less if you fashion ones yourself out of found materials. Street sweeper bristles and the metal shafts found inside of windshield wiper blades are two popular sources for such bare stock. The "featherweight" tensioner is sold for 10 dollars. Do you really feel the need to buy something that costs one *thousand* percent of the price of a tool that does the same job in a better way?

Bogotá jiggler rakes

One style of tool that has become *very* popular with a growing segment of lockpickers in recent years is a style of raking and jiggling tool known as a Bogotá. Created by a remarkable individual by the name of Raimundo (the three mountains surrounding the capitol city of Columbia were the inspiration for this design), this family of tools has the appearance of a rake (and, indeed, they can be used as such) but would be more properly called jiggler tools. I know that back in Chapter 2 we discussed jigglers and I asserted that one key feature is that they can often act as both a picking tool and a tension tool all in one unit. Do not consider that feature alone to be the key distinction of a jiggler, however. When a tool is most suited to be used in a punctuated up-and-down motion or elliptical pattern, (as seen in Figures 3.37 and 3.38, respectively) that, to me, is what defines it as a jiggler.

The Bogotá family of tools (the original design has since been augmented with related designs such as the Sabana and Monserate picks, all of which appear in the Appendix) are crafted in such a way as to be a constant size and thickness across their entire working tip; this distributes loads and pressures very evenly regardless of how violently the tools are worked in a lock (see Figure 4.15).

FIGURE 4.15

Bogotá lockpicks from my personal kit.

The high-polish, mirror-like finish that is characteristic of this type of tool also aids in movement of the pick within the keyway as it is worked in multiple directions rapidly. There are individuals out there, including people whom I know and respect as lockpickers, who claim that Bogotá tools are some of the best ways of tackling pick-resistant locks (and locks with difficult high/low pinning combinations) without setting every pin stack individually. While conventional raking can get hung up on the lips of pick-resistant pins, jiggling is more about trying to approximate a number of different bitting lines in rapid succession and therefore can result in some fortuitous good luck, particularly with Bogotá picks.

PRACTICE EXERCISES

So, if one doesn't own (or doesn't want to rely exclusively on) specialized jiggler tools, what is the best method of learning how to tackle locks that feature pick-resistant pins? Well, by now it may come as little surprise to readers that I am a devoted fan of taking a progressive approach to learning about these sorts of locks.

Spooled progressive practice locks

Starting with a lock that features just a single pin stack (which includes a spooled driver pin as shown in Figure 4.16), try to observe the significant "wiggle" of the plug, and experiment with applying tension and pressing on the pin stack. Add a maker line like the one referenced in Figure 4.9 and try to observe the same movement shown in the subsequent diagrams. If you can feel or see the "counter rotation" that was discussed earlier in this chapter, try moving on to additional progressive locks featuring spool pins. I would suggest the following progression:

- Progressive Spool Number One—A single pin stack featuring a spooled driver pin. (see Figure 4.16)
- Progressive Spool Number Two—A pair of pin stacks, only one of which needs to feature a spooled driver pin. (see Figure 4.17)
- Progressive Spool Number Three—Three working pin stacks, in which two of the drivers are spooled. (see Figure 4.18)
- Progressive Spool Number Four—This lock can have four functional pin stacks, but I'd stay with only two spooled driver pins at this time. (see Figure 4.19)
- Progressive Spool Number Five—A lock featuring five working pin stacks can represent a "real world door" rather effectively, and if you still just have two spooled driver pins, it will be a decent

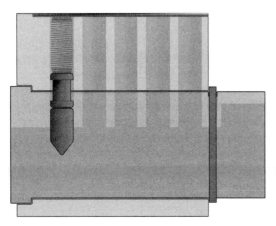

FIGURE 4.16

Progressive Spool Number One—A single pin stack featuring a spooled driver pin.

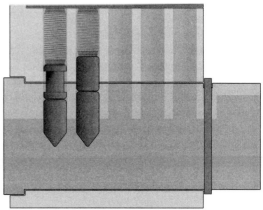

FIGURE 4.17

Progressive Spool Number Two—A pair of pin stacks, only one of which needs to feature a spooled driver pin.

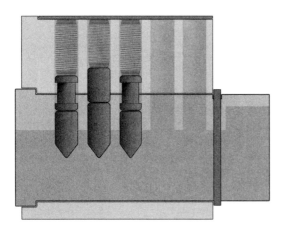

FIGURE 4.18

Progressive Spool Number Three—Three working pin stacks, in which two of the drivers are spooled.

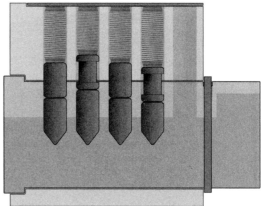

FIGURE 4.19

Progressive Spool Number Four—This lock can has four functional pin stacks, two of which feature spooled driver pins. These spooled pins have changed position in comparison to the Progressive Spool Number Three lock, to offer greater variety and challenge.

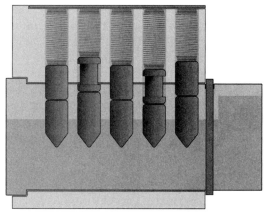

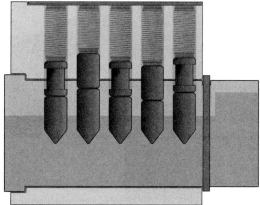

FIGURE 4.20

Progressive Spool Number Five—A lock featuring five working pin stacks, two of which include spooled driver pins.

FIGURE 4.21

Progressive Spool Number Six—A lock featuring five working pin stacks, three of which contain spooled driver pins. This lock exceeds the difficulty level of nearly all products you could find at a local hardware store

challenge but capable of offering you an educational experience instead of simply frustration. (see Figure 4.20)
- Progressive Spool Number Six—Try that same five-pin lock again, but this time allow three of the five pin stacks to be assembled with spooled driver pins. This will now exceed much of what you are likely to encounter on a day-to-day basis where typical "hardware store" locks are concerned. If you can master this lock, you're in very good shape with your "pick-resistant pin" skills. (see Figure 4.21)

Do not expect this series of progressive training exercises to go quite as quickly as those that were encouraged in Chapter 2. Remember that patience and repeated practice is what will make all the difference. If you have successfully opened, say, the Progressive Spool Number Three a couple of times but have had no success with the Number Four lock, I would say that it is actually more beneficial (in my view) to spend 30-60 min opening the Number Three lock repeatedly. Try picking it in both directions. Try picking it using various tension tools in both center-of-plug and edge-of-plug positions. An hour spent having success and building up muscle memory can often be far more helpful than an hour (or even 2 or 3 hours) of unsuccessful frustration.

Pick-resistant keyways

One other feature that manufacturers will often introduce into their "basic" locks in order to make picking somewhat more difficult is additional warding and angular cuts in the profile of the keyway. The protrusions of metal that one can see within the keyway (they are known as wards) have multiple functions. As was discussed back in Chapter 1 in the section where the plug of a pin tumbler lock was first introduced, the warding of a keyway not only serves as a means of distinguishing the proper brand of key and holding it in the correct position. . . it also can frustrate the process of lockpicking on occasion.

The more angular a keyway, the more likely it is that pick tools will encounter difficulty when attempts are made to move them up and down. Additionally, if the keyway is particularly narrow and features numerous curves, it will be difficult to position a single, solid shaft of metal up at an angle (for instance, a lockpick being used with the "rocking" motion described in Chapter 2).

Figure 4.22 shows a series of various popular keyways. As you look from left to right, notice how they become both narrower and more angled.

When a keyway's profile contains angles and wards that are so substantial as to negate any single, straight, unobstructed line down the middle of the keyway, it is called paracentric. Observe the same five keyways in Figure 4.23 and consider the additional guiding lines drawn in as visual aids to better understand this definition.

In Figure 4.23, the first two keyways are clearly rather wide and open. The third keyway shown has curves that are more substantial, but it is still possible to draw a straight line down the middle without coming up against any obstruction (although it does come remarkably close at two points). The fourth lock features a paracentric keyway. There is no angle at which a straight line can be drawn from the top of the keyway to the bottom without encountering wards of metal. The fifth lock is dramatically paracentric and would offer significant hindrance to anyone attempting to manipulate it with pick tools. (This lock *does* exist... by the way, it is a Gege lock, a product line that is now offered by the Kaba company. The Kaba Mas name is well respected in the world of locks and safes, and their products are well-engineered and generally very resistant to attacks of all kinds.)

NOTE

You may now be asking yourself, "If those advanced designs are possible, then why aren't *all* locks manufactured with such pick-resistant features?" The answer pertains to cost and ease-of-use. Consider the Gege lock shown at the far right in Figures 4.22 and 4.23. All of those hard-angled curves are introduced into the keyway by repeated passes with cutting jigs of increasing size as the plug material is forced pneumatically through fabrication machines. All of those harsh angles mean that the key will fail to insert if there are any deformities on its surface or if excessive wear and tear develops over time in the lock. A customer is not likely to approve of a lock that suddenly stops operating with little to no explanation, particularly if it costs more than other options they saw on a store shelf.

Now, I am *not* saying that the Gege lock is likely to become unreliable due to its design. In fact, I'd pit this or any Kaba product up against the generic "hardware store" brands we have here in North America any day. What I *am* saying, however, is that if all of these "common" manufacturers were to start trying to produce highly paracentric locks of this nature, they would have a hard time competing (in terms of both price and quality) with the few designs that are already on the market. Other major brands see no substantial pay-off to engineering products of this nature.

There is also the consideration of technological determinism. Market penetration is a force with considerable momentum. The sheer, huge number of locks that are already in use today featuring typical KW-1 or SC-1 keyways (originally designed by the Kwikset and Schlage companies but which have each lapsed into the public domain) means that most of the keys copied at hardware stores and locksmith shops are of that design. Customers buying new products often want to acquire ones that are similar to what they already have (perhaps they even ask for them to be keyed alike to an existing lock that they own) and this perpetuates the trend further.

No matter the particular reasons, suffice it to say that you are likely to encounter weaker, easier-to-pick locks out in the real world for a very long time. There are quite a few locks available at retail outlets which do incorporate some of these pick-resistant features, of course. Identifying them and acquiring them for purposes of practice is the topic of the last section in this chapter.

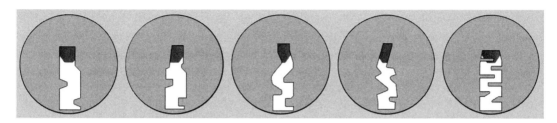

FIGURE 4.22

A series of increasingly difficult keyways.

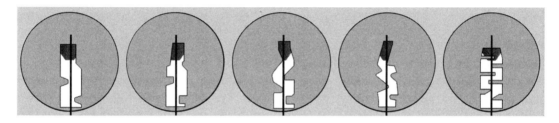

FIGURE 4.23

A series of keyways, the right-most two of which are paracentric.

REAL-WORLD LOCKS THAT OFFER GREATER CHALLENGES

So, by now you've perhaps made at least one trip to your local hardware store and have been astonished at the ease with which you have been able to pick most of the products you found on the shelves. (You took them *home* first, right? Because it's bad form to pick locks on a store shelf. You don't own them, after all... and one of the two golden rules is "Never pick locks you don't own.")

If you are interested in finding locks at local retail outlets which can offer you the challenge of experiencing pick-resistant pins, allow me to suggest a number of options to you.

Defiant brand door locks

I'm not promoting them here simply because of their name, hah. I like suggesting this product line to people who are learning about picking because they strike a healthy balance between cost, quality, and security. These are Home Depot's "generic" companion to the name-Brand Kwikset locks (which they also stock and whose keys are the same KW-1 profile (see Figure 4.24)). I like these locks for beginner practice because they do not cost an arm and a leg to acquire, but they aren't made *so* cheaply as to result in malfunctions and jamming. Defiant locks almost always feature five pins stacks; the middle one invariably contains a spooled driver pin. With the "double sided deadbolt" entry pack you can obtain a pair of these lock cylinders, keyed-alike. They are easy to service, so you can field-strip them and make pairs of progressive locks representing difficulties within your

FIGURE 4.24

A Defiant brand deadbolt.

range, and the pair of spool pins that you will have acquired in this purchase will allow you to create the first five levels of my suggested Progressive Spool locks.

Master Lock color-plated series and fusion series

There are two styles of padlock lock offered by the Master Lock company that can be deceptive in their level of difficulty. The small, plastic "Color Plated" models in the 130 and 140 family (see Figure 4.25) are available at most hardware stores, often in keyed-alike multipacks. The plastic and metal "Fusion" models (see Figure 4.26) aren't seen as often, but they are still available at many retail stores. Both of these products tend to be four-pin locks with medium difficulty bitting configurations and include at least one spool driver pin somewhere. The Color Plated line, in my experience, will frequently have *two* spool driver pins. I even observed a pseudo-serrated pin inside of one once. With their small size, light weight, and low cost, these locks often take novices by surprise with their difficulty.

American Lock padlocks

The offerings from American Lock (see Figure 4.27) present a very formidable challenge to anyone seeking to tackle pick-resistant pins. While the range of products from this company varies greatly in terms of resistance to brute force attacks (they have small, aluminum body padlocks for lockout/tagout purposes all the way up to heavy-duty shackle-less puck padlocks), all of their offerings tend to rely on the exactly same lock cylinder. (Indeed, the ease with which most

FIGURE 4.25

A Master brand padlock in their "Colored Cover" line. These will typically feature one, if not two, spool driver pins.

FIGURE 4.26

A Master brand padlock in their "Fusion" line. These will typically feature one spool pin and a slightly smaller keyway, making for a slight challenge beyond a purely "basic" padlock.

FIGURE 4.27

Padlocks from American Lock. This company has a wide range of models which offer varying degrees of physical strength, but the internal lock cores in every one of these products are equally formidable.

American Lock products can eject their core is a great benefit to those who are still learning. With the lock's core ejected, you can easily field-strip the cylinder and remove some of the pin stacks, if needed.)

American locks always feature serrated pins (usually it is the key pins that are serrated in these products) and often include spooled driver pins in at least one chamber. These are significant obstacles to most lockpickers at first, but use what you learned about field stripping and rekeying in the beginning of Chapter 3 to prune them down to a more reasonable level on your first attempt.

You should be able to have three-pin American locks open with relative ease if you're patient. From there, with enough time and patience, four pins and even five pins should eventually yield to your tools and your skills.

WARNING

While I am a big fan of certain aspects of the American Lock design, it should be known that older versions of their padlocks (particularly the 700 series, 1100 series, and 5000 series) had a glaring weakness that would allow for fast, simple bypassing in most situations. This has been addressed in the shackle-less 2000 series, and was never an issue on many of their U.S. Government models, but it should be understood if you are using this lock for high security purposes. We will discuss this attack in greater detail in Chapter 5.

Advanced security pin cylinder

Perhaps my favorite lock, as far as learning about pick-resistant pins is concerned, is one that I found in Norway. It can be seen in Figure 4.28. I understand that these euro-profile half cylinders are popular across much of Scandinavia, and from what I have seen in the collections of other

FIGURE 4.28

The "Advanced Security Pin Cylinder" that I occasionally find in Scandinavia.

friends and associates, my supposition is that many of them are clones of a design by ASSA in Sweden.

I wish I had a proper make and model name for these locks; however, I encounter them sold under various banners in numerous stores. The *best* version of this lock that I have ever encountered was marketed under the name Dejo and featured a menacing seven-pin configuration. The lock had only *one* standard driver pin. Three of the drivers were typical spool pins, while the remaining three were *double spool* pins similar to the "sneaky pins" described by Han Fey and seen in this chapter in Figure 4.8.

There is no end to the degree of challenge that this one lock can present. My friends and I have *never* been able to successfully pick it with more than five pin stacks installed. I was able to bump the lock in a number of advanced configurations, but as far as picking those monstrous spool pins... four is my usual limit. I only achieved the five-pin attempt once. (And, as we say in the lockpicking world, once is luck. Only when you've picked a lock *twice* does it truly count. Three times means you finally win the beer/kissing/bragging rights.)

If this lock is such a monster, why do I give it such praise as a training aid? I love it because of the multitude of ways in which it can be reconfigured and repinned. Again, this is a process best handled by a friend or associate who is willing to help you learn. Have someone field-strip the lock and assemble it in a two- or three- or (when you're ready for it) four-pin configuration. Allow them to choose at random which driver pins they will use in which positions. You will never know what to expect, given that the lock often comes with such a wide range of pin designs right off the shelf.

SUMMARY

This chapter has provided an overview of some of the basic styles of pick-resistant designs that manufacturers will seek to introduce in certain products. These solutions for making locks slightly more secure are popular due to their low relative cost and the fact that suppliers will rarely have to retool their whole factory or change their overall product design to make use of them.

Pick-resistant pins like spooled, mushroomed, and serrated drivers are common in medium-grade products available on store shelves. Higher quality locks take this type of engineering a step further, with fancier designs and sometimes additional milling inside the pin chambers within the plug.

Attempts at picking these locks may fail initially, but with dedication and patience, it should be possible for those learning about lockpicking to grasp the mechanics of what is happening within these locks and ultimately overcome such obstacles. While certain specialized tools may help in this process, many are (in my view) a waste of money. You are best served creating progressively pinned locks in order to gain experience with how these pick-resistant pins behave. When you have become comfortable enough, there are a number of inexpensive and easily accessible products on your local store shelves that you can use to try your new skills on real-world hardware.

Reference

1. Fey H. Cutaway cylinders and their locking technique (Part 1) [document on the Internet]. The Open Organisation of Lockpickers (TOOOL); 2005 May [cited 2010 Apr 6]. Available from: http://toool.nl/images/f/f9/Cutaway1.pdf.

Quick-entry tricks: Shimming, bumping, and bypassing

5

INFORMATION IN THIS CHAPTER

- Padlock shims
- Snapping and bumping
- Comb picks
- American Lock bypass tool
- Door bypassing

Purists in the world of lockpicking consider the act of using covert entry tools with finesse as the only "proper" way to open a lock without using a key. When competitions are held (and they are, many times per year, in fact... it's quite a sight to behold, seeing people feverishly and rapidly opening all sorts of high-security locks in record time), lifting picks, raking picks, and tension tools are just about the only items you see contestants using.

However, in the world of penetration testing, one is not limited exclusively to the use of "sport legal" tools. Whatever works, however it works... that's the name of the game during a physical assessment or red team breach. Many times, it's *far* more efficient and a great deal easier to *bypass* locks instead of picking them. The term bypassing does not refer to the act of, say, finding a particular door to be locked and then going a window instead. No, bypassing is the act of triggering the release of a locking mechanism without manipulating the pins or combination mechanism in the traditional "picking" sense. Bypassing is often faster, easier, and indeed, used with greater frequency in the real world than most of the techniques described in Chapters 3 and 4.

While it might not win you a top prize at LockCon or any of the other lockpicking championships around the world, knowledge of bypassing can often make the difference between getting past a locked door possible in 5 seconds as opposed to 5 minutes.

PADLOCK SHIMS

The use of shim material is a common practice in the locksmithing trade. Thin sheet metal can slip into various thin crevices on a lock and be used to force pins to behave in a specific manner (this is used sometimes during the act of field stripping a lock), or it can be used to trigger the release of a latch mechanism (in order to pop open a padlock with minimal effort).

The most common type of shim that can be seen in a covert entry toolkit is a butterfly shim. Designed to be inserted into the body of a padlock near the shackle, these products are easily ordered from locksmith supply catalogs and on the internet. Instead of acquiring these items through traditional channels, however, one of my absolute favorite tricks is homemade production of these incredibly useful items. Using scrap aluminum sheet metal from soda or beer cans, it is possible to fabricate your own padlock shims in under a minute. This is a technique that has been known for some time, but over the years this technique has somehow become very much associated with my name.

To set the record straight, I am most assuredly *not* the first person who has ever thought to use a metal can to attack a lock. I sometimes accept the credit for *popularizing* this particular technique that will be demonstrated in Figures 5.2–5.19, and I happen to believe that my "M shape" shim pattern is one of the easiest to attempt, but there are plenty of other padlock shimming procedures that work very well. My associates who are involved with Survival, Evasion, Resistance, and Escape (SERE) training are well-versed in improvising shim tools from bobby pins and hair clips. I have seen their techniques work just as well as this one. You may discover an entirely different technique by searching the internet or just experimenting on your own. That is perfectly fine. As always, do whatever works best for you.

The Deviant beer can shim

Using metal from a beer can is my favorite means of quickly shimming open weak padlocks. Metal from any beverage can often works, but thicker cans are often superior. Tall cans holding 16 ounces of liquid are often of a more robust construction than smaller ones. This can help. There is also the natural advantage of having more raw material with which to work when starting out with a tall can (see Figure 5.1). It is possible, with careful cutting, to turn a can of 16 ounces into a pack of 16 shims. Cans of 12 ounces or less yield considerably fewer shims.

This guide will show you, step-by-step, how to fabricate your own padlock shims from aluminum cans. You can use this text as a reference, naturally, but if you need to fabricate these shims in the field, it is possible to work totally from memory if you can remember just a single, simple starting dimension.

The specific starting size
Begin by cutting a rectangle of metal that measures 2.5 in. long and 1 in. wide (see Figure 5.2). For those of you accustomed to the Metric system, that would be 5 cm × 2 cm. If you start with this size piece of metal, everything else you do should work very easily and smoothly.

Making your mark
With a piece of metal cut to the requisite starting size, the rest of the process is a series of simple estimates, all of which involve dividing segments in half. It is entirely possible to do this simply by eye, but if you wish to use a felt tip marker to assist you (this is especially helpful when starting out), flip the metal over to expose the blank side. Divide the metal in half across both dimensions. Figure 5.3 shows this process performed with guidelines drawn using a felt-tipped marker.

With that done, now divide each of these halves in half... resulting in a series of quartering lines running in both directions, as shown in Figure 5.4.

With this grid shape applied to the metal, five key points are now apparent. Three of them are located where the shorter lines meet one edge. The other two are at the intersection where two of the short lines cross the middle long line. These five points are identified clearly in Figure 5.5.

FIGURE 5.1

Metal from beer and cider cans makes the finest improvised shims. The taller 16 ounce cans will naturally yield greater numbers of these useful tools, but both sources are equally effective. Sodas and energy drinks often come in smaller cans that not only produce fewer shims, but they are also often thinner and weaker. Expect mixed results on stubborn locks if your metal isn't robust.

FIGURE 5.2

The best starting size for a homemade shim is a piece of metal 2.5 in. long and 1 in. wide.

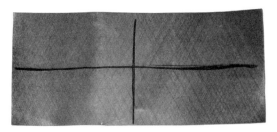

FIGURE 5.3

Divide your piece of shim metal (either visually or manually with a magic marker) in half, both along the length and width.

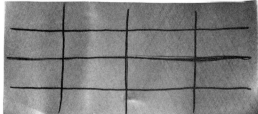

FIGURE 5.4

The shim metal is now divided into fourths across both the length and width.

The magic "M" shape

By connecting these five points with a curved line, it is possible to create a shape that is more or less like a capital letter "M" on the metal. If you have been using a marker to draw on the aluminum up to this point, continue to do so now. Mark a curved letter "M" as shown in Figure 5.6.

Cut this "M" shape out of your piece of aluminum. I caution you, however, do not be tempted to make a series of four, independent, simple cuts. That may be an easy way to cut a letter "M", but it is *far from* the best technique. Try to cut this "M" out of the metal using *one long, curved cut*. It may take some practice, but using a singular cut—particularly one that has curves as opposed to sharp points—will make the shim much more robust. Curves will help to evenly distribute loads and stresses across the whole segment of metal. Sharp angles where two distinct, separate cuts meet can be potential points of weakness. Figure 5.7 shows a piece of homemade shim metal in the "M" pattern with nice, curved cuts.

With the "M" cut made, all that remains is to fold and bend the shim into a proper shape.

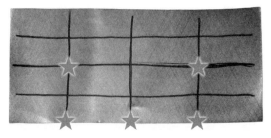

FIGURE 5.5

The five key points that will help us in the next step.

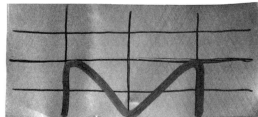

FIGURE 5.6

The "letter M" that will serve to guide your next cut into the aluminum.

A series of simple folds

Recall the "longer" lines that were drawn on this piece of metal during the initial phase of the process. These now become our folding points. Starting with the long line that is the farthest away from the "M" cut that was made in the metal, fold along that line so that the "top" edge of metal (top

FIGURE 5.7

A piece of homemade shim metal that has been cut into a proper "M" shape.

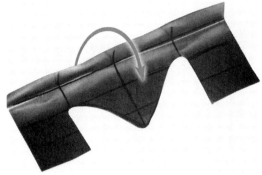

FIGURE 5.8

The first fold takes place along one of the "longer" lines, bringing the top edge down to meet the midline of this rectangle.

being a relative term that applies to the shim as we are viewing it in this example) comes down to the midline. See Figure 5.8 for an explicit representation of where this fold takes place. The result should look like the metal seen in Figure 5.9.

Now all that remains is to deal with finalizing the "wing" pieces on each side. Some people will just cut them off, but I feel they are much better left intact. Folding them around, as shown in Figures 5.10 and 5.11, makes the finished product more robust.

The last thing that remains to be done is to work the shim metal into a proper, rounded shape. This can be performed directly on the padlock you wish to open, or—if you have a pen or other rounded object handy—you can round the shim that way, as shown in Figure 5.12.

Insert and twist

You should now have a shim that *very closely* resembles the "professional" products you would normally be able to buy in a locksmith supply catalog (see Figure 5.13). This tool is now ready to be used in the opening of a padlock.

FIGURE 5.9

After the first fold, your homemade shim should look like this.

FIGURE 5.11

Folding the end pieces one further time around. The shim is now almost fully formed.

FIGURE 5.10

Fold each of the two end pieces upwards. Some people call this stage of shim fabrication the "moose" in that the upward-facing ends look like antlers framing an animal's head.

FIGURE 5.12

Using a ballpoint pen to give the shim a rounded shape.

Insert the tip of the shim into the lock on the *outside* edge of the shackle. It is necessary to know which side the shackle latches within the lock body. This can naturally be observed if the lock is open... wherever there is a notch cut into the shackle, there is a retaining mechanism. In this example, we will be demonstrating with a Master Combination Dial lock (shown in Figure 5.14) that retains the shackle only on the left side (from the perspective of someone facing the operating dial of the lock).

Insert your shim into the lock and get the tip seated into position, as shown in Figure 5.15. It will not be possible to insert the shim too deeply at this time, since the "wings" of the shim will strike the lock body, as seen in Figure 5.16.

FIGURE 5.13

A fully formed, properly shaped homemade padlock shim.

FIGURE 5.15

A shim that has been properly seated into position.

FIGURE 5.14

A Master brand combination dial lock is perhaps the easiest to attack with a padlock shim. I recommend that people attempt this technique for the first time using this padlock. In particular, the aluminum version of this lock (that is almost always colorized, not silver like the original steel combination dial locks) is weaker and tends to have wider crevices. It is the most forgiving of novice errors and the best learning tool for those who are learning how to shim.

FIGURE 5.16

The shim cannot be inserted further into the lock at this time, since the wing pieces are striking the lock body.

Now the magic happens. Pinch the wings of the shim together as tightly as you can. This will give the shim strength and rigidity during the next step. Keeping a tight hold on the wings, rotate the shim around (in either direction) so that the wings now face out, away from the lock body. While rotating the shim, apply downward pressure so that the tip sinks further inward. If you've done everything right (and had a bit of good luck, perhaps), things should appear as they do in Figure 5.17.

If you believe that you have inserted the shim fully, try to pull up on the shackle. Do not grip or disturb the shim during this process, leave it alone completely. Simply pull upon the shackle and the padlock's body. More often than not, the lock will pop open completely with ease (see Figure 5.18).

This process is usually not damaging to the lock. Occasionally, if you're lucky, it won't even result in much damage to your shim. However, it should be understood that all padlock shims are disposable tools. Even proper, factory-made units, which tend to be fabricated out of steel, will not last forever. Homemade shims crafted from aluminum have an even shorter service life. After one or two attempts, it is normal to see deformations and cracks forming near the tip (see Figure 5.19). Most aluminum shims will not last beyond a half-dozen uses; many crumble or tear after just one or two attempts.

Double shimming

The padlock shown in this first example (in Figures 5.14–5.18) only retained the shackle by means of a latch on a single side. Many padlocks, especially those which operate with keys, have retaining notches (and, thus, internal latches) on *both* sides. When a lock is open, it is possible to observe the shackle and see if it is a single-sided or dual-sided mechanism (see Figure 5.20).

FIGURE 5.17

A padlock that appears to have been properly shimmed. Notice how far "down" into the lock the shim has sunk. That is a good thing.

FIGURE 5.18

The end result after the successful use of a homemade padlock shim.

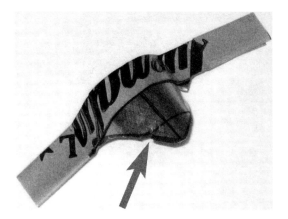

FIGURE 5.19

After just one attempt, this shim is already showing signs of wear. I would not expect it to survive beyond a few more uses.

FIGURE 5.20

Padlocks with two different latching designs. The padlock on the left latches on only one side of the shackle. The padlock on the right latches on both sides.

It is often still possible to use a shimming attack against a padlock that latches on both sides of the shackle. Two shims are needed, of course. They do not have to be operated simultaneously (at exactly the same moment), however. A shim can be applied on one side, twisted down into position, and then a second shim can be applied moments later. The order in which this is done rarely matters.

TIP

Interestingly, homemade shims fabricated from thin metals like beverage can aluminum are often the best tools for the job on dual-latching padlocks. Factory-made metal shims are often much thicker, which can result in difficulty during insertion and twisting. Some locks simply don't have enough "wiggle room" between the shackle and the lock body to accommodate two thick steel shims. The thin aluminum shims often fit into these sorts of crevices with ease, however.

Unshimmable padlocks

Not all padlocks can be attacked with shims. In fact, in my view, a lock isn't a "proper" padlock, worthy of your money at a retail outlet, if it is not protected against shimming. The most common method of designing a padlock such that it cannot be shimmed is with the use of a "double ball" mechanism. The lock shown in Figure 5.21 has such a mechanism; even though it is a very small, very cheap padlock, it is still resistant to this attack.

FIGURE 5.21

This padlock features a "double ball" mechanism, which is described (and even diagramed) prominently on the packaging.

Double ball mechanisms rely on a central control cam (attached to the tail side of the plug) that either allows or blocks the movement of two solid ball bearings. If that cam is not turned, the ball bearings *cannot* move. A shim is not going to be able to apply any sort of meaningful pressure within the lock and bypass the pins, leading to a quick and easy release.

If you are purchasing supplies from a proper locksmith, you can always just inquire directly as to whether or not a particular padlock is protected against shimming. If you do not have an expert with whom you can speak, it is often possible to look at the notch cuts on a lock's shackle in order to determine what mechanism is holding it shut. As seen in Figure 5.22, there are various styles of notches that are cut into padlock shackles. Notches that feature any "straight" lines are often used to engage weak, spring-loaded latches. Notches that are entirely curve-shaped are usually a sign that a double ball mechanism (or some other unshimmable retaining piece) is used in the lock.

Please know that the size of a lock rarely correlates to how effectively it can resist shimming. Some of the largest locks in the market (often marketed under terms like "commercial grade" or other robust-sounding names) are designed to resist brute force attacks (as with a crowbar or bolt cutters) but are wholly unprotected against shimming. Conversely, some very small padlocks (like the Argentinean lock in Figure 5.21) are unshimmable. Look at the two locks in Figure 5.23. Both of these locks are completely resistant to shimming and have the same internal construction, despite appearing quite different.

Much more information concerning padlock shimming can be found on the internet, especially if you search Google or YouTube. Indeed, my own instructional video regarding shimming (that covers all of this material and more) can be found here... http://www.youtube.com/watch?v=U8Cj47hFtx4.

FIGURE 5.22

Notches on the shackles of three different padlocks. The first two are from locks that can be attacked with a shim, as evinced by the straight edges that appear in the notches. The third shackle, on the far right, has a notch that is entirely curved. This is almost always a sign of a proper, double ball mechanism.

FIGURE 5.23

Two different models of lock by the Finnish company Abloy. Despite appearing quite distinct, these locks have almost identical internal construction and each one uses an unshimmable double ball mechanism. Note the curved shape of the notches on both sides of each shackle.

SNAPPING AND BUMPING

Lock bypassing isn't just a technique that can be used on padlocks. The intricate pin tumbler mechanisms in many door locks can also be bypassed entirely, often with highly simplistic tools. The techniques of snapping and bumping have been known to locksmiths for years and rely on very simple laws of physics to quickly spring a lock open.

Snap guns

Occasionally featured on TV programs about crime or espionage (and often found listed in the back pages of spy publications and soldier-of-fortune catalogs) are tools known as pick guns, also known as "snap guns" or "lock snapping guns." These tools feature a long trigger handle which, when pulled, will retract and then quickly release a needle-like arm. This arm is designed to be inserted into the keyway of a pin tumbler lock and held such that it will smack into the exposed surfaces of the key pins when the "snap" takes place, as shown in Figure 5.24.

In an ideal world, the resulting strike against the pin stacks will take place simultaneously across all key pins in the same instant and with relatively the same force, as depicted in Figure 5.25.

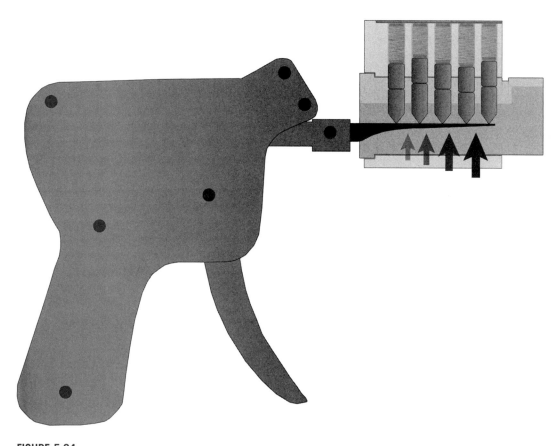

FIGURE 5.24

A pick gun or snap gun is designed to be held such that the long needle-like arm flies toward the pin stacks, contacting the key pins.

Newtonian laws of motion tell us that, like balls on a billiard table (such as the ones seen in Figure 5.26), energy should transfer through the key pins (see Figure 5.27) and result in movement of the *driver* pins. If you're lucky, the driver pins will fly "upward" (see Figure 5.28) allowing you to turn the plug if you time everything perfectly.

Bump keys

As mentioned in the description of Figure 5.25, those attempting to use pick guns will often experience difficulty if the needle arm doesn't contact all of the key pins at exactly the same moment and deliver adequate force. It is quite possible, however, to replicate this same physical force using a device that is much smaller, more reliable, and (in my opinion) easier to operate. I am speaking about a bump key.

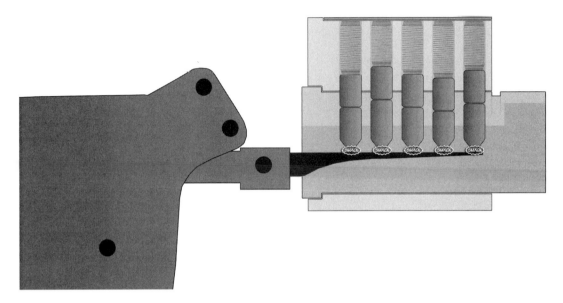

FIGURE 5.25

When using a pick gun, one attempts to make the needle arm contact all the tips of the key pins simultaneously. This is often very difficult. Not only must the pick gun be held perfectly level, but there has to be enough room within the keyway for the arm to travel. This is less and less common in modern, well-engineered keyways.

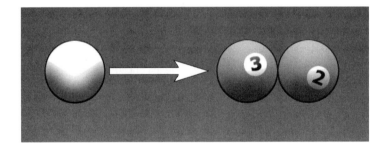

FIGURE 5.26

Lock snapping (and bumping, for that matter) rely on basic principles of Newtonian physics, which can be illustrated via the transfer of energy between balls on a billiard table.

What makes a key a bump key?

A bump key, in its most basic form, is nothing more than a key that is designed for the keyway profile of a specific lock and that has had each of its bitting positions (see Figure 5.29) cut down to a particularly deep level (see Figure 5.30). Occasionally, this type of cutting can result in a particularly large rise of metal out near the tip of the key blade (also visible in Figure 5.30). If this ever happens, it is often advisable to make an additional bitting cut (at an equally deep level)

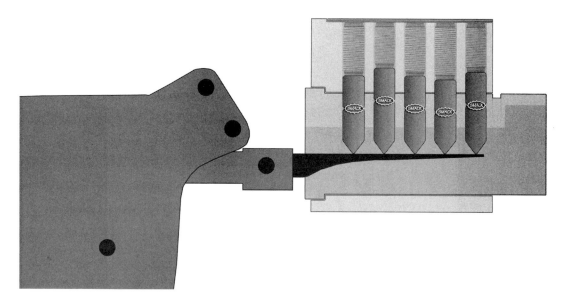

FIGURE 5.27

Ideally, energy that is delivered to the key pins will transfer through the driver pins.

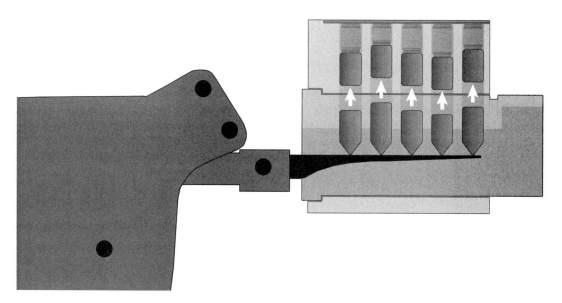

FIGURE 5.28

If all goes well, the driver pins will fly out of their default positions for an instant, allowing the lock's plug to turn.

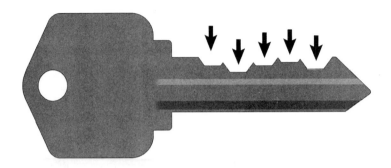

FIGURE 5.29

The bitting positions on a normal key are all evenly spaced along the blade.

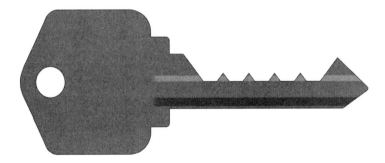

FIGURE 5.30

On a bump key, those same bitting positions (as seen in Figure 5.29) are used, but the cuts are made to a much deeper level. Typically, each position is cut to its factory-deepest setting, usually depth "9" on a code-cutting machine.

in one further position (as shown in Figure 5.31). If you have access to a locksmith's code-cutting machine, this type of key fabrication is often achieved by programming the cuts to be at a depth of "9" in every position. (It is for this reason that a bump key is sometimes called a "999" key.)

The keys shown in Figures 5.30 and 5.31 are of a type typically called "pull" bump keys. The "pull and bump" technique with which they are used is depicted in Figures 5.34–5.36. Some people, however, choose to modify their bump keys even further. By removing additional metal around the shoulder and the tip of the key (see Figure 5.32), it is possible to make a "push" bump key. Taking off approximately 0.03 in. (just shy of 1 mm) of metal from the shoulder and tip will result in a key like the one seen in Figure 5.33. This type of key can be used to perform a "push bump" technique.

The "Pull" bump method

The two methods by which bumping can be performed are related, but vary enough that separate diagrams will be used to demonstrate them. The first technique we will examine is the "pull" method. This is widely believed to be the "original" style of bumping that was popular with locksmiths for

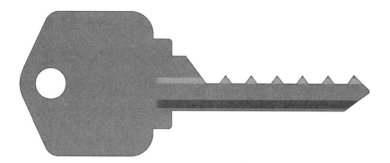

FIGURE 5.31

To eliminate the large "hump" of metal that is sometimes seen on the tip of a bump key (one is visible in Figure 5.30), an additional bitting position can be cut into the key blade out near the tip.

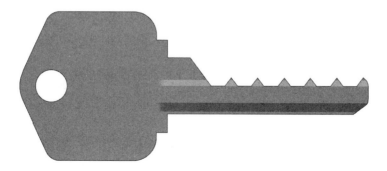

FIGURE 5.32

Additional metal is removed at these points on a "pull" bump key to turn it into a "push" bump key.

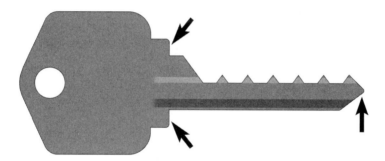

FIGURE 5.33

A "push" style bump key, also known as a "negative shoulder" or "minimal movement" bump key.

decades, long before the amateur lockpicking world and the hacker community (and, through them, the public) gained widespread knowledge of bumping.

Even though it has been cut down considerably, a bump key's blade (particularly the protruding points) will still make contact with all of the key pins in a lock as it is inserted into the keyway. With each passing stack there is a noticeable "click" that can be felt and heard. To perform a "pull" bump, the key is inserted all the way into the lock, then pulled out by "one click" (see Figure 5.34). It is then struck directly and squarely on its head, driving it into the lock. As it travels inward, the small ridge points will smash across the key pins, delivering a forceful blow to them (see Figure 5.35). Since the pins are being held in chambers and thus cannot travel laterally, the only direction in which this force can travel is "upward" toward the driver pins. The driver pins will then receive all of this energy and fly upward, leaving the plug free to rotate for a split second (see Figure 5.36).

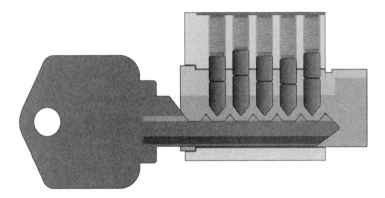

FIGURE 5.34

A bump key in position for a "pull and bump" attempt. It has been pulled out by "one click" and is ready to be struck.

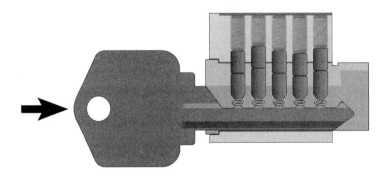

FIGURE 5.35

As the strike comes, the bump key moves into the lock, smashing across the key pins as it does so.

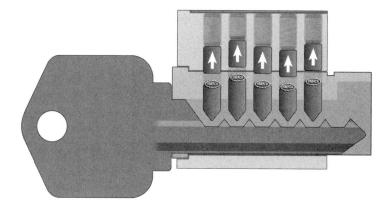

FIGURE 5.36

This looks to be a successful bump attempt; the driver pins are moving out of their default positions, hopefully allowing the plug to rotate if everything is timed just right.

The "Push" bump method

A different type of bumping attack is possible if one is using a key of the type shown in Figure 5.33. Known as a "push" technique, it is performed with the bump key fully inserted into the lock (see Figure 5.37). The key is not, in other words, "pulled out by one click" at the start of the procedure. The removal of extra metal near the shoulder (and tip) of the key will allow it to over-insert into the lock. This small amount of extra wiggle room is often enough to allow the small ridges of the bump key to contact the key pins and deliver adequate bumping force.

Like with the "pull" method, a solid blow is delivered directly upon the rearmost protruding part of the key's head, knocking the key inward. The ridges will contact the key pins (see Figure 5.38) and the resultant force will likely be transferred up to the driver pins, thus causing them to jump out of position (Figure 5.39) so that the plug can be turned.

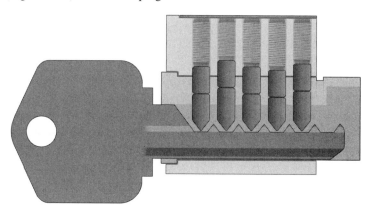

FIGURE 5.37

A "push" style bump key in position.

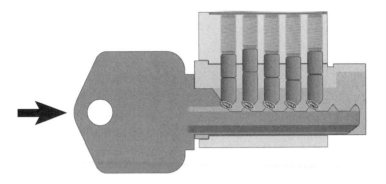

FIGURE 5.38

A "push" style bump hit being delivered.

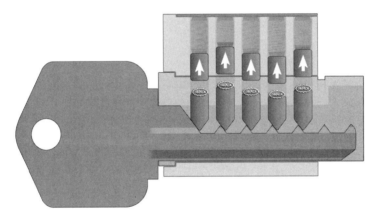

FIGURE 5.39

With the energy transferred to the driver pins, they should hopefully all jump out of position and leave the plug free to turn.

A few tips about technique

Bumping may appear to be quite a brutal tactic (and, indeed, it is not very good for the lock... it generally leaves clear visual indications after one or two attempts and can seriously degrade the lock's functionality over time), but it is also one where some degree of finesse is necessary.

There isn't much thought that goes into delivering the blow upon the bump key (the advice I always give to people is, simply, try to hit the key hard enough that it will hurt if you miss), but your timing when attempting to turn the plug is critical. Some people advocate applying slight turning pressure to the key before you make your strike. While this has been known to work sometimes with the "pull" method, I do not recommend it personally. After all, any such turning force is likely to cause at least one of the pin stacks to bind, and that means that at least one driver pin won't be easily able to fly upward and out of the plug.

I advise people to keep their fingers in position, near the bump key, but to not apply any turning pressure until the exact moment that the hit has landed. I believe this gives you the best chance of success. In truth, it's all a matter of timing. I have seen great frustration on the faces of many people who are attempting to bump a lock... then, when it works for them one time, they suddenly cannot figure out what was so hard, and they repeat the process with success from that point on.

Having the right tool for striking the key makes some difference. Plenty of improvised bump hammers exist (I have seen everything from butter knives to screwdrivers to other locks used successfully in bumping), but some of the best tools are often purpose-built. Sadly, the one bump hammer that is the most commercially available (developed and sold by Peterson Tools) is, in my mind, the most difficult to use. Other tools, like the legendary Tomahawk hammer and Ke-Bump hammer, have been made in limited quantities by the leadership of The Open Organisation Of Lockpickers in the Netherlands and the United States, respectively, but aren't in widespread distribution.

Regarding which *technique* is more effective... as with most aspects of lockpicking, that varies for each individual. If I had to generalize, I would say that the "pull" method might be a little bit easier to perform, but it is slower if you wish to make repeated attempts. Because the key has to be manually pulled "out" by one notch each time, an unsuccessful bump must be followed by a pause while one resets the key, then takes a position nearby with fingertips, and tries again. The "push" bump key, on the other hand, will naturally "reset" itself after every strike, allowing for repeated attempts, one after the other. I will caution you, however, that if the lock hasn't opened after a half-dozen blows or so, it is usually best to remove the key (and possibly inspect it to see if there is any noticeable damage or deformity), reinsert it, and start again.

No matter what technique is used, over time this type of attack tends to degrade the lock's internals as well as its front face. It will be quite obvious to even casual observers if a lock has been bumped repeatedly.

Bump-resistant and bump-proof locks

The vast majority of pin tumbler locks in use today can be bumped.* What then, you might be wondering, makes some locks immune (or at least resistant) to this problem? There are two ways of mitigating the threat of bump key attacks. One is very expensive (and impractical for most manufacturers), the other is more achievable but has not seen major market penetration at the time of this publication's first edition.

Certain high-security locks are outright immune to bumping because their mechanisms either do not operate with pin tumblers or because their pin stacks are augmented by additional components that wholly eliminate the risk of bumping. A list of high security locks that simply cannot be bumped under any circumstances would be as follows:

---

*I do not mean nearly all *models* of pin tumbler lock are vulnerable, although *most* of them are. Rather, my assertion that the "vast majority" of locks are vulnerable is due to the fact that cheap locks with little to no protection have much greater market penetration than competing locks that offer some degree of protection. Until manufacturers simply *stop producing* locks that are susceptible to bumping, it is likely that consumers will continue buying and installing locks that can be bumped.

- Rotating disk locks such as those offered by Abloy and Abus
- Locks that feature "sliders" such as the Evva 3KS and the latest generation of Mul-T-Lock products (their MT5 series)
- Magnetic key systems like the Evva MCS and many products from Miwa

This is, of course, by no means an exhaustive list. It should also be understood that most of the locks on this list retail for close to (if not more than) 100 USD. Interestingly, some locks which I would not consider high security for other reasons are, in fact, almost entirely immune to bumping attacks. Wafer locks and the "Smart Series" line by Kwikset are two such examples. I would not trust them to protect seriously sensitive areas, but you can rest assured that no one will bump these open. How, then, is bump protection achievable in typical, everyday situations where one also desires resistance to covert entry?

The answer lies in the ways that some manufacturers are retooling their processes in order to produce basic, cheap pin tumbler locks that can withstand bump key attacks. As we saw in Chapter 3, it is often possible to change the *pins* in a lock without dramatically reengineering the rest of the lock's machining process and in doing so change how the lock performs against potential attacks.

In Chapter 3, we saw how spool pins, serrated pins, and other such pins can frustrate picking attacks. Well, some manufacturers today are experimenting with bump-resistant pins in the same fashion. Two of the most successful designs to date have been pins designed by Master Lock and Ilco.

Master Lock's Bump Stop technology

The Master Lock company has done extensive studies on the physics of bumping and devised a new way of pinning their lock cylinders that can often eliminate a great deal of the risk that this attack poses. By changing the shape of one of their driver pins and not allowing it to drop into the plug completely (as seen in Figure 5.40), it is possible to make a bumping attempt highly impractical. With a substantial gap between the key pin and the driver pin, energy cannot transfer and the driver pin (at least in one chamber) will not move.

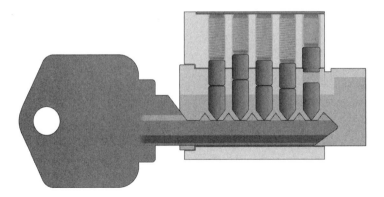

FIGURE 5.40

A lock that includes one antibump pin of the Master Lock Bump Stop design. The driver pin in chamber five does not contact the key pin and thus cannot easily accept a transfer of energy during a bump attempt.

One aspect of the Master design that makes it not 100% adoptable is the fact that this differently shaped driver pin has a *slightly* larger diameter than the others in the lock. That necessitates a wider pin chamber in the housing and prevents such a pin from being installed in an aftermarket fashion.

The Ilco antibump pin

The Ilco company is not usually recognized as a manufacturer of locks (although they do offer a line of replacement lock cylinders) but is instead famous for being a major supplier of lock components and locksmithing supplies. Recently, they began marketing a series of pins and springs that they have designated as their "Bump Halt" solution. Instead of attempting to prevent a driver pin from dropping completely into the plug (as Master Lock does), Ilco offers locksmiths the ability to use pins of widely varying mass (along with high-strength springs) that can dramatically interfere with the physics of bumping. By installing an Ilco antibump driver pin (and accompanying high-strength spring) into one or two chambers (see Figure 5.41), one can drastically shift the manner in which pins behave during a bump attempt.

Because of the Ilco pin's greatly reduced mass and the higher-strength spring that sits on top of it (and, indeed, surrounds it), this pin will not travel up and down at the same speed as the other pins in the lock during a bump attempt. It is still possible to get a Bump Halt pin to jump slightly during bumping, but it is likely to have reached the crest of its leap and already be returning downward toward the key pin before the other "standard" driver pins have leapt up out of the plug.

My associates and I have tried installing Ilco Bump Halt pins and springs into locks and then bumping them. I was able to successfully bump a lock with a single Ilco driver pin just once (and, as we say in lockpicking. . . something must be repeatable at least twice or else it doesn't count), and once we started trying locks with *two* such driver pins, *no one* was able to bump the locks at all.

This is, in my view, a splendid low-cost solution to the problem of bumping. It does not *eliminate* the physical risk, mind you. . . it just makes bumping attempts *incredibly unlikely* to succeed. An additional benefit of this Bump Halt style of pin is that no modification to the lock's plug, housing, or key is needed. It can be retrofit into just about any pin tumbler lock with ease.

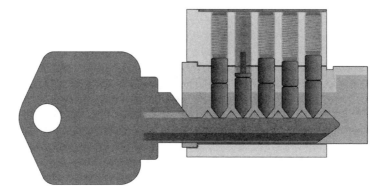

FIGURE 5.41

An Ico Bump Halt pin and high-pressure spring has been installed in the second chamber of this lock.

COMB PICKS

Like bump keys, comb picks (a set of which can be seen in Figure 5.42) are another very old type of attack tool that had fallen out of fashion for a time, but which are now receiving attention again. This is due to the fact that most manufacturers had eliminated the risk of the overlifting attack (which is what comb picks do) some time ago. However, like a virus that hasn't surfaced for an outbreak in years, overlifting has started to appear again... due to the fact that (to continue our infectious disease analogy) the "immune systems" of some lock manufacturers have degraded over time due to lack of use.

Overlifting

Most pin tumbler locks are manufactured with rather limited room in the plug chambers. There is enough space for the pins and springs, of course, and some room for the stack to traverse up and down in order to operate... but beyond that there is little else. Indeed, this is—in a way—one of the security features of such locks. Pin stacks, whether they are very tall (see Figure 5.43) or very short (see Figure 5.44), cannot be pushed entirely up into the housing of the lock.

Of course, that is how locks are *supposed* to work... but that's not always how they are designed and manufactured. Sometimes, because of poor planning or fabrication shortcuts, locks are produced with excessive space in the housing and, thus, extra-long pin chambers (see Figure 5.45).

A lock such as this is susceptible to an overlifting attack. By raising all of the pin stacks beyond their normal operating heights, it could be possible to rotate the plug freely without actually "picking" the pins.

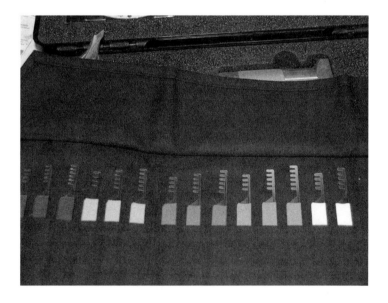

FIGURE 5.42

A set of comb picks.

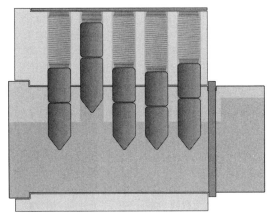

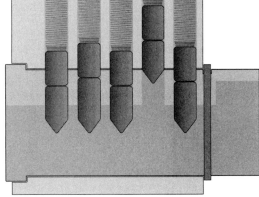

FIGURE 5.43

Attempts to lift the second pin stack of this lock beyond the functional height are ultimately stopped by the top of the pin chamber.

FIGURE 5.44

Attempts to lift the fourth pin stack of this lock beyond the functional height are ultimately stopped by the top of the pin chamber. Even though the key pin is much smaller than the pin in the second position (which was seen raised in Figure 5.43), it still cannot leave the plug... there isn't enough room in the pin chamber within the housing.

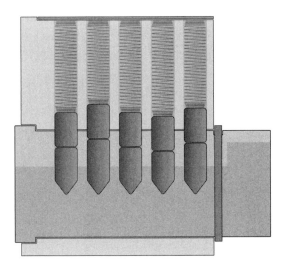

FIGURE 5.45

A poorly produced lock that features too much space in the portion of the pin chambers that runs through the housing.

Using comb picks

Comb picks are inserted into the keyway of a lock, moved deep enough that they can contact all of the key pins simultaneously (see Figure 5.46), and then lifted vertically in order to push the entire length of each pin stack completely out of the plug, as shown in Figure 5.47.

Comb picks come in large kits because of the varied pin spacing and different number of pin stacks (not to mention differing degrees of lift necessary) in locks today. Fortunately, the majority of name-brand locks tend to be not vulnerable to this attack, but with increasing marketplace competition driving prices ever-downward, some suppliers (particularly no-name vendors who manufacture their parts in the developing world) do not consider the risk of overlifting when producing their locks.

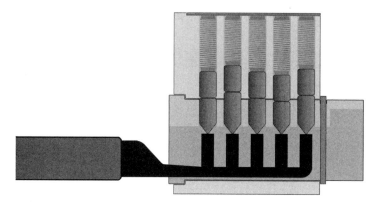

FIGURE 5.46

A comb pick inserted into the plug of a vulnerable pin tumbler lock.

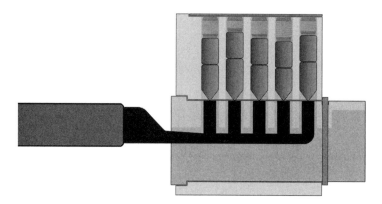

FIGURE 5.47

A comb pick that has successfully lifted all the pin stacks up into the housing. The plug can freely rotate now. (A tension tool could be employed to assist in the turning motion.)

AMERICAN LOCK BYPASS TOOL

One of the craftiest bypass products I have ever seen is developed by Peterson Tools and is used to attack some of the most popular offerings by the American Lock company. It is also effective against some of this brand's competing products. For a time, American Lock had developed a fix that would frustrate (although not totally prevent) this attack. However, American Lock is now wholly owned by Master Lock. The latter company has now started producing Master-branded products which directly compete with American Lock goods (which are also still produced and sold under their original name). Despite appearing virtually identical on store shelves (see Figure 5.48), there are significant differences between these locks. The methodology behind the "American Lock Bypass Tool" can potentially work against both of these brands.

The unique bypass tool offered by the Peterson company looks at first glance like it could be a conventional lockpick (see Figure 5.49), but it is in fact something quite different. It is not a hook pick, and it is not inserted into the keyway facing toward the pin stacks. It is inserted facing *away* from them, and it is pushed all the way *through* the entire plug and out the tail side. As you can see in Figure 5.50, the shackle release mechanism in these locks is a control cam (these locks use a high quality double ball mechanism) that features a quarter-circle type edge on one side. That quarter circle interfaces with the tail side of the plug. This bypass tool can reach beyond the plug (because this lock, like most others if you recall from Chapter 1, has the keyway milled *entirely through* the plug) and apply pressure to the control cam directly.

FIGURE 5.48

Competing products from Master Lock and American Lock (which are now owned by the same company) in the "square body padlock" line. Despite looking similar and having virtually identical price tags, the internal components are strikingly different.

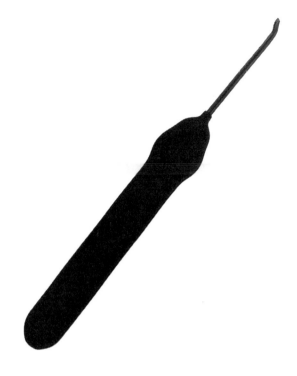

FIGURE 5.49

An "American Lock Bypass Tool" from Peterson Tools. Contrary to how it may appear in this photo, it is *not* a conventional hook pick.

FIGURE 5.50

A bypass tool reaching through the plug in order to contact the control cam. (This is a disassembled lock, of course. During actual operation, the cam would be pressed directly up against the tailpiece of the plug.)

What is ironic about the American Lock/Master Lock pairing is the fact that while these two product lines appear similar (indeed, they both feature this style of lock core and control cam which can be exploited by this style of attack), there are actually many distinctions internally between the two products.

American Lock was aware of the bypass problem in the past. They began engineering their newer models in ways that could not be exploited[†] and retro-fitting existing locks with something known as a "blocking wafer" that would prevent the use of the bypass tool. Now, the folks at Peterson eventually devised a companion product (known as a "wafer breaker") that would defeat this upgrade, as well... but it became much harder to perform the bypass. All modern American Lock products on store shelves today *should* have this "blocking wafer" installed from the factory. The Master Lock variant of the square body padlock, however, does *not* seem to ship from the factory with this protection.[‡] One other key distinction between the American Lock and Master Lock versions of this style of padlock is the lack of pick-resistant pins. As was mentioned in Chapter 4, American Lock products are routinely constructed with a healthy assortment of spooled and serrated pins (see Figure 5.51) that

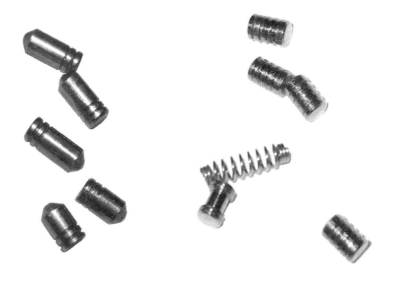

FIGURE 5.51

Pins from a modern padlock produced under the American Lock name. Serrated key pins (shown on the left) are paired with serrated driver pins (shown on the right). There was even a spool driver pin in one chamber (shown in the middle, nearest to the spring).

[†]Hence, the American 2000 series, also known as the "puck style" or "shackle-less" padlock. This lock cannot be bypassed and is a very solid, robust unit. Indeed, the publicity of the bypass attack was part of the evolution that led up to this lock being produced. That story is wonderfully illustrative evidence of the fact that independent security research and responsible public disclosure of vulnerabilities, ultimately results in better security for all of us.

[‡]The Master Lock design places the "half circle" on the tail of the plug and the "quarter circle" on the control cam in a slightly different alignment, making Peterson's original tool quite difficult to use; however, the same *weakness* is present in the lock. With some additional dedicated research and engineering, it is likely that the Master Lock product could be exploited in the same way.

can thwart many picking attempts. The Master Lock version of this line of products has no such protection... they are all standard, cylindrical pins in every chamber.

Of course, in my view, the real tragedy here is that locks are *still* shipping from the factory vulnerable to an attack that has been known and discussed publicly[§] for years. This vulnerability would be *totally* eliminated if the padlocks were made to be key retaining, much in the way that the US Government version of the American Lock line of products all are.

DOOR BYPASSING

The previous three sections (discussing bump keys, comb picks, and padlock bypass tools) involve methods of defeating pin tumbler locks by inserting nonstandard tools into the keyway. One should never discount the ability to open doors without ever interacting with anything *near* the lock mechanism itself, however. Perhaps the purest form of bypassing is when one completely disregards a keyway entirely and attempts to simply spring a door open.

The word "spring" is particularly relevant in this context, as many of the most basic "door bypasses" involve the exploitation of weak, spring-controlled mechanisms. The two most common styles of door bypass that this section will discuss are the popping of spring-loaded latches in the doorjamb and manipulation of spring-loaded door handles.

Slip attacks against latch bolts

There is a reason that anyone serious about security will insist that a deadbolt be installed on any door which is protecting a sensitive area. Deadbolts (as we have seen in Chapter 1) derive their name from the fact that the locking bar remains in a static position until it is acted upon by the turning of a lock plug... it is a "dead" mechanism with no forces or pressures of its own that can cause movement. Not all doors feature a deadbolt, but nearly *every* door has some manner of simple latching mechanism.

Door *latches* (also sometimes called *catches*) are designed to hold a door shut until a handle is turned. These devices are almost always spring-loaded and typically involve a small protrusion of metal (the latch) clicking into place upon a strike plate mounted to the doorjamb. For the user's convenience, a key is typically not needed to operate a latch; simply pulling the door shut is sufficient to engage it. Often, it is possible to *lock* a doorknob or handle but this merely prevents the knob itself from turning, it does nothing to secure the latch itself. As anyone who has watched old spy-themed TV shows knows, slipping of thin material (on television and in films a credit card is a popular device for this purpose) into the crack near the doorjamb can often result in the latch becoming disengaged temporarily.

While credit cards and similar thin materials can sometimes work on doors that open *inward* (where all that is needed is simple pushing pressure applied to the side of the latch that *faces you* in the doorjamb), it is also quite possible to attack doors that require pressure from the other, less

---

[§]I demonstrated the American Lock bypass during a lecture at the DEFCON security conference in the summer of 2005.

FIGURE 5.52

A physical penetration tester's "lucky number seven."

accessible, side. One of my favorite stories about the tools and supplies carried by certain penetration testers during red team audits was told to me by an individual who participated in the Discovery Channel program *Tiger Team*. Luke McComie is often heard praising the virtues of having a "lucky number seven" in his tool bag on many physical penetration tests (McComie Luke, oral communication) (see Figure 5.52).

A house number seven digit (made out of metal, preferably as thin as possible) is often a *very* effective doorjamb shoving tool. It is capable of not only triggering the release of a door latch with direct, frontal pressure but can also be used to hook and grab the *inward* side of a door latch in many instances. It may seem inelegant (and wouldn't be allowed in a professional lockpicking competition, of course), but during penetration testing, you should always use whatever means available. If that means bypassing a door using a lucky number seven as opposed to picking your way in... by all means go with whatever is fastest!

Triggering door handles and push bars

In order to comply with the Americans With Disabilities Act, businesses no longer equip office doors with round knobs. All door handles now tend to be of the type seen in Figure 5.53, long and easily grasped. Many office doors also feature push bars (sometimes called crash bars, see Figure 5.54) which similarly allow for greater ease-of-use.

These technologies allow doors to be operated more easily, yes... but they also facilitate a number of attacks that can be executed if there is any room to reach around or underneath the door (due to less

FIGURE 5.53

An ADA-compliant door handle.

FIGURE 5.54

A push bar (also known as crash bar or panic bar) installed to comply with fire codes.

than ideal mounting, lack of weather-stripping, or other gaps that can naturally occur when security is not considered during a door's installation). Such hardware is almost always found in facilities of all shapes and sizes, except those rare instances when an institution is working with material that is highly sensitive enough to bypass the "safety-of-life" requirements that are codified in law.

Some of the best and simplest additions you can make to a physical penetration tool bag are available at your local hardware store. Browse any display of metal rod stock that you come across; often you'll find that some of the items there (see Figure 5.55) are well-suited to being bent and formed into various useful shapes. Another utterly fabulous (and often cheaper) source of bendable metal rods are "sign holders" designed to be inserted into the earth and to display messages concerning an Open House or the location of a backyard party, etc. Not only are these items *very* affordable (I routinely acquire them for less than a dollar each) but as you can see in Figure 5.56, they come by default with a few convenient loops already in place. These can serve as effective and helpful handles; all that is needed (typically) is to bend the tip into an "L" or "U" shape in order to reach through a doorjamb and either grab a latch or impact a push bar.

Perhaps one of the best (and most entertaining) examples of just how easily security can be defeated using metal rods as bypass tools was demonstrated by Barry Wels and Han Fey at the IT-Defense conference in Brühl, Germany in February of 2010. In their video (a screenshot of which can be seen in Figure 5.57), Barry successfully opens a hotel room by inserting a long metal rod under the door, grabbing the handle on the inside. This attack is particularly interesting, given that the method of entry bypasses not only a mechanical lock, but also an electronic one. The full video can be viewed here... http://youtube.com/watch?v=WAkJRpKeyYg

FIGURE 5.55

Metal rod stock... incredibly useful when trying to engage handles from the opposite side of a door.

FIGURE 5.56

Metal "sign holders" can also be incredibly effective and useful bypass tools. The prefabricated loops make excellent handles.

FIGURE 5.57

Barry Wels demonstrating the "under door metal rod" attack in a video presented at the 2010 IT-Defense conference in Germany.

Courtesy of Barry Wels

Many facilities engineers pay great attention to protecting the crevices around and beneath their doors, of course. (This is not typically due to concerns of security, but rather in the interest of keeping out the elements, reducing heating and cooling costs, and muffling noise.) My associates and I have discovered a rather unique avenue of attack, however, that is often available in office and hotel settings on doors which might otherwise appear to be protected from typical attempts to reach the inside handle.

In professional spaces used for meetings, it has become a popular trend to install peepholes on doors to conference rooms. This allows passers-by in the hallway to unobtrusively inspect a room and see if it is occupied before attempting entry. This is a nice feature that can help avoid interrupting any business that may be taking place, but it introduces a security flaw. As you have no doubt noticed (and can see in Figure 5.58), the optical element within a peephole does not perform equally in each direction. In order to achieve the necessary field-of-vision, peepholes such as this tend to be mounted *backwards*. This exposes the "insecure" side of the door (the side facing out into a hallway or other common area) to the mounting threads and tool slot on the peephole.

At a pinch, it is sometimes possible to unscrew and pop a peephole out of its door, resulting in an exposed hole nearly a half inch in diameter. Through this hole it could be possible to attempt attacks against handles on the inside of the door. Metal rods or even loops of strong cord can be used, if one has a good sense of where the handle is positioned on the other side. This attack was demonstrated to great effect by noted security researcher CP during the seventh NotACon conference in Cleveland, Ohio. Do I expect this vulnerability to be exploited numerous times in the real world? No, I do not; but it is worth considering if you are assessing a company's security posture... or evaluating your own.

FIGURE 5.58

Peepholes are not bidirectional devices. The field-of-vision often dictates that when installed in office meeting rooms, the insecure side of a peephole faces a common area, such as a hallway.

SUMMARY

In previous chapters of this book, we have focused exclusively on finesse attacks against lock mechanisms themselves. It is always important, however, to remember that as a penetration tester, your goal is not to exploit only the most *difficult* flaws in security using only *advanced* techniques. Rely upon whatever gets you in quickly, easily, and cleanly. A solid grasp of bypassing techniques can often be the difference between being spotted by security personnel and slipping past a defensive perimeter before anyone has time to notice or react.

They all come tumbling down: Pin tumblers in other configurations

6

INFORMATION IN THIS CHAPTER

- Tubular locks
- Cruciform locks
- Dimple locks
- The secret weakness in 90% of padlocks

From the start of this book, we have spent a great deal of time focusing on pin tumbler locks. Chapters 1 and 2 dedicated a great many diagrams to illustrations of how these locks are constructed and function. Chapters 3 and 4 contained many guides and exercises on how to use basic lockpicking tools in order to manipulate and open these locks. However, thus far the material presented has focused almost entirely on pin tumbler locks of the common "bitted blade" variety... which feature a "vertical" keyway and a row of pin stacks running along a single, uniform vector such that the key pins ride along the thin edge of a key.

Not all pin tumbler locks are of this style, however. Indeed, there are a number of other popular methods of orienting pin stacks within a lock. The styles of lockpicks and techniques that may be used when attempting to exploit these products are also rather varied and unique. This chapter will present an overview of some of the most common "alternative" designs of pin tumbler lock and summarize the tools and tactics which can be effective against them.

TUBULAR LOCKS

Many of you may have encountered tubular locks at some point in time. Sometimes they are also called "Chicago Locks" or "Ace Locks" due to the fact that the original lock in this style was the *model* named "Ace" *produced by* the Chicago Lock Company. However, presently the design has been adopted by a number of other manufacturers around the world, most of whom have no affiliation with the original designers. It is for that reason that the name "tubular lock" is the best designation for this style of hardware. An assortment of tubular locks can be seen in Figure 6.1

While these locks might initially appear to be *very* different from all of the hardware that we've been discussing thus far in the book, in fact they operate by means of simple pin tumbler mechanisms the likes of which were first seen at the start of Chapter 1.

Let's look more closely at the components and construction of tubular locks. The similarities to the basic "blade key" design will become apparent.

Practical Lock Picking. DOI: 10.1016/B978-1-59749-611-7.00006-4

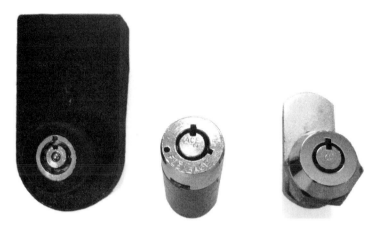

FIGURE 6.1

Three different tubular locks. The first is a gun lock by Dac Technologies, the second is the venerable Ace lock produced by Chicago, and the third is a no-name generic copy of the original Chicago design. Notice that while all three locks feature the "key centering" notch in the top dead center position, only the Ace lock has an additional notch that allows the key to be removed with the plug turned and the unit "locked open."

Inside a tubular lock

Nearly all tubular locks have a round housing, often one featuring a prominent lip or collar that helps to align the lock flush against a mounting surface. The left side of Figure 6.2 shows a photograph of a typical tubular lock housing; the right side shows a cross-sectional diagram of this same piece of metal.

 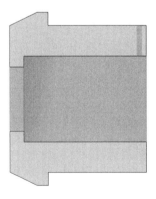

FIGURE 6.2

A tubular lock housing. The round hole cut into the front face of the housing is of a somewhat smaller diameter than the larger chamber found within.

Tubular locks have plugs, much like other pin tumbler locks. They are circular, allowing rotation, but naturally they have a distinct appearance unlike anything we have examined thus far in this book. Perhaps most distinct is where the pin chambers are drilled. Figures 6.3 and 6.4 show a tubular lock plug and the creation of these chambers.

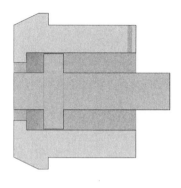

FIGURE 6.3

A tubular lock plug. It is inserted into the housing from the tail side during the assembly of a lock.

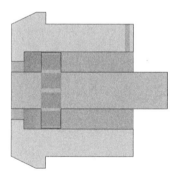

FIGURE 6.4

A tubular lock plug with the pinning chambers drilled. They are drilled completely through the middle flange section of this piece of metal.

There is an additional component to a tubular lock's housing, called a "barrel," which is inserted into the lock after the plug during assembly. It is often held in place by means of a small screw or pin which is inserted in a hole at the tail side of the housing. Figure 6.5 shows this additional piece of housing being inserted into place and Figure 6.6 calls attention to the retaining pin. Naturally, however, the pin would not be pounded into place at this moment, given that there are no pins in place

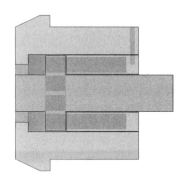

FIGURE 6.5

The barrel component of a tubular lock's housing. Can you see where it has been inserted in the diagram on the right side? This is where the rest of the pin chambers exist in a tubular lock.

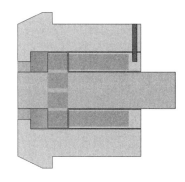

FIGURE 6.6

Showing where a retaining pin would be installed in the housing of a tubular lock. This locks the barrel (which is shown in the photo on the left) to the overall housing. Normally the lock would not be fused together at this point, as no pin stacks are present. Key pins, driver pins, and springs would normally be inserted into the plug and barrel, then the whole affair would be installed and fused in place with this retaining pin.

just yet. The pins are omitted in those two figures as to keep the diagrams less busy; Figure 6.7 shows a tubular lock fully assembled.

When a tubular lock is at rest, the springs push all pieces of the pin stack toward the front face. In each chamber, driver pins are sitting partially within the plug and partially in the barrel. For the plug of a tubular lock to turn freely, the pin stacks must be pushed back away from the front face, to varying degrees, in order to allow the pin stacks to meet the shear line in between the plug and housing insert (see Figure 6.8).

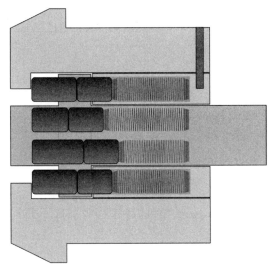

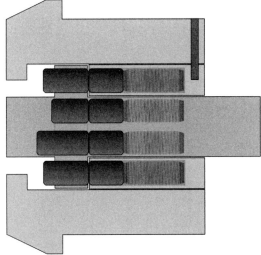

FIGURE 6.7

A diagram of a fully assembled tubular lock. Naturally, this image cannot represent the complete array of pin stacks, as some of them would be "behind" others, on the "far" side of the plug, in this side-view perspective.

FIGURE 6.8

A tubular lock with its pin stacks pushed to the various depths necessary in order to free the plug and allow rotation. All of the driver pins have been pushed out of the plug and are set exactly at the shear line.

Users of tubular locks are able to quickly and easily push all of the pin stacks simultaneously by means of the simple and yet elegant design of a tubular key. Notches are cut into the metal of a tubular key around its circumference. These notches vary in size (see Figure 6.9).

All of this might seem daunting, but remember... this lock typically relies on basic pin stacks, the likes of which we have encountered before as far back as Chapter 1.

Pick tools for tubular locks

Now, it may seem to some people that such a lock would be easy to pick, given that every single pin stack is exposed to the user. Indeed, some people do try to pick tubular locks by applying slight tension to the plug (often by inserting a small, squared tension tool into the key-centering notch) and stabbing straight at the pins with a small, thin tool... often a half diamond pick.

This technique will often work as a means of setting the pin stacks at the shear line, but such success is often short-lived. Yes, the plug will be free to rotate... but it can only be turned slightly (usually between 45° and 50°) before the pin chambers of the plug and the barrel line up (not in their original pattern... of course, now *new* chambers of the plug and the housing will align) and most of the pin stacks will snap back into place. In order to pick a tubular lock in this manner, tension would have to be consistently applied and the attacker would have to meticulously push upon the pin stacks as many as seven or eight times!

FIGURE 6.9

Tubular lock keys. Notice the bitting notches cut to various depths around the tip of the key.

Fortunately, there are more efficient ways of picking tubular locks. A specialized pick tool is needed, however (see Figure 6.10).

A tubular lockpick tool can simulate the various bitting cuts on a tubular key by means of a series of scalloped channels on its tip which contain movable feelers (see Figure 6.11). Depending on where the feelers are positioned, the channel can simulate anything from a total non-cut (blank key) to a very deep cut (typically a depth of seven).

FIGURE 6.10

A tubular lockpick tool. Many vendors produce variants of this tool, but the overall design remains the same in almost all cases.

FIGURE 6.11

The working tip of a tubular lockpick tool. Notice the channels and the movable feelers (the strips of dark metal) which can be adjusted to any position.

The feelers reside in small channels cut into the tool's cylindrical shaft. While simple versions of this type of pick do not offer any level of sophistication beyond that, most high-quality tubular pick tools in the market today incorporate some means of controlling how "tight" the feelers are. Often, this is achieved by means of a screw collar. The various components of such a collar are shown disassembled in Figure 6.12.

It is possible to completely disassemble and remove the adjustable collar on this style of pick tool. If you wish to modify your tool's feelers or otherwise customize your pick, then this is often achieved by removing a small screw or hex nut that holds the collar in place (see Figure 6.13).

One of the most common modifications (one which I perform upon every new tubular lockpicking tool that I acquire) is the removal of a "reset washer" that is often installed by default. This washer, which you may have seen on such tools in the past, serves almost no useful function and (in my opinion) gets in the way. By removing the adjustable collar you can get that washer out of there.

WARNING

While there are a number of useful modifications that can be performed on a tubular pick, take care when disassembling one of these tools. The feelers are likely to all pop out of their channels and fall onto the table. Do not worry too much, as they are all typically uniform and can be reassembled in any manner. Still, take care you don't lose them. Also, when reassembling a tubular pick, do not retighten the screw or hex nut too much. Move each of the feelers in its chamber... they all should have uniform and equal "tightness" at any given time. Overtightening of the assembly screw will often cause the feelers on the opposite side of the pick's shaft to become immovable. Back the screw off until all feelers have uniform movement.

FIGURE 6.12

The various components of a tubular lockpick's adjustable collar. Often, the largest ring (shown on the far left) rides upon a threaded screw surface. Beneath it sits a small metal flange. Beneath the flange is a rubber O-ring. As the large ring is screwed down upon the collar, this puts pressure on the flange, which in turn squeezes the O-ring. The more the rubber O-ring is sandwiched, the more it presses up against the metal feelers, restricting their movement.

FIGURE 6.13

The retaining screw that holds this tubular pick tool's adjustable collar in place. By removing it, the entire pick can be disassembled.

I am often asked exactly what the best setting is for this adjustable collar component on a tubular pick tool. Like many aspects of lockpicking, there is no single hard-and-fast rule upon which you can rely, but I have found what I believe to be a decent "average" standard that you can at least use as a benchmark. Try the following... unscrew the adjustable ring somewhat on your tubular pick. Now, using just a single finger, spin it back in the "tightening" direction until it stops. From this point of slight friction, turn the ring *an additional quarter-turn tighter*. That is a healthy baseline. Many simple locks will require less tightness than this. Some advanced locks (which we will discuss in the upcoming section, "Picking Tubular Locks") require additional stiffness in the feelers.

> **NOTE**
> _____
> Some individuals speak of adjusting a tubular pick tool's overall "tension" and while I suppose this term applies, I tend to shy away from it given that the concept of "tension" is already an integral part of lockpicking and that term is used in other ways unrelated to adjustments on a tubular pick tool. In this book, the "tightness" of the feelers will be referenced. The term may sound slightly more pedestrian, but I feel it is perhaps the best word to use.

It is a common misconception about tubular lockpicks that because these feelers feature "handles" down by the large, main grip it somehow means that the user manipulates these individual feelers when using the tool. That is not the case.

> **TIP**
> _____
> The one exception to the above rule is in the use of the PRO-1 Tubular Lockpick manufactured by Peterson Tools. This is a highly advanced device (with a price tag to match) that can be used to manipulate pin stacks individually. It also features adjustable tensioning/locking controls for each feeler and various interchangeable heads so that the tool can be used in a wider variety of tubular locks.

Picking tubular locks is a process that requires finesse, and one that can be infinitely easier with the right tool. The next section describes two different ways that people sometimes choose to use a tubular pick.

Picking tubular locks

For the most part, the process of using a tubular pick tool involves pushing all of the feelers up flush with the tip of the tool, then operating the pick in the lock in such a way as to slowly inch the feelers into the correct positions. As referenced in the previous section, "Pick Tools for Tubular Locks," the feelers are not manipulated manually. Rather, through actions within the lock, the pin stacks themselves will naturally tend to push the feelers into the correct positions.

Zeroing the pick

There may be multiple ways of *using* a tubular lockpick, but *preparing* the tool is always performed in the same way. In order to "zero" the feelers they are traditionally pushed upward, beyond the tip of the tool's working shaft (see Figure 6.14) and then the tool itself is pressed against a hard, flat surface (see Figure 6.15) in order to make the tips of the feelers perfectly flush with the tip (see Figure 6.16). While this is often referred to as "zeroing" the tool (in that a bitting code of zero is typically representative of no cut at all on a key), the term is not 100% accurate in this context, given that by some standards a bitting code of *eight* represents no cut at all. Still, given the prevalence of the term, I would not consider it improper to speak of "zeroing" a tubular pick tool when this process is performed.

As mentioned at the start of this section, there are two main ways of using a tubular pick tool. In each case, however, it is important to be mindful of how this tool should be inserted into the lock.

FIGURE 6.14

A tubular pick with all of its feelers pushed upward, beyond the working tip.

FIGURE 6.15

Pressing a tubular pick into a flat, hard surface in order to "zero" the tip of the feelers.

FIGURE 6.16

The pick tool is now fully reset and ready to be used in a lock.

Inserting the pick

Tubular pick tools rarely, if ever, feature a prominent point of metal sticking outward from the cylindrical shaft (the "outer centering bit") as seen on tubular keys, but they almost always feature a small bump or protrusion of metal upon their inner surface (an "inner centering bit") which can align with a slot on the plug of the lock.

Align the pick tool properly at the face of the lock. Insert the tool directly into the lock as far as it will travel. Take care to position and move the pick in a direct parallel with how the lock is oriented (see Figure 6.17). If you attempt to insert the tool at an off-center angle (as shown, perhaps a bit exaggeratedly, in Figure 6.18), this can disturb the feelers and push them out of position accidentally.

In general, a tubular pick should feel relatively smooth and unobstructed when being inserted into a lock. Occasionally, the "key centering notches" on a plug will be a bit small, and the first time your pick is inserted it might seem a bit stiff or resistant. If you are unsure as to whether or not you inserted your pick properly, remove it and observe the feelers. The next section, "Working the Pick," offers some advice as to how the appearance of the feelers can indicate whether a mistake has been made.

Working the pick

As we begin discussion of how to manipulate a tubular lock with this style of pick tool, it is a good idea to examine some specifics of how the feelers move on this pick tool. Observe the three companion images shown in Figure 6.19.

- On the left is an image showing a feeler that has moved partway down in its working space. You are likely to see many feelers that move in this fashion.

FIGURE 6.17

A tubular pick should always be inserted in a straight, direct manner.

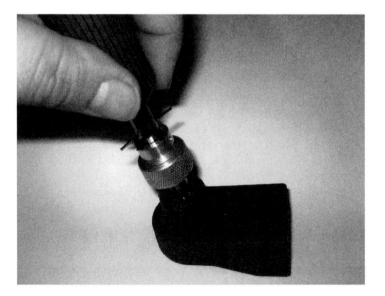

FIGURE 6.18

Take care to NOT ever insert the tubular tool at an off-angle. This can disturb the position of some of the feelers.

FIGURE 6.19

Three possible positions where a feeler can move during the use of a tubular pick.

- In the middle is an image showing a feeler that has moved all the way to the maximum cut depth for a particular position on a tubular key. You won't encounter this quite as often when picking most locks. Super-deep cuts like that don't occur as frequently on keys. Encountering a feeler moved to that position on your pick can sometimes be a sign of a problematic pin stack (usually one with a very stiff spring) that will require extra attention.
- On the right is an image showing a feeler that has been moved *deeper* than the deepest cut position. This is a sign that something has gone wrong, more than likely the pick tool snagged the edge of the lock's housing when it was being inserted into the plug.

It is my hope that these three distinct feeler movements are clear to you. They will be referenced as we discuss the two primary methods of using the tubular pick.

The side-to-side rocking technique

The first method of tubular picking that I ever learned was the side-to-side rocking technique. This is straightforward to understand, easy to perform, and has a relatively decent success rate against tubular locks that feature no special protections.

Begin by "zeroing" the feelers as shown in Figures 6.14 and 6.15. Insert the pick directly and completely into the plug as shown in Figure 6.17. With the pick tool all the way in, rock it by attempting to rotate the plug clockwise and counterclockwise with a motion indicated by Figure 6.20. The plug won't be able to move very far, and you may believe that you're not accomplishing anything at all. If you were to remove the pick tool, however, chances are you'd notice that many of the feelers have moved. How is this possible?

The reason has to do with how binding pins cause movement of a pin stack. Recall Chapter 2 when we first discussed pin stacks and the binding of driver pins in the shear line. Figure 2.7 showed the motion of a driver pin as it became wedged in the shear line when the plug was exposed to a rotational force. What may not have been as obvious back then (given that it was immaterial at the time and therefore not discussed) was the fact that the driver pin's becoming slightly angled to the side also puts additional pressure upon the key pin. This has essentially no effect when working with conventional pick tools inside of a blade-key-style pin tumbler lock... the pin stacks are already resting in the "bottom" of their chambers when the process begins. In a tubular lock, however, the pin stacks are sitting atop

FIGURE 6.20

Rotating the pick tool both clockwise and counterclockwise in an attempt to cause pin stacks to bind. Do not let the size of the arrow mislead you, initially you will not be capable of a great deal of rotational movement, but keep at it. It will have an effect.

the feelers of the pick. These feelers are capable of *moving*, of course. Thus, when you rock the pick tool in alternating directions as shown in Figure 6.20, some of the pin stacks will be binding. The pins in these binding stacks will be "wiggling in place" slightly, and this will bring pressure upon the feelers of those chambers. The feeler of a binding stack will move slightly, but (in theory) it should only slide to the depth at which the pin stack above it is no longer binding. Why is that? Because if the pin stack is at the proper height and no longer binding, the pins of that chamber should no longer be "wiggling" in place. Continued oscillation of the pick tool back and forth should bring about similar movement by pins in other chambers as they start to bind.

In tubular locks that feature no special protections against picking and manipulation, this technique will often produce results in a matter of minutes.

The in-and-out pressing technique

A rather different technique than the one described in the previous section, this is a method somewhat in between an overlifting attack and an impressioning attack. Some of my associates have had great success attacking tubular locks by inserting their pick tool (properly zeroed, of course) into the lock all the way, applying some rotational turning force in one direction, and then moving the tool out slightly and then pressing it back in again. Figure 6.21 attempts to indicate the series of motions that are involved in this process.

Ultimately, what one is trying to accomplish by this technique is to push all of the pin stacks out past the shear line, then allowing them to slowly fall back toward the face of the lock while the plug is under tension. The alternative movement can also work in the same way... pushing the tool

FIGURE 6.21

An attempt to diagram the In-and-Out Pressing Technique. The pick tool is fully inserted, rotated to one side, and then moved in and out to very small degrees.

further into the plug while it is under tension. In both cases, the notion is to hopefully catch the split between the key pin and the driver pin at the shear line. This technique (in my view) takes a little more getting used to than the "Side-to-Side Rocking Technique", but I have seen it produce successful results in a matter of *seconds* as opposed to minutes.

Be aware that a tubular pick tool can be removed from the lock at any time and from any position, because it does not have an outer centering bit like most keys. Because of this, it is possible to deny other users easy operation of a tubular lock. If you have successfully picked a tubular lock and remove your tool with the plug turned to any position other than the default, resting position, the result will be similar to what is seen in Figure 6.22. Yes, this is a successful opening attempt... but now the lock is inoperable, even with the proper key. The only course of action at this time (other than filing the outer centering bit off the key) would be to use the pick tool to manipulate the lock shut again.

Pick-resistant tubular locks

As was seen in Chapter 4, some manufacturers make changes to the components of their pins stacks in order to produce locks that are harder to attack. This is as common a practice with tubular locks as with flat-blade-key locks.

Varied spring strength

The most typical difficulty that I have encountered when picking tubular locks is the use of different styles and strengths of springs in various chambers. The Chicago Lock Company, originator of the tubular lock design, has been incorporating this feature in their locks for quite some time. The second-generation Ace locks are particularly hard for novices to pick for this reason.

FIGURE 6.22

A tubular lock that has been picked open and can now no longer be operated by the key. It will remain "stuck" like this until a tubular pick tool is used to rotate the plug back to the default position again.

It would not be such a problem if *all* of the pin chambers had high-strength springs. One could merely calibrate the tubular pick tool for *excessive* stiffness (by tightening the adjustment collar considerably) and proceed. However, in a lock with *assorted* spring strengths, that method will not work. Too much stiffness will all but prevent the pin stacks featuring "average" springs from moving. Too little stiffness will result in way too much movement by pin stacks featuring "high-strength" springs. So what is the solution?

Often, the best approach is a two-stage approach. Begin by zeroing your pick and adjusting the stiffness to what I described as a decent, average level. Thumb-tighten the ring until it stops, then grip it firmly and provide an additional quarter-turn.

Insert the pick directly into the lock and then remove it. Observe the feelers. In an ideal world, a few of them might have moved (perhaps quite significantly, down to the bottom of their bitting cuts as seen in the middle photo in Figure 6.19) while others have remained stationary. That's what you want to see. The chambers where the feelers have moved significantly contain high-strength springs. Ignore those for now; we will come back to them in a moment.

Proceed with oscillating movement as shown in Figure 6.20. (I find the "Side-to-Side Rocking Technique" to be of greatest use in these cases.) After a time, remove the pick from the lock. Observe the feelers. Some of them should have moved partway down, and of course the ones that moved *completely* down (as seen in the previous paragraph) will still be in that position. Figure 6.23 shows an example of this... the feeler identified as #1 was facing a high-strength spring and is likely out of position at this time; feeler #2 was facing a conventional spring and may have rocked into the correct position now.

If you encounter this, all hope is not lost. On the contrary, you may be halfway there. Use this time now to *reset* the feelers but *only* in pin stacks that you suspect have high-strength springs.

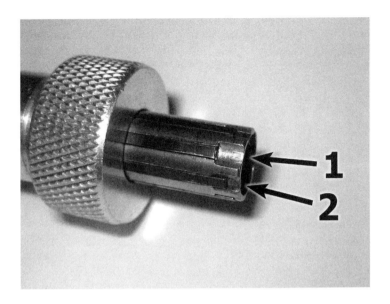

FIGURE 6.23

Comparing the difference between high-strength and conventional springs within tubular pin stacks. After some rocking back and forth, it appears that the lower feeler (#2) may have moved into the proper position. The feeler seen above (#1) is all the way at the "deepest" depth and has likely encountered a high-strength spring behind the pin stack where it was pressing.

Observe the photo in Figure 6.24. Feeler #1 has been reset back to its "zeroed" position. Feeler #2 has been left undisturbed.

With some selective resets performed, it is now time to *increase* the stiffness of your feelers. Turn the adjusting ring an additional quarter-turn or perhaps even a half-turn. This will effectively lock in place the feelers that were facing conventional springs (these feelers do not need to move any further, since they are likely in the correct positions already) and now you should have enough stiffness to try to tackle the high-strength pin stacks a second time.

You can check if you have dialed up the stiffness enough by inserting and removing the pick one time. Have any of the feelers moved all the way back to their deepest position again? If they have, reset them again and adjust to even greater stiffness.

For tubular locks whose only protection is varied spring strength, this technique is often the most effective.

Higher security pins in tubular locks

Some tubular lock manufacturers incorporate changes not just to the *springs* but also to the *pins* within their locks. These changes are also geared towards making the locks more secure. One interesting feature that I have encountered to a great degree could be called, for lack of a better term, "long posts" on the driver pins. Did any of you notice back in Figure 6.7, when we first saw the diagram of an assembled tubular lock that the pin chambers were cut rather deeply into the barrel? In

FIGURE 6.24

Feeler #1 has been reset to its starting position, but feeler #2 has been left where it was. The pick tool is nearly ready for a second pass.

some locks, this can result in the potential for an overlifting attack. Seen in Figure 6.25, if there is too much room in a pin chamber, the entire pin stack can be pushed out of the plug, allowing it to rotate freely.

In order to prevent this, some manufacturers will incorporate long posts on the tail side of their driver pins (see Figure 6.26). These posts also have the virtue of helping to guide and align the springs during the assembly and operation of the lock.

Beyond the "anti-overlifting" posts, some manufacturers will incorporate specially shaped key pins and driver pins which attempt to frustrate the two styles of attack described in this chapter. Some of these pin shapes are shown in Figure 6.27.

Attacking a tubular lock that features antipick features such as this in every chamber would likely prove to be quite difficult. It is quite likely that picking attempts would fail with anything other than a tool like the Peterson pick.

Odd styles of tubular locks

I have occasionally encountered some rather strange (perhaps some would simply say "unique") tubular locks. A variant that I have encountered with greater frequency than any other is a tubular lock without any "key-centering" notch on the plug. Such a lock is shown in Figure 6.28. During usage, the plug obtains all of its turning force simply from the portions of the key pins that are sticking up into the bitting cuts of the key. It is quite difficult to attack such a lock with conventional tubular picks, given that the normal method of using these tools is to begin with all feelers out at the "blank key" position. It is not possible to "grab" onto the plug like this. Additionally, the lack

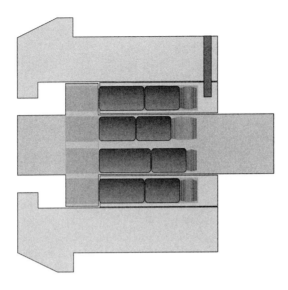

FIGURE 6.25

Overlifting the pins of a tubular lock.

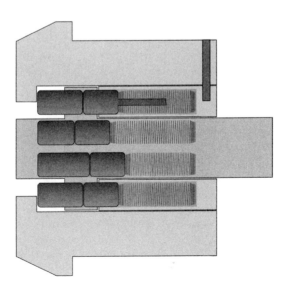

FIGURE 6.26

The pin stack shown at the top of this diagram includes a driver pin that features a long post on its tail side.

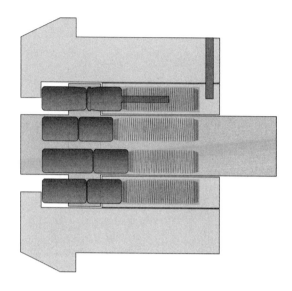

FIGURE 6.27

Additional protections in a tubular lock. Again, direct your attention to the top pin stack in this diagram. The key pin has a tapered edge and the driver pin has a mushroom lip.

FIGURE 6.28

An unconventional (by our standards here in North America) tubular lock. Notice how there is no key-centering notch on the plug.

FIGURE 6.29

An assortment of multipiece tubular pick tools I obtained when traveling in Malaysia. These are the only tools I own which can successfully attack the lock seen in Figure 6.28. As you can see, they operate in a similar fashion to the pick tools seen earlier in this chapter (they have a series of "feelers" that can move independently), but they are much more complicated to use.

of a key-centering notch on the plug often will prevent a tubular pick tool from even seating properly in the lock. The only way to attack such locks is with specialized tools, often ones developed in the part of the world where the locks are prevalent. The lock in Figure 6.28 is from Southeast Asia. It can only be attacked with the pick tool shown in Figure 6.29, which The Open Organisation Of Lockpickers obtained from a locksmith in Kuala Lumpur.

CRUCIFORM LOCKS

There is a style of lock that some people in North America may not have encountered very often (if at all) but which is very popular in other parts of the world (specifically Asia, the Pacific Rim, and South America) and therefore deserves mention here. I am speaking about cruciform locks, also known as cross locks or Zeiss locks.* While the keys of these locks may look intimidating at first glance (see Figure 6.30), they are, in fact, nothing more than a unique style of pin tumbler lock. Each blade surface of the key rides along its own separate channel in the plug and can interact with its own unique row of pin stacks. Typically, these rows are three or four pin stacks deep. Also typical of this style of lock is the presence of a "blank" channel in the plug. In spite of having the appearance of four bitted sides (indeed, the keys to the lock shown in Figure 6.30 do have bitting *cuts* on all four surfaces), the lock itself is only pinned in *three* of the four channels.

Cruciform locks are produced by a number of different manufacturers. As we have seen when exploring other types of pin tumbler locks (flat-blade-key style, tubular key style), it is possible

---

*While the terms cruciform and cross are relatively interchangeable, depending on how fancy one chooses to be in referencing the shape of the keyway, the name "Zeiss lock" is less accurate. Much in the way the name "Chicago lock" is no longer a suitable term for tubular locks (since that original manufacturer has now been joined by numerous others in the marketplace), the name "Zeiss lock" is a reference to one of the pioneers of this design...but that company is no longer the sole producer of this style of lock. I highly recommend that people use terms that reference the shape of the keyway instead.

FIGURE 6.30

A cruciform lock and its keys. Some people seem intimidated by the multiple blades appearing at perpendicular angles to one another, but the locks themselves tend to be relatively simple.

to add antipick features to pin stacks, but such measures are only employed by companies who wish to specifically focus on security. Many times, in an attempt to lower production costs, locks are produced using the simplest components and assembled as quickly and cheaply as possible. The pin stacks inside of most of the cross locks that I have encountered have no special protections to make them resistant to picking. The only obstacle (and it is minor) comes from the fact that the keyway and pin orientation requires the user to have a nonstandard approach.

Manually picking a cruciform lock

It is often possible to manually pick this style of lock using conventional tools. If you have a tensioner that can effectively apply turning force to the plug and a pick tool that can reach inside (in these small, tight spaces, a half-diamond pick tends to work well), one can feel around, seeking binding pin stacks, setting pins, etc. This can be a little bit more of a tedious process than with single-blade style pin tumbler locks, given that the pins may have a binding order that makes you traverse around between the various channels multiple times. Still, it is possible. Personally, I enjoy using specialized cross picks instead.

Cross lock picks

There are a few variations of the specialized tool that is often used in attacking cruciform locks, but nearly all of them involve very similar features. There is a tubular shaft that can be used to apply some manner of turning force to the plug, and there are a series of picking tips (often in the form of half-diamond picks or bits of stiff wire bearing diamond-shaped bumps at their ends) which can move in and out of the shaft. A typical cross lock pick is seen in Figure 6.31.

As can be seen in Figure 6.31, the central shaft of this tool (which the user controls by means of the large, round handle) applies tension to the plug by means of small rods on its tip that fit into the keyway. Many cross lock picks come as kits with interchangeable shafts (see Figure 6.32) that allow the user to select different size rods in order to obtain a better grip in the keyway. Longer rods are sometimes necessary due to the fact that some cruciform locks have an extra "curtain" of metal built into their front face, which can spin freely (see Figure 6.33). Attempting to engage this bit of metal and turn will not have any effect on the plug, hence the need for a tool that can reach more deeply into the keyway.

NOTE

There are some highly specialized cross lock picks which do not utilize small rods at the end of their tensioning shaft. Fabricated with large, flat blocks of metal (which often protrude out *past* the picking arms), these picks are often designed for use in very specific locks, often automotive locks. Using a cruciform key to start your car or motorcycle may seem strange to individuals in North America, but in other parts of the world this can be seen. Pick tools for this type of lock are often highly specific and not of great use when attempting to open common padlocks or door locks that use cruciform keys.

FIGURE 6.31

A typical cross lock pick. The four picking arms are attached to the rear plunger and can move in and out of the shaft. The central shaft has small rods on its tip that can grip the keyway, allowing the user to apply tension to the plug using the large, round handle.

FIGURE 6.32

Interchangeable components of a cross lock pick. The round tensioning handle can be attached to a tubular shaft featuring either large or small rods, in order to engage various types of keyways.

FIGURE 6.33

A cruciform lock on the front of a safe. The very first piece seen in the keyway is a free-spinning plate of metal. Applying tension to that would have no effect, thus a cross pick with longer "rods" at its tip is needed.

In my opinion, cross picks are among the easiest lockpicking tools to use. Begin by extending the picking arms out beyond the tubular shaft. Align the diamond tips with the channels of the keyway as shown in Figure 6.34 (their position doesn't matter, as all four arms should be fabricated equally from the factory). Insert them completely into the lock as shown in Figure 6.35 (you may need to pinch them together slightly when guiding them into the keyway). Then, bring the tubular shaft toward the lock face, aligning the rods with the keyway and inserting them into each corner (see Figure 6.36).

Telling someone how to use a cross lock pick is about as easy as telling someone how to use a rake pick. Do you recall how in Chapter 2 when raking was introduced I expressed regret that there was no formalized process to raking that I could explain in a step-by-step manner? The same holds true for using a cross lock pick. Indeed, this is because of the fact that you essentially use the tool to perform a raking attack against all of the chambers simultaneously.

Apply gentle rotational tension to the plug by turning slightly with the pick tool's large handle. Remember, as with many types of picking, light to moderate tension is the key... don't turn too hard. With tension applied, grab the plunger and punch the picking arms in and out of the lock very quickly. Figure 6.37 attempts to illustrate these two actions, although nothing but a live-action video is likely to capture the speed with which you can punch in and out... not to mention the speed with which this attack can open the lock if you are successful.

Sometimes, the lock will open almost instantly (see Figure 6.38). Sometimes it will take a dozen passes or so. In my experience, however, it should not take more than that. If you have not experienced success after ten or twelve scrubbing movements, I would suggest the following... slowly remove the tool from the lock, taking care to notice exactly how the picking arms are aligned with the chambers of the keyway. With the tool removed, rotate it 90° and reinsert it in the manner shown in Figures 6.34 through 6.36. What can you hope to accomplish by this?

FIGURE 6.34

A cross pick being prepared for use, with its four arms extended outward beyond the tubular shaft.

FIGURE 6.35

A cross pick with its picking arms fully inserted into the lock.

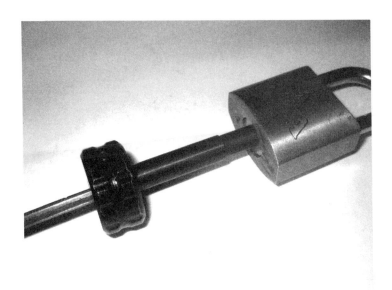

FIGURE 6.36

A cross pick with the tensioning piece inserted into the keyway.

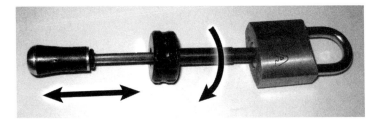

FIGURE 6.37

A cross lock pick is used by applying slight rotational tension to the plug and then punching the pick arms in and out very rapidly.

FIGURE 6.38

A cross lock that has been picked open; you should find that it's often *quite* easy to do.

Well, remember how I said that the position at which you insert the tool (initially) should not matter, because all four picking arms are fabricated to be uniform? As you have seen time and time again (predominantly when we discuss the manufacturing of various components of a lock), nothing coming from a machine shop is ever produced with *absolute* uniformity and perfection. The various arms of a cross pick may have slightly differing degrees of flex and stiffness. How they perform in each chamber may not be perfectly equal. By exposing the picking arms to *different* chambers and rows of pin stacks, perhaps you'll get lucky and find one orientation more suitable than another. This has happened to me a lot, in fact. I'll try to use a cross pick without success for a couple of attempts, then turn the pick by 90°, and my next attempt will open the lock almost immediately. Remember, in penetration testing, it doesn't matter if you get in by skill, luck, or some combination of the two!

Before we bring this section to a close, I should say a word about the varying styles and brands of cross lock picks. The term "brands" is perhaps a bit generous, as many of these tools are produced by fly-by-night companies and sold on web sites and in catalogs known more for rock-bottom prices than high-quality products. I have found cross lock picks that I absolutely love. I have also come across ones that were manufactured so badly as to break practically on the first attempt made to use them. In my experience, most cross lock picks are based around two different companies' designs. (The market is flooded, of course, with no-name knock-offs copying each of these designs in great quantity.)

The KLOM company (and all those who have copied their design) produces a cross lock pick with a nice array of interchangeable tension tips, but the tensioner handle of their tool is made of plastic. I managed to completely strip the channel for the retaining screw when I attempted to switch tips and tighten the handle in place. An alternate design, offered by the GOSO company (and all of their competitors who are copying *their* design) has a much higher quality tension handle made of steel; however, this pick tool doesn't always come with varied tensioning tips.

Figure 6.39 tries to give you an impression of the differing handle shapes, which can serve as a way of distinguishing which type of tool you may be purchasing if you shop online or through supply

FIGURE 6.39

Two different tensioning handles for cross lock picks. The handle on the left is all plastic and potentially weak. The one on the right is steel, and (in my experience) is much stronger and of a higher quality.

catalogs. The KLOM plastic handle is shown on the left. The GOSO steel handle is shown on the right. In the end, if you are *really* interested in cross lock picks, perhaps the best plan is to acquire both... and use the KLOM tips with the GOSO handle. As with all lockpicking tools, some of the best ones are those that you fabricate and tweak yourself.

DIMPLE LOCKS

Some people may find it odd that this book has not covered the topic of dimple locks until now. Perhaps that's a symptom of my being from the United States... while this style of lock may be quite common in other parts of the world (indeed, I have even heard this lock called a "Euro key" style, a name I am not crazy about due to the obvious implications of geographic narrow-mindedness), it is not very typical where I come from.

Dimple locks bear this name because of the manner in which the bitting cuts are formed on their keys. Instead of notches cut into the thin edge of the key blade, holes are drilled into the flat surface of the key blade. A simple dimple lock that perfectly represents this style of manufacturing can be seen in Figure 6.40. While this may appear to be a very innovative design (and to some degree it is; I don't want to discount the multitude of dimple locks out there that are very well-engineered

FIGURE 6.40

A dimple style lock. This particular lock is from Japan, although dimple keys can be seen in a number of regions around the world. They are less common in North America, however.

FIGURE 6.41

While the key and keyway may seem highly unconventional, holding the lock at the right angle (and shining a light in the right spot) can often reveal the simple, regular pin tumblers found within.

and monsters to pick), it is important to understand that the underlying mechanism within such locks is still just plain pin tumbler stacks. (If you peer into the keyway at the right angle and with good lighting, the pins can be seen, as shown in Figure 6.41.) Without any additional precautions taken by manufacturers, these locks can be picked in the same manner as pin tumbler locks with "vertical" keyways.

Because of the orientation of the keyway on dimple locks, traditional lockpick tools are rarely useful. There is a whole wide range of specialized tools that exist for the purpose of picking dimple locks. Most dimple picks have the look of small flags or golf clubs (see Figure 6.42), and they are

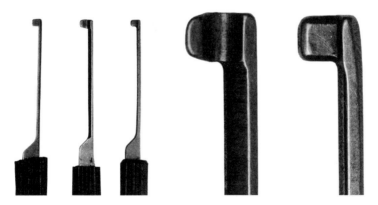

FIGURE 6.42

A series of dimple picks. On the right is a closer look at the tips on two of these tools.

Courtesy of datagram

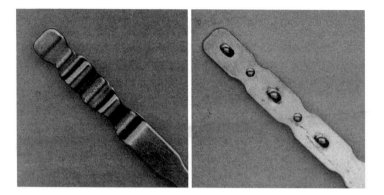

FIGURE 6.43

A closer look at the tips of two dimple rakes.

Courtesy of datagram

used not by *rocking* or *raising*, the techniques that were first seen in Chapter 2, but are instead inserted into the lock and *rotated* along their long axis. This allows the small "flag" tips to catch and lift some of the pin stacks. There are also rake tools designed for dimple locks; the tips of two such tools can be seen in Figure 6.43.

I stated that these locks can be often picked when manufacturers do not take "any additional precautions" like the ones we have seen before, most typically in Chapter 4. It should be understood, however, that *many* manufacturers of dimple locks *do* take security quite seriously. Pick-resistant pins are quite common in dimple locks, and (in my experience) they tend to be fabricated with great imagination and creativity. (The styles of pins that Han Fey calls "sneaky pins"[1], which were also referenced in Chapter 4, would be right at home in many dimple locks.) Furthermore, the overall fabrication of dimple locks and dimple keys tends to be handled in a manner that shows great attention to tight mechanical tolerances and precision machining.

Dimple locks are not impossible to pick, but they will often give you a very significant challenge. Even with specialized pick tools such as those seen in Figures 6.42 and 6.43, it can be difficult. Tackling a dimple lock that lacks any special pick-resistant features, however, is likely to be well within your skill range if you have proceeded through all of the exercises that this book has suggested thus far. It can even be done without the purchase of expensive, specialized pick tools. My associates and I have attacked cheap dimple locks with entirely improvised tools in the past. A half-diamond pick makes an adequate dimple lifter at a pinch. Some people will even carve a spare half-diamond pick slightly to make it more effective in this vein. I also have one broken pick with me in my large tool kit that I bent into a wave shape in order to make an impromptu dimple rake. Such improvised tools can be seen in Figure 6.44. While they aren't very pretty, they can still be effective from time to time.

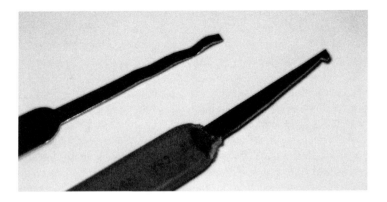

FIGURE 6.44

Improvised dimple picks. The wavy rake was made from a broken tool and the lifter pick is a half-diamond that I carved slightly with a hand file.

THE SECRET WEAKNESS IN 90% OF PADLOCKS

There is one last secret tip I want to share with you. I didn't choose to reveal this early-on in the book, because I wouldn't want anyone taking a shortcut method to opening every lock they see. I wanted you to learn, I wanted you to practice. However, having read this far... you can now discover the secret vulnerability present in the vast majority of padlocks on the market today. Often, all that is needed is a paper clip or stiff piece of piano wire to attack locks with this weakness.

How often have you seen small holes in the body of a padlock? These are visible on *many* popular makes and models. They may be in different positions, but they are almost always present. Many such holes are shown in Figure 6.45. Would you like to know what these are, what purpose they serve, and what weakness they provide?

FIGURE 6.45

Small, nondescript holes are found on the body of *many* padlocks. Do you know what they are for?

I am so sorry to disappoint you, my dear readers. These are simply drain holes, and nothing more. When exposed to the elements, padlocks can accumulate water due to rainfall or even condensation running down the shackle. This water could pool inside the lock, potentially resulting in jamming or fouling... particularly in cold climates. By having holes such as this in the body of the lock, water is able to drain out.

I do hope you can pardon me for this bit of dark humor at the end of the book. However, it is here with a twofold purpose. First of all, I wanted a fun and amusing way to dispel all of the rumors that circulate concerning these holes. I have heard highly uninformed people make incredibly grand claims over the years concerning drain holes. I have heard them described as places where "master override keys" can be inserted. I have heard them linked to theories about how a lock might be disassembled. I have heard them described as "anchoring points" used by factory machinery to hold and align work pieces during production. None of these theories has any basis in fact.

SUMMARY

The second reason that I chose to close with this humorous notion is to reinforce a universal truth about lockpicking... the only tried-and-true means of opening most of the locks that you come across is to practice, practice, practice. Becoming a great lockpicker is no different than becoming a talented musician or a skilled athlete. It develops over time, with hard work and dedication. I truly hope that that this book has given you a solid foundation of knowledge upon which you can build and that the suggested techniques and exercises offered in these chapters can help you to become comfortable with your tools and tactics. If you have had fun reading these pages and trying my suggestions, hopefully you have developed a new hobby and you'll keep at it. Over time, this unique and fascinating skill set can become a part of your vocational life if you perform penetration testing work... and it can be a very entertaining leisure diversion for you and your friends.

Reference

1. Fey H. Cutaway cylinders and their locking technique (Part 1) [document on the Internet]. The Open Organisation Of Lockpickers (TOOOL); 2005 May [cited 6 April 2010]. Available from: http://toool.nl/images/f/f9/Cutaway1.pdf.

Guide to tools and toolkits

INFORMATION IN THIS CHAPTER

- Guide to differentiating pick tools
- A note about tension tools
- Pick kit suggestions

This final section in the book is devoted to discussions of lockpicking tools... what we call them, how to choose them, and how to carry them where they're needed. There are a number of different companies producing lockpicks. The quality of tools on the market today can vary a great deal... however, it should be understood that much of the variation from one supplier to the next pertains to very intricate details of metallurgy. Often, it's not so much a matter of *quality* as of *suitability*. Tools that one person may find useful might not be popular with someone else. It's a matter of taste, which is often tied to individual skill.

People who are just starting out learning to pick tend to do well with tools produced using spring steel. This metal has some flex and give to it, and it is a little more forgiving of rough handling, even when thin stock is used to produce equipment. Lockpickers with more experience are usually fans of pick tools that are stiffer, as this can offer better tactile feedback when someone has learned to "see with their hands" during lockpicking. Tools made of hardened steel are often popular with professional lockpickers. One vendor, Peterson Tools, touts their "government steel" tools as being particularly stiff. The company Southern Ordinance (commonly known as SouthOrd), which is usually known for selling medium-quality spring-steel equipment to novices, breaks from their normal routine with their "Max Yield" line of picks. Designed for finely skilled hands, these tools are also quite stiff. My favorite vendor of pick tools is the Chicago-based company HPC. Their distribution network tends to be more restrictive, with only locksmiths and recognized security professionals able to obtain HPC picks (the Rytan company has a similar policy), but to me the quality is second-to-none. Both the spring steel and the stainless steel line of HPC tools are particularly stiff, due in part to slightly greater thickness of material on their spring steel equipment. This is a smart tradeoff, in my mind. By thickening their picks slightly, HPC offers equipment in a forgiving spring steel that still performs like a "stiffer" hard pick.

Most lockpicks are made from metal that is 0.020 inches thick. Southern Ordinance, Rytan, and a wonderful (but lesser-known) outfit named Southern Specialties, all produce picks of this size. The HPC Company's line of stainless steel picks also tends to be 0.020 inches thick. HPC's spring steel picks are offered in 0.022 and 0.028 inch thicknesses. If you are doing much of your work in North America (where keyways tend to be less narrow and with less challenging warding), their thicker picks are terrific, in my view. When designing their "Emergency Credit Card pick" (which will be discussed

Practical Lock Picking. DOI: 10.1016/B978-1-59749-611-7.00016-7

in the section on pick kit choice later in this chapter), The Open Organisation Of Lockpickers opted to use metal that is 0.025 inches thick... a fine average that serves all needs rather well.

As you become more skilled you may find yourself wishing for stiffer lockpicks that offer greater tactile feedback. You can seek out supplies fabricated with harder materials, purchase thicker picks, or you can try to modify your existing tools. Heat-treating your steel picks by tempering them with a torch until the metal glows a deep red color, then quenching them in oil is an effective way of increasing stiffness somewhat. Another solution is to seek out picks with metal handles as opposed to plastic or rubber ones. (The exception to this rule is lockpicks that are fabricated by Legion303. If you are lucky enough to come across one of his custom-made sets somehow, it will be instantly obvious to you that the handles are made of a baked plastic material yet they perform like ceramic or metal. That is part of the magic of his process.)

GUIDE TO DIFFERENTIATING PICK TOOLS

One thing that has been a significant source of confusion among lockpickers (both within the sport-picking and hobbyist community and those who are professionally in the locksmithing trade) are the multitude of names that exist for all of the pick tools in common use today. Some pick tools are known by as many as five separate names... a fact that can cause no end of headaches when discussing tool kits among friends or attempting to place orders for picks from suppliers.

If you don't think it too presumptive of me, I am going to attempt to bring some order to the chaos. I have done a lot of traveling, lecturing, and collaborating with lockpickers and locksmiths around the world, all the time paying close attention to what names they used when referring to their tools. I have asked my friends and associates what the most typical and/or most appropriate names are for all of the picks in our tool kits. The results of these years of dialog are assembled here. This list shall (hopefully) represent some of the most-accepted names for common lockpicking tools.

I have no wish to impose a draconian ultimatum across the lockpicking world, but it would be *really* nice if some of the vendors out there would *consider* referring to products using the terms that the *community* has adopted, as opposed to relying exclusively on the arcane series of model numbers and product codes that continue to appear in catalogs.

Thick and thin shafts

One often sees some tools described as "Euro" or "Thin" in contrast to others referred to as "Standard" or "Plain" in some fashion. Due to how these terms are worded, many people come to believe that vendors use metal stock of differing thicknesses when fabricating such equipment. That is *rarely* the case. As mentioned in the above section, most manufacturers of pick tools have a very specific thickness of metal and they use it for all products. Most "thick" and "thin" tools (when they're offered by the same vendor) are distinct only in terms of the size of their *shafts* (i.e., the portion of a lockpick in between the handle and the working tip).

Look at the two tools shown in Figures A.1 and A.2. The difference in their profiles is the only thing that makes them either "euro thin" or "standard size," the metal stock used is the same in both cases.

FIGURE A.1

A "plain"-sized pick, which would work in most locks but could encounter some difficulty when facing a lock with a very thin keyway with tight warding.

FIGURE A.2

A "thin" or "euro" style pick. Everything about this pick is exactly the same as the pick above, save for the thickness of the shaft.

Hook picks

Sometimes called "lifter" picks or "finger" picks, the most common and widely accepted name for such tools is just the term "hook." These tools appear in Figures A.3–A.8.

FIGURE A.3

Short Hook (flat top variant)—The name "Short Hook" (or "Small Hook") gets tossed around a lot with no official standard attached to that title. I would propose that to be a "short" hook, the working tip must have an overall rise that is no more than 150% the thickness of the shaft where it meets the tip. This short hook features a flat top and the tip rises to a height that is 100% the thickness of the end of the shaft.

FIGURE A.4

Short Hook (rounded tip variant)—I would still call this a "Short Hook" due to the fact that its tip (despite being rounded and having a little more size than the pick shown above) still does not rise more than 150% of the thickness of the end of the shaft.

FIGURE A.5

Medium Hook—Any hook tool whose tip rises between 150% and 200% of the thickness of the end of the shaft I would call a "Medium Hook."

FIGURE A.6

Gonzo Hook—Particularly popular among the European sportpicking community, the "Gonzo Hook" is named due to its particularly deep curve and rounded tip (giving it the appearance of the nose of the popular Muppet character). A Gonzo Hook, in my definition, has a tip which rises between 200% and 250% of the thickness of the end of the shaft.

FIGURE A.7

Long Hook—I do not have much love for hook tools that are any larger than a Gonzo. This tool (which is also often called a "Large Hook," a "Deep Hook," or a "Useless Hook") might help you out if you are attacking certain types of Post Office locks or attempting to pick your way out of handcuffs. Other than that, it serves little purpose and should really stop showing up in beginner tool kits. *(Full Disclosure—when I was just starting out giving lectures and such, this tool would sometimes appear in pick kits that I had with me. I tried to make up for that over the years by teaching people how to modify it into a passable Gonzo. You grind about one millimeter off the tip and round the edges.)*

FIGURE A.8

Gem Hook—A hook pick whose tip is neither flat nor rounded, but instead has a pointed rise sticking upward. This pick is highly popular among some people in Peterson's "Slender Gem" variant.

Diamond picks

Useful as either individual lifting tools *or* for raking across pin stacks, diamond-shaped picks come in a handful of sizes and styles. Diamond tools are shown in Figures A.9–A.12.

FIGURE A.9

Small Half Diamond—Every kit should have at least one half diamond. In my view, to be a proper "half diamond", a tool must have a straight, flat undersurface. This particular tool is a "small" half diamond because its working tip rises no more than 50% the thickness of the end of the shaft.

FIGURE A.10

Medium Half Diamond—This tool is similar in shape to the one above, but its working tip rises between 50% and 100% of the thickness of the end of the shaft. Some people might mistakenly call this a "large" half diamond, but I do not feel that term applies.

FIGURE A.11

Large Half Diamond—Besides the fact that the working tip rises more than 100% the thickness of the shaft (I've seen up to 150% the size in terms of tip rise. Anything beyond that seems silly to me), what makes this tool distinct is the different shape of the head. A "large" half diamond often has a steeper slope on its front face than the "medium" and "small" variants.

FIGURE A.12

Diamond Head—I used to see this tool in catalogs once in a while. Thankfully, I do not see it anymore. Utterly no one with whom I have ever spoken has considered this a useful tool.

Rake picks

I have heard some individuals insist that one should not call these tools "rakes." The *motion* used with these tools is "raking" they will insist, but the tools themselves go by other names. Ignore this argument, please. People who are recognized and respected in the lockpicking world totally disregard this assertion. The term "rake" is the most appropriate name for such tools. There is a huge market for one-off, experimental concept rakes, but Figures A.13–A.18 represent the vast bulk of rake tools that one will see in catalogs or in lockpickers' kits.

FIGURE A.13

Snake Rake—consisting of an "up, down, up, down" shape in smooth, curved profiles with a rounded tip; this is one of the most popular raking tools and is produced by essentially every vendor. Southern Ordinance confusingly calls this a "C Rake", while Peterson Tools designates it as a "Double Rake."

FIGURE A.14

Three-Quarter Snake—Similar to the classic snake rake tool shown above, but this rake pick only features an "up, down, up" shape. HPC and Rytan are some of the only vendors of which I am aware that produce this tool.

FIGURE A.15

Half Snake—This is not nearly as common a rake tool. It's based on the main "snake" design but features only a single "up, down" curvature in its shape.

FIGURE A.16

Double Snake—As far as I know, Peterson Tools is one of the few prominent manufacturers of this tool, which they call a "Quad Rake."

FIGURE A.17

Stretched Rake—Taking the "up, down, up, down" motif in a new direction, this tool makes an appearance every so often. Some people call this an "S Rake" due to its stretched size, but that label is used by SouthOrd for a different tool.

FIGURE A.18

Batarang—Named so in homage to one of the Caped Crusader's most useful tools, this very pointy rake is called an "S Rake" by SouthOrd. Southern Specialties calls this a "Camel Back" tool. Trust me, however, to the lockpicking community this will always be a "Batarang." It is not a highly popular rake, however, given the particularly bad weakness in its design. I've seen the tip of this rake snap off a number of times when someone handles it too roughly.

Jagged lifters

Many people would simply classify the tools shown in Figures A.19–A.23 as "rakes"; some can indeed be used as rake tools quite effectively in many instances. However, the original purpose of most of these designs was to approximate some of the most common key bitting patterns. By inserting one of these tools into a lock and lifting it into the pins vertically (perhaps at varied angles), one can sometimes get lucky and catch most (or all) of the pin stacks at the shear line. Nowadays, most people use the combined rapid lifting/raking technique of "jiggling" which is explored in the subsequent section.

FIGURE A.19

Wedge Rake—This tool is definitely a contender for the "least useful lockpick" award, in my opinion. Often called a "W Rake," I know of no one who likes this tool or who uses it with any regularity at all. In the Brockhage catalog, this is referred to as a "Short Jag." Southern Specialties calls it a "Ramped" tool.

FIGURE A.20

Long Rake—Some people call this an "L Rake" or "Computer Generated Rake" (but I know of no evidence that this design is a product of algorithms or crazy math). Some people like it. I don't have one in my kit, but I don't think it's particularly horrible or anything. Brockhage calls this a "Long Jag," while Southern Specialties refers to it as a "Saw Tooth."

FIGURE A.21

Falle Slope—Unlike the "Long Rake" shown above (which some people consider to have been designed using computer modeling, without evidence to that effect), we have it on good authority that John Falle designed his jagged lifter tools after *extensive* research and computer modeling. This tool and the two that follow in Figures A.22 and A.23 are specialized items that attempt to mimic common key bittings.

FIGURE A.22

Falle Valley—Another John Falle tool that can be lifted into a pin stack at varied angles in the hope of setting all the pins.

FIGURE A.23

Falle Hump—Known affectionately as the "Long Rimple" by my Dutch friends, this is a John Falle design that I particularly like. Unlike the Slope and Valley, this Falle tool can be an effective rake as well as a lifter. *This nickname should not be confused with the term "Long Ripple" which is used by Peterson to refer to a tool that is similar to either a Long Rake or a Falle Slope.*

Jiggler picks

Many of the tools in this section are creations of the wildly talented individual known as Raimundo. The "Bogotá" pick that he created years ago spawned a whole family of related tools which are typically used with the elliptical raking/jiggling motion described in Chapter 3 in Figure 3.38. To be a proper "Bogotá" pick, however, a tool must be fabricated using Raimundo's unique process of rounded edges, high polish, and feature an unconventional, angled handle. Figures A.24–A.31 represent the Raimundo family of Jiggler picks along with some affiliated items.

FIGURE A.24

Bogotá—The new design that started quite a trend, three humps with undercutting and a consistent, even overall thickness. High polish and rounded edges on all surfaces are a characteristic of all "proper" attempts at duplicating the Raimundo style.

FIGURE A.25

Wave Jiggler—This is basically a knockoff of the original Bogotá design, with similar spacing between humps but fabricated just from stamped, flat metal with no high polish. These tools are often incorrectly called "Bogotás" (that name is truly reserved for the tools that get the Raimundo finishing treatment). Since the name "Wave Jiggler" can seem a bit awkward, I am ok with people calling this a "pseudo Bogotá" or "knock off Bogotá"... sometimes, the tongue-in-cheek term "Faux-gotá" is used.

FIGURE A.26

Raimundo Single Hump—Sometimes called a "Bogotá half diamond" or "Raimundo half diamond," I don't like that term. A half diamond is a pick with a fully flat underside, in my view. When produced as a simple, flat pick, the vendor Southern Specialties calls this a "Hollow Half Diamond."

FIGURE A.27

Raimundo Double Hump—Another popular variation in the Raimundo family. I once heard this called a camel pick. Hah, does that make the pick in Figure A.26 a dromedary?

FIGURE A.28

Raimundo Quad Hump—Yet another Raimundo variation. Both the "Two Hump" and "Quad Hump" are far less common than the original three hump Bogotá.

FIGURE A.29

Sabana—In a review* by John King, this tool seemed to perform about as well as the "Single Hump," the "Four Hump" outperformed it somewhat.

FIGURE A.30

Monserate (Fore)—In that same review referenced above, this pick performed very well, for both experienced pickers and novices. The Monserate picks are unique in the Raimundo family being that they don't have undercuts in the rearward positions.

FIGURE A.31

Monserate (Aft)—The companion piece to the one above, this is just a slight shift. It has been said that these Monserate picks are a variation on the King and Queen design (described in the last entry of this section of the Appendix).

---

*http://theamazingking.com/bogota.html

Ball picks

Ball picks are sometimes used to attack wafer locks. While I can appreciate the means by which a Snowman style ball pick can be employed in this manner, personally I tend to rake such locks or use wafer jiggler tools, as described in Chapter 2. The handful of ball picks that one sometimes encounters are shown in Figures A.32–A.35.

FIGURE A.32

Ball Pick—This tool appears in all sorts of kits and on the popular "jackknife" tool kit. Some people claim they use it on wafer locks. I tend to think there are far more useful tools that could be part of your inventory.

FIGURE A.33

Snowman—Also called a "Double Ball" pick, this tool is popular for attacking wafer locks. I prefer to just rake such locks, but if you want to try to "lift" individual wafers, this tool can help you do that.

FIGURE A.34

Half Ball—It really seems like sometimes people who get into the business of making pick tools produce whatever picks they can copy from existing designs, then try to "set themselves apart" by scratching their head and saying, "Well, I suppose we could make *this*." I all but guarantee that someone took an existing CAD diagram and just drew a straight vector line, cutting off part of the tool, and said, "Hey, look! I just made a new pick." I have never seen anyone use this tool... ever.

FIGURE A.35

Half Snowman—Like a full-size Snowman, this tool can also help to "lift" individual wafers in a lock. Again, I would think that there are far superior tools out there, but some people like to keep at least one Snowman-type pick in their kits.

Curve picks

A unique type of design which is difficult to classify, these are essentially "hook" picks designed for rocking-style lifting, but their shape is so distinct that I felt they merited their own category here in this guide. These picks are shown in Figures A.36 and A.37.

FIGURE A.36

Deep Curve—For the longest time, tools of this profile were unique to Falle sets. Other outfits are producing them nowadays, however. Peterson seems to make a version of this which they call the "Reach" tool.

FIGURE A.37

Hybrid—Something in between a typical hook and a curve tool, this is a pick which I saw once in someone's kit that had been designed by an individual known as LockNewbie. The craftsmanship was terrific and great care had apparently been taken in the fabrication, polish, and finishing.

Offset picks

A number of vendors offer pick tools that appear to have traditional shapes at the tip of a shaft which has been bent at approximately 20° at a point maybe a half inch back from the tip. My friend Scorche pointed out that these are also called Deforest picks. They are shown in Figures A.38–A.40.

FIGURE A.38

Offset Diamond—A half-diamond top on the end of an offset shaft. The Peterson company calls these "Hooked Diamonds."

FIGURE A.39

Offset Ball—A half-ball tip at the end of an offset shaft.

FIGURE A.40

Offset Snake—It would seem to me that this could make raking more difficult, but I've seen this tool out there.

King and Queen

These are two very interesting styles of lockpick. They are instantly recognizable, due to their having an appearance unlike any other you are likely to see. These are "bitting approximation" tools much like the items described in the "Jagged Lifters" section above. However, unlike those previously mentioned tools, the King and Queen picks (which appear in Figures A.41 and A.42) are *never* really suited for any kind of raking attempt. Their sharp, extreme angles can jam within the lock and they are not robust enough to withstand such feverish movements.

FIGURE A.41

King Pick—Used as a key approximation tool, a King pick is lifted into the pins and then turning force is applied to the plug using a tension tool. If the lock opens, great. If it doesn't... one totally releases pressure, aligns the pick differently, lifts it slightly, and tries to turn again. The same tactic is used with the Queen pick shown in Figure A.42.

FIGURE A.42

Queen Pick—The complimentary tool to a King pick. These two tools were developed by taking all available data about common key bittings and distilling it down to merely a pair of picks. These are often thought of as "last chance" tools, but sometimes they do indeed work. Locksport key figure Schyuler Towne used one to great effect during his first ever attempt in the Gringo Warrior lockpicking competition.

Extractors

This last entry of this section does *not* show a lockpicking tool. Tools such as the one shown in Figure A.43 are, rather, *extractor* tools. Please understand what these are. They are not used for picking locks, but rather they are designed to help locksmiths remove broken keys and other fouling from within a lock's keyway. While these tools may make an appearance once in a while in a prepackaged tool kit (after all, they are useful to certain professionals working in the field), they are of very limited use to penetration testers, hobbyist pickers, etc. It may be a good idea to keep

FIGURE A.43

Broken Key Extractor—This might look like a half-diamond tool at first glance, but it is not. Unless you are a practicing locksmith, there is almost no chance that you need this in your kit.

one around in your kit just in case you snap a pick during a live pen test, but don't accidentally reach for it when you're starting out and learning, because it is not a pick and should not be used to lift or scrub within a lock.

A NOTE ABOUT TENSION TOOLS

As was touched upon in Chapter 2, I would like to again take a moment to point out the multitude of terms that abound for a relatively simple piece of equipment and seek to begin a dialog among lockpickers regarding what phrasing could be most appropriate. Throughout this book, the text has made reference to "tension tools" or just "tensioners." (I use those two terms interchangeably.)

Many locksmith supply catalogs will refer to these pieces of equipment as "tension wrenches" and therefore this term has been adopted by many in the lockpicking community. Particularly savvy individuals are keen to point out that while this particular tool can *cause* tension within the lock, you're not really *applying* tension with it... when picking a lock, you are in fact applying *torsion*. The term "torsion tool" and also "torsion wrench" therefore is commonly heard, particularly in debates about naming conventions.

Due to the fact that "torsion" is a far more obscure word, particularly to nonnative English speakers, occasionally you may hear some people voice support for a more accessible term, calling this a "turning" tool. I believe that the debate regarding how to most appropriately describe the physics of what is happening has merit, and I appreciate those who would devote time and energy toward making "torsion tool" a more accepted and understood label. However, it is the word "wrench" which I feel does the greatest disservice to those who are learning to pick locks... and it is *this* term that draws the bulk of my criticism and efforts for reform. In addition to sometimes being a catalyst for *really* muddled terminology (as I said once before in Chapter 2, every so often you'll hear a person mistakenly say "torque wrench" which is a *wholly* inappropriate term... that would never happen if "wrench" weren't a part of the dialog to begin with), the word "wrench" simply gives a wrong impression to novices.

In the public mind, a wrench is a tool that is used to grip something tightly and apply *considerable* turning force. That is just not the case in the world of lockpicking. In the interest of discouraging excessive manual pressure on the part of those who are learning how to pick, I ask you to join me in trying to expunge the word "wrench" from the lockpicking vocabulary. The debate over "tension versus torsion" is still a good one, and should continue over time, but that's a matter of much finer degree. Ultimately, as long as people know what you're talking about, the public is well served. The problem with the word "wrench" is that so often, particularly among new learners, people do *not* understand your exact meaning and this leads to frustration and headache that we can all help to avoid.

PICK KIT SUGGESTIONS

Lockpickers carry their equipment around in toolkits of widely varying sizes and styles. As you become more experienced and come to appreciate specific tools, your personal kit will undoubtedly evolve and grow over time. My own toolkits have undergone a great deal of evolution over the years. However, I feel that I have settled into something of a helpful routine and wish to share my discoveries with you in the hope that you might be able to develop your own tool collection with minimal cost and wasted investment.

Most pick kits, I feel, can be thought of in specific categories. Some might travel with you almost all of the time, while others can remain with your work supplies exclusively. The following list shows the lockpick kits that I rely on in daily life.

Typical kit

The kit shown in Figures A.44–A.46 is the one that travels with me everywhere, but which is not always directly *on my person* 100% of the time. It's typically in the small backpack that I always carry, which contains my laptop, MP3 player, camera, etc. For a basic "everyday" kit, my favorite design is the zipper-style case offered by a number of vendors. Personally, I believe the best one to be manufactured by HPC, since their kit contains additional foldout flaps that offer a few extra pockets. The kit I own was custom-made, but in the HPC style.

I know some people who claim that a selection such as mine shows a lack of commitment to efficiency. Some lockpickers are fans of pushing people to consider a "small" pick case (the most common ones in this style have only one or two pockets and typically snap shut, see Figure A.47) because it forces them to choose *only* the tools that are *absolutely* necessary. I can respect that line of thinking.

FIGURE A.44

My basic, everyday kit. It measures about 6 in. × 2½ in.

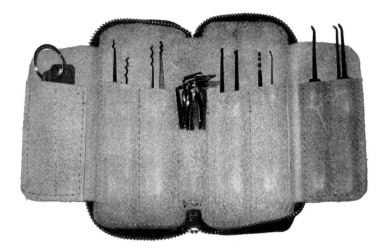

FIGURE A.45

The assortment of tools that I carry in my everyday kit. The additional flap pockets are invaluable.

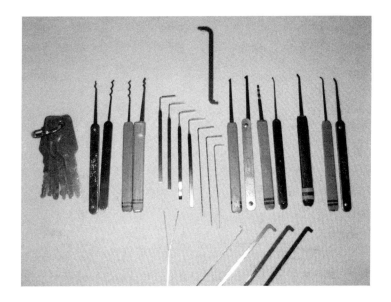

FIGURE A.46

I carry a small assortment of hooks, rakes, and a couple of half diamonds. A wide range of tension tools are also with me (that double-ended tool shown at the top middle of this figure is known as a "Peterson Prybar" and it's outstanding) along with a set of jigglers.

FIGURE A.47

This is a smaller kit, featuring the barest essentials that I would choose to carry. A short hook, a Gonzo hook, a half diamond, a snake rake, and a Bogotá... next to about eight tension tools. Among them is that fabulous Peterson Prybar.

Car kit

If you are interested in using a "small" kit as your everyday tool set, the best way to resist the urge to cram as much as possible in there is to pair this with a larger kit that you keep nearby, but not with you all of the time. I would call this a car kit, since I typically have something like the tool pack shown in Figures A.48 and A.49 in my truck wherever I go.

Big kit

If you get *seriously* into lockpicking, you're going to eventually reach a point where you have so many tools that traditional kits don't work for you. I've seen some folk address the situation by putting a series of smaller kits (sometimes with labels on them) inside of a travel case otherwise designed for sundries. Many modern consumer electronic products like MP3 players and high-end mobile phones come with their own "travel" cases which also work well for this task. I, along with many of my lockpicker friends, eventually just wound up sewing custom-made kits. I like that solution the best, because it offers me room for *exactly* what I want and nothing needs to get left out (see Figure A.50).

FIGURE A.48

A nice bifold or trifold pocketed case works well as a car kit.

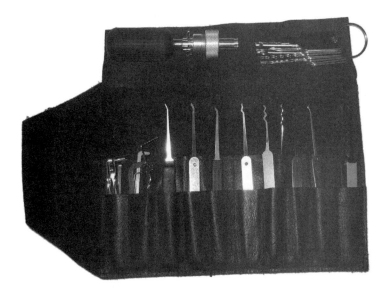

FIGURE A.49

In a car kit, I would typically recommend carrying a few extra hooks and rakes. Perhaps add in a spare half diamond if that's a tool that you treat with some rough handling at times. Give yourself extra tensioners, especially if you loan them to friends on occasion. In the extra room afforded by a car kit, I'd say it's a good idea to keep a set of jiggler tools as well as a tubular lock pick.

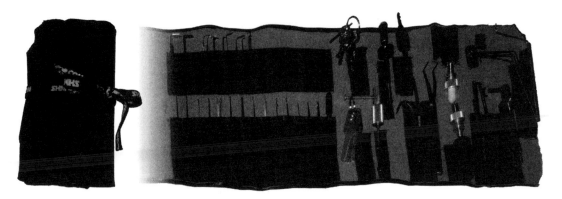

FIGURE A.50

A large "pick roll" that I custom made for myself. There's still some room for growth, and it also can accommodate many of the strange tools that I would never need on a daily basis. This is the tool kit that I carry with me to conferences and lockpicking competitions.

Pocket/emergency kit

Sometimes, despite how small you make your "everyday" kit, you might find yourself not wanting to bring it along with you. Maybe you're out at a fancy evening party and you think that the extra bulk will ruin the lines of your outfit. Maybe you're outside enjoying lovely seasonal weather in just a pair of shorts and a T-shirt. Or maybe you're just a victim of the tech revolution and already carry a personal cell phone, an office Blackberry, an MP3 player, etc... and you just don't want one more bulky item in your pockets. Whatever the reason, some people choose to equip one additional kit, in a super small size, that they can always have on them without fail.

One of the most innovative methods of creating this was shown to me by a locksmith friend of mine named Ed. Ed discovered that *small cigar travel cases* can make *excellent* miniature pick cases. He has a small leather case with only two hollow chambers that measures only 4 in. long and is less than 2 in. wide. In it, he carries a single hook, a single half diamond, and two modified Peterson Prybars. Being a devotee of escape artistry and handcuff trickery (he routinely attends "Houdini"-type conventions), his mini case also contains a specialized handcuff pick, some shim tools, and a miniature pen light.

For those who don't want to cut and grind their existing pick tools down to four inches in length, there is one other option. The Open Organisation Of Lockpickers produces an "Emergency Pick Card" which is exactly of same dimension as that of a credit card (see Figures A.51 and A.52). It is made of 0.025 inch steel (and newer versions are being created as thin as 0.020 inches thick thanks to stronger alloys) and can snap. Some people would think that the small handles make it difficult to use, but in fact it will do the job quite nicely in a pinch. There are even small holes that allow you to add the picks to your key ring once they have been broken apart.

FIGURE A.51

Tucked behind the first two pockets in this wallet is something that looks like a credit card, but is not.

FIGURE A.52

The TOOOL Emergency Pick card is exactly of the same size as that of a standard bank card, but it actually contains a nine-piece tool kit (six pick tools and three tension tools which are built into the frame) that can come in *very* handy if you're in a tight spot. It's the one lockpicking tool kit you can count on to always have with you, no matter what.

CONCLUSION

Lockpicking is a very entertaining pastime and can quickly become a hobby to which you dedicate significant time and resources. However, please understand, you do not need most of the items available for purchase when you're just starting out. As discussed in this Appendix, there are many tools which I feel almost *no one* needs to purchase *ever*.

I encourage you to develop your skills. Invest in tools and practice locks. However, please always try to remain mindful of the virtues of efficiency and simplicity. Less is often more. Do not be tempted by the biggest pick kit that you see for sale. Some of the nicest assortments of tools that I've ever encountered were simple eight- or ten-piece kits that were crafted lovingly and with care by people who chose their tools from a variety of sources, customized some of them along the way, and kept them in a small, modest pouch.

However you choose to equip yourself, take care to always be ethical and responsible with this knowledge, and keep on practicing in order to be the best that you can. Enjoy!

Index

Note: Page numbers followed by *f* indicate figures.